A History of

Childhood

A History of

Childhood

Children and Childhood in the West from Medieval to Modern Times

Colin Heywood

Polity

First published in 2001 by Polity Press in association with Blackwell Publishers Ltd.

Editorial office:
Polity Press
65 Bridge Street
Cambridge CB2 1UR, UK

Marketing and production:
Blackwell Publishers Ltd
108 Cowley Road
Oxford OX4 1JF, UK

Published in the USA by
Blackwell Publishers Inc.
350 Main Street
Malden, MA 02148, USA

ISBN   0-7456-1731-X
ISBN   0-7456-1732-8   (pbk)

A catalogue record for this book is available from the British Library and has been applied for from the Library of Congress.

Typeset in 10½ on 12 pt Times by Best-set Typesetter Ltd., Hong Kong
Printed in Great Britain by TJ International, Padstow, Cornwall

This book is printed on acid-free paper.

Contents

Acknowledgements

The author would like to thank his Nottingham University colleagues Dr Ross Balzaretti, Dr Margaret Walsh and, above all, Dr Julia Barrow, for supplying references and reading parts of the typescript. Thanks also to Dr Olena Heywood, who commented on the entire work and provided support at all times, to M. Jean Murard, for help with the illustration from Troyes, and to editors Lynn Dunlop and Sally-Ann Spencer at Polity. Finally he would like to mention inspiration from his own children, Sophie and Joe, and from Nottingham students who took courses in this area.

Introduction

> My name is Etienne Bertin, but I've always been called 'Tiennon'. I
> was born in October 1823, at a farm in the Commune of Agonges, near
> Bourbon-l'Archambault. My father was a *métayer* on the farm in part-
> nership with his elder brother, my uncle Antoine, called 'Toinot'.[1]

So began *The Life of a Simple Man* (1904), in the world of a share-
cropping family in the Bourbonnais region of France during the early
nineteenth century. Its first few chapters gave a vivid account of the
ups and downs of childhood in this milieu. The author, a sharecrop-
per himself, acknowledged that there was 'nothing remarkable' in this
poor, monotonous life of a peasant. Yet he was determined that his
novel would 'show the gentlemen of Moulins and Paris and elsewhere
what the life of a *métayer* really is'. Drawing on the reminiscences of
his grandfathers, he recounted his experiences as a child of family
feuds, his work as a shepherd boy, the Spartan meals, the nightmares,
and a visit to a fair, catechism with the local priest and the double
wedding of his brothers.[2] Numerous autobiographies written in
modern times by people from very ordinary backgrounds, no less
than memoirs and biographies of leading figures in public life, also
took it for granted that readers would wish to know something of
their early experiences. A few devoted the whole work to recollections of a peasant or working-class childhood.[3] Like Tiennon, they
routinely apologized to their readers for the humdrum circumstances
of their existence, but persisted in telling their life story none the less.
Such authors often asserted their identity with a particular region or
neighbourhood. Lucy Larcom opened her memoirs by observing that
'It is strange that the spot of earth where we were born should make

such a difference to us. People can live and grow anywhere, but people as well as plants have their *habitat'* – in her case, the Cape Ann Side in north-eastern Massachusetts.[4] Some writers emphasized their family identity, however humble or even dissolute their ancestry. Fritz Pauk, from Lippe in Germany, dismissed his grandfather as a heavy drinker, never knew his father (a cabinetmaker who disappeared before he was born), and so shuttled back and forth between an aunt and his 'good mother'.[5] Others dwelt on their games and fantasy life as children, or, at the other extreme, bitter experiences of poverty and oppression. Autobiographies written by German workers for some unknown reason stand out by their *misérabiliste* outlook. Today one might go as far as to assert that childhood reminiscences are generally the most successful part of an autobiography. They certainly satisfy our curiosity about a stage of life commonly assumed to shape the character and destiny of an individual.[6]

Yet this fascination with the childhood years is a relatively recent phenomenon, as far as one can tell from the sources available. During the Middle Ages there was no question of peasants or craftsmen recording their life stories, and even accounts of the highborn or the saintly did not usually show much interest in the early years. A St Augustine (354–430) or an Abbot Guibert of Nogent (*c*.1053–1125) might give some details of their childhood experiences, but these were the exceptions that proved the rule.[7] Ottokar von Steiermark, writing in Middle High German, made his position perfectly clear, 'greeting the birth of a future king of Hungary with "I don't want to write any more about him now; he'll have to wait until he gets older"'. Similarly, during the early modern period in England, children were largely absent from the literature, be it Elizabethan drama or the major novels of the eighteenth century. The child was, at most, a marginal figure in an adult world.[8]

For the medievalist James A. Schultz, this change in perspective is easily explained. His contention is that for approximately 2,000 years, from antiquity down to the eighteenth century, children in the West were merely thought of as imperfect adults. As they were considered 'deficient', and entirely subordinate to adults, he reasoned that their stage of life was likely to be of little interest for its own sake to medieval writers. Only in comparatively recent times has there been a feeling that children are special as well as different, and hence worth studying in their own right.[9] Such a massive generalization over periods and places is unlikely to withstand close scrutiny. Nevertheless, it is instructive to compare the 'imperfect' child inherited from antiquity with the mystical child of the nineteenth-century Romantics. On the one hand, Dante (1265–1321) echoed the classical tradition when he divided a man's regular life span into a period of growth (*adolescenzia*, up to the age of 25), a period of maturity (*gioventute*, from 25 to 45, peaking at 35) and a final period of decline (*senettute*, from 45 to 70). In this scheme it was the moral superiority of middle age that was most in evidence. Youth and old age were conspicuous merely for their departure from the ideal moral mean in their own contrasting ways. Aristotle felt that only men in the prime of life could judge others correctly, youth exhibiting too much trust, old men too little. The Aristotelian concept of the child, then, saw him (and it was a male they generally had in mind) as 'important not for himself but for his potential'.[10] On the other hand, for the German philosopher Richter, writing in 1814, the world of the child encapsulated the future, which 'like Moses at the entrance to the Promised Land, we can only look upon, without ever penetrating'. The Romantics idealized the child as a creature blessed by God, and childhood as a source of inspiration that would last a lifetime. The way was open in the nineteenth century for scientists and educators to study childhood on the grand scale.[11]

Yet, even in the twentieth century, old ways of thinking about childhood died hard.[12] Social science research on child-rearing was slow to escape the narrow boundaries of psychological behaviourism. Until the 1960s, according to Hans Peter Dreitzel, researchers saw the child as an 'incomplete organism' which developed in different directions in response to different stimuli.[13] Again, adulthood was the critical stage of life for which childhood was merely a preparation. All the emphasis in anthropology, psychology, psychoanalysis and sociology was on *development* and *socialization*. What mattered was finding ways of turning the immature, irrational, incompetent, asocial and acultural child into a mature, rational, competent, social and autonomous adult. This conception of children as essentially deficient vis-à-vis adults, according to Robert MacKay, had the effect of deterring research into children as children.[14] In addition there remained the lingering feeling that childhood was a 'natural' phenomenon, which could hold little of interest for researchers. The temptation was for members of any society to consider their own particular arrangements for childhood as 'natural', having been steeped in them all their lives. At the same time, it was easy to assume that the biological immaturity of children would be the overriding influence on this stage of life.

Such ways of thinking about childhood and children have barely survived the last few years. In 1990 the sociologists Alan Prout and Allison James argued that a new paradigm for the sociology of childhood was emerging, based on six key features. In 1998 they (together with Chris Jenks) returned to the fray with another paradigm, this one revolving around four sociological approaches. Given the slippery nature of the customer, they wisely presented it as necessarily a matter of interpretation, 'inviting engagement and simultaneously forbidding closure'.[15] Three of their propositions stand out as potentially fruitful for historians. The first is that childhood is to be understood as a social construction. In other words, 'child' and 'child-hood' will be understood in different ways in different societies. To quote Prout and James, 'the immaturity of children is a biological fact of life but the ways in which this immaturity is understood and made meaningful is a fact of culture'.[16] An influential study by William Kessen in 1979 noted the futility of efforts by American child psychologists to discover the fundamental nature of the child in their laboratories. He countered that the American child, like any other, was a cultural invention. Common themes in child psychology, such as a belief in the purity and innocence of children, were therefore to be explained by historical developments in nineteenth- and twentieth-century America rather than by 'eternal science'. Today in the West we do indeed generally associate childhood with such characteristics as innocence, vulnerability and asexuality, whilst people in, say, the slums of Latin America or a war-torn region of Africa, will probably not do so.[17] The second strand to the new paradigm is that childhood is a variable of social analysis, to be considered in conjunction with others such as the famous triad of class, gender and ethnicity. In other words, an age category such as childhood can hardly be explored without reference to other forms of social differentiation which cut across it. A middle-class childhood will differ from a working-class one, boys are unlikely to be raised in the same way as girls, the experiences of the young in an Irish Catholic family will diverge from those in a German Protestant one, and so on. The novelist Frank McCourt understood this all too well:

> When I look back on my childhood I wonder how I survived at all. It was, of course, a miserable childhood: the happy childhood is hardly worth your while. Worse than the ordinary miserable childhood is the miserable Irish childhood, and worse yet is the miserable Irish Catholic childhood.[18]

The third contention is that children must be seen as active in determining their own lives and the lives of those around them. A key weakness of the earlier neo-behaviourist emphasis on socialization was, arguably, its reduction of children to passive receptacles of adult teaching. Recent research in the social sciences indicates that it is misleading to allocate parents the role of model and children the role of followers. As Dreitzel notes, 'beginning with the first smile or the first cry, parents react to their child's behaviour and respond with warmth or hostility, encouragement and satisfaction – depending on their child's character no less than on their own attitudes.' Relations between adults and children can instead be depicted as a form of interaction, with the young having their own culture or succession of cultures.[19]

This new line of thinking on children and childhood raises problems of its own, as its exponents readily acknowledge. If childhood is to be seen as a social construction, what role is there left for biological influences? How can one discover general insights into childhood when the emphasis is on the plurality of social constructs: at the extreme, on what is unique to each society rather than what is common to all? Accepting that other societies will have conceptions of childhood different from our own, how do we react to practices such as infanticide and child prostitution, which we would judge abusive? Is there not a danger, as Diana Gittins observes, of dismissing 'real problems, real pain, real suffering of real embodied people'? And in focusing on the language and lore of children, or the 'tribal child', is there not a risk of casting the young into a ghetto on the margins of society?[20] Even so, the 'new paradigm' in the social sciences has both influenced and been influenced by historical writing about childhood to good effect.

Historians of childhood have in fact been rather thin on the ground for a long time. As late as the 1950s their territory could be described as 'an almost virgin field'.[21] Much of the early work was in any case heavily institutional in character, outlining the rise of school systems, child labour legislation, specialized agencies for juvenile delinquents, infant welfare services and so forth. Ideas about childhood and children themselves were hardly in the frame.[22] Yet gradually historians have contributed to a recognition of the social construction of childhood, cross-time comparisons being as instructive as cross-cultural ones. The work of Philippe Ariès in the 1960s was particularly congenial to social scientists. They readily latched on to his famous assertion in *Centuries of Childhood* (1962) that 'in medieval society the idea of childhood did not exist' to demonstrate the shifting nature of childhood.[23] This work sparked off a whole series of strictly historical debates: on whether the medieval period did in fact have an awareness of childhood, on the key periods in the 'discovery of childhood', on the nature of parent–child relations at various periods, and on the role of the schools, to name a few.[24] The growing volume of monographs in the historical literature over the last thirty years or so also makes it possible now to grasp the diversity of experience among young people in the past. The American experience lends itself particularly well to this approach, but European historians have also engaged with the impact on childhood of class, gender and so forth.[25] No less importantly, certain historians have eagerly taken up the challenge of moving children centre stage for their part in shaping the past. David Nasaw, for example, demonstrated how poor children in the cities of early twentieth-century America used their purchasing power to encourage the lurid offerings of penny arcades, cheap vaudeville halls and moving-picture theatres, in defiance of adult reformers. Similarly Miriam Formanek-Brunell noted how some American girls used dolls for their own purposes rather than those of their parents, cutting them to pieces or running them through a clothes wringer.[26]

A particular problem for historians is to unearth source material on past childhoods. Children themselves leave few records, and even artefacts designed for them, such as books and toys, have a poor survival rate. Historians have displayed considerable ingenuity in their use of sources, turning to official reports such as those produced by factory and schools inspectors, polemical works generated by debates concerning childhood, literary accounts in novels and poetry, 'ego documents' in the form of diaries, autobiographies and oral testimony, folklore collections, advice manuals for parents, visual evidence from portraits and photographs, not to mention toys, games, furniture and the like. Some aspects of childhood have proved easier to document than others. Accounts of philanthropic and state initiatives to improve child welfare can rely on the extensive archives normally maintained by institutions. This doubtless helps to explain the massive scale of the literature available in this area.[27] Studies of the representation of childhood also have a solid base in the literary and visual texts available to them. 'Classics' from such authors as Goethe, George Sand, Wordsworth and Dickens have emerged as an abiding source of inspiration to specialists in a number of disciplines. However, as Roger Cox warns, a discourse, as defined by Michel Foucault, can never be read off in straightforward fashion from a text: an act of interpretation must intervene.[28] Medievalists face these problems in a particularly acute form. They risk gaining a seriously distorted impression of ideas on childhood at this early period because they are forced to rely on a small number of texts, many of them fictional in character. They have made extensive use of sources such as hagiography, law codes, encyclopaedias, penitentials, romances and illustrations on manuscripts. All the same, these works were produced by a tiny minority of the population, who were above all male, clerical and close to the narrow circles of the aristocracy and the urban patriciate. Moreover, authors of literary works at all periods, in following the conventions of a particular genre, were not necessarily providing a direct reflection of contemporary ideas on childhood.

The 'sentiments approach' to the family and parent–child relationships also faces acute problems in finding evidence to answer the questions posed. What historians like Philippe Ariès, Edward Shorter and Linda Pollock want to know is how parents felt about their children in the past. This is by no means a hopeless task, given the survival of sources such as diaries and autobiographies, but it is difficult to achieve any precision over the timing of changes in attitudes and regional or socio-economic variations. The most daunting obstacles arise when historians look beyond the literate minority to the masses, a point where, according to one authority, source problems become almost insuperable. Information is available from the writings of clergymen, doctors, folklorists and other educated observers, but these of course are all outsiders to the groups being discussed. Hence critics routinely condemn Ariès for the vagueness of his account, Shorter for pontificating on half a continent with 'a few scraps of evidence', and Pollock for losing sight of the seamier side of parent–child relations, as she relied on the inevitably self-censored testimony of diaries and memoirs.[29] Attempts to recreate the experience of childhood also have to be wary with their sources and methods. Children have left traces in various places, ranging from Anglo-Saxon burial sites and medieval coroners' reports to modern records of their heights, deaths, school attendance and employment in a factory. Adults too have attempted to recall their childhood years, in autobiographies and during interviews with specialists in oral history. Yet Ludmilla Jordanova is persuasive in warning against any search for an 'autonomous, authentic voice of children', on the grounds that the very languages, mental habits and patterns of behaviour of the young are learned from adults.[30] Furthermore, there is once again the risk of treating various texts as windows into reality. Autobiographies, for example, might appear a secure point of entry to the world of the child. Closer inspection reveals that one is dealing with a literary form, complete with its own conventions. Above all, it is 'a review of a life from a particular moment', and hence it inevitably involves some shaping of the past. One can hope for some interesting insights, but they are likely to reveal as much about the author at the time of writing as about his or her past.[31] There are also various models for working-class autobiography, differentiating it from the classic 'spiritual autobiography' of the middle classes. Regenia Gagnier discerns six 'rhetorical genres' in nineteenth-century Britain which workers could follow: conversion and gallow tales, storytellers and politicians, and self-examinations and confessions.[32]

This book is divided into three parts. The first focuses on childhood as a social construct, and the deceptively simple question of 'what is a child'? In particular, it considers the question of how medieval societies might have perceived childhood, the key turning points in the history of ideas in this sphere between the early medieval and modern periods, and the long-running themes discernible in the debates. Not everyone would agree with Carolyn Steedman that claims for a history of adult attitudes towards children are 'much more compelling' than those for a history of children.[33] Even so, there is no disputing that these abstract ideas are worth studying because sooner or later they have an impact on real children. The second part of the book traces the process of growing up in the past, concentrating on the relationships between children, their families, and their peers. This takes us into a long list of topics ranging from infanticide and child abandonment to games and folktales. The final section considers aspects of children in the wider world, above all their work, health and education. The periods covered run from the early Middle Ages to the First World War, stopping before one becomes embroiled in the mass of institutional developments characteristic of the twentieth century, and the countries are those of Europe and (from the early modern period) North America. The general aim has been to focus on the child's perspective as well as the adult ideas and institutions that affected their lives. What matters is the *interaction* of children with parents, neighbours, teachers, doctors, employers, policemen and the like. It is also the intention to give at least a hint of the varied experiences of growing up in the past, and to concentrate on ways of interpreting the material rather than the details of what happened. For this reason the work takes a thematic rather than the more conventional chronological approach. This means zooming to and fro across the centuries, as well as across two continents, in what may appear at first sight a disconcerting approach. However, the aim is to highlight key issues in the history of childhood and children.

PART I

Changing Conceptions of Childhood

Childhood, according to the seventeenth-century French cleric Pierre de Bérulle, 'is the most vile and abject state of human nature, after that of death'.[1] It is tempting to agree – not least as an antidote to all the sentimental nonsense surrounding the supposedly pure and innocent child of the Victorian era. Such extremes serve to remind us that childhood is a social construct, which changes over time and, no less importantly, varies between social and ethnic groups within any society. As noted above, it is always tempting to think in terms of a 'natural' and indeed universal child, whose path to development is largely determined by its biological make-up. Biology does of course play a part in the psychological as well as the physical development of a child. The psychologist Jerome Kagan informs us that the most important biological influences spring from the maturation of the central nervous system structures during the first dozen or so years of life. These permit the emergence of motor and cognitive abilities such as walking, speech and self-awareness. At the same time, Kagan takes the now-familiar line that experience counts as well as biology.[2] Any idea of a purely 'natural' child becomes difficult to sustain once it is realized that children readily adapt to their own particular environment, the product of assorted historical, geographical, economic and cultural forces. To the extent that human beings can construct their own nature, as Nicholas Tucker recently noted, one might anticipate varying outcomes in what passes for childhood in different societies. Childhood is thus to a considerable degree a function of adult expectations.[3]

It follows that if historians wish to recreate the way day-to-day experiences of children in the past (what might be called the social history of children) they must in the first instance understand how adults thought and felt about the young (the cultural history of childhood).[4] Childhood is of course an abstraction, referring to a particular stage of life, as opposed to the group of persons implied by the word children.[5] What we will be looking for in various societies is some understanding at a theoretical level of what it is to be a child, rather than mere descriptions of individual children. It may be useful at this point to follow philosophers in making the distinction between a *concept* and a *conception*. David Archard suggests that all societies at all times have had the *concept* of childhood, that is to say, the notion that children can be distinguished from adults in various ways. Where they differ is in their *conceptions* of childhood, which specify these ways of distinguishing the two. Thus they will have contrasting ideas on the key issues of how long childhood lasts, the qualities marking out adults from children, and the importance attached to their differences.[6]

1

Conceptions of Childhood in the Middle Ages

And in the beginning was Ariès. His wide-ranging and dramatic account of the 'discovery' of childhood was a truly seminal work. Briefly stated, Ariès made the startling assertion that the medieval world was ignorant of childhood. What was missing was any *sentiment de l'enfance*, any 'awareness of the particular nature of childhood, that particular nature which distinguishes the child from the adult, even the young adult'. The moment children could survive without the care and attention of their mothers or nannies, somewhere between the ages of 5 and 7, they were launched into the 'great community of men'. They joined adults in their games and pastimes and, whether they were courtiers or workers, acquired a trade by throwing themselves into its daily routines, living and working with those who were already fully trained. According to Ariès, medieval civilization failed to perceive a transitionary period between infancy and adulthood. His starting point, then, was a society which perceived young people to be small-scale adults. There was no idea of education, medieval people having forgotten the *paideia* of classical civilization, and no sign of our contemporary obsessions with the physical, moral and sexual problems of childhood. The 'discovery' of childhood would have to await the fifteenth, sixteenth and seventeenth centuries. Only then would it be recognized that children needed special treatment, 'a sort of quarantine', before they could join the world of adults.[1]

Critiques of Ariès's work

Centuries of Childhood (1962) has enjoyed mixed fortunes among professional historians. (For what it is worth, Ariès was an amateur 'weekend historian'.) Some, including a few medievalists, accepted its interpretation of childhood with enthusiasm, using its insights as an inspiration for their own researches.[2] Others were more measured in their appreciation, or downright hostile. Jean-Louis Flandrin 'marvelled' at its impressive documentation but was 'concerned' about weaknesses in its methods of analysis. Adrian Wilson, one of Ariès's most systematic critics, concluded that it was riddled with logical flaws and 'methodological catastrophes'.[3] The book was far more favourably received among psychologists and sociologists. Indeed, they had an alarming tendency to treat it as a 'historical report' rather than a highly contentious thesis. Judith Ennew observed that all sociologists return to it 'as if to Scripture'.[4] Why, then, has it enjoyed such renown, in some quarters at least? The answer must surely be the challenge presented to the reader by the counter-intuitive character of its argument. Most people assume that their own ideas and practices concerning childhood are 'natural', and are shocked to discover that other societies diverge from them. But once childhood is perceived as being culturally constructed, whole new fields for study are opened to scholars. It also becomes easier to mount a radical critique of thinking about children in their own society. For example, in 1979, Martin Hoyles attacked the present 'myth of childhood', and its desire to exclude children from the worlds of politics, sex, work and culture, by exposing its shallow historical roots.[5]

Sniping at Ariès is all too easy. His sweeping assertions on childhood may dazzle the intellect, but they also give numerous hostages to fortune. In the first place, critics accuse him of naivety in his handling of historical sources. They are particularly scathing of his approach to iconographic evidence. Ariès famously asserted that, until the twelfth century, medieval art did not attempt to portray childhood, indicating that there was 'no place' for it in this civilization. All that artists came up with was the occasional tiny figure resembling a man on a reduced scale: a 'horrid little dwarf' in the case of the infant Jesus.[6] No one disputes that children are generally missing from early medieval art. However, as Anthony Burton remarks, the concentration on religious themes means that many other things are missing too, notably 'virtually all of secular life'. This makes it impossible to single out childhood as a significant absence. As for the miniature adults, they are not necessarily a 'deformation' inflicted on children's bodies. If, for example, the child in a twelfth-

Virgin and Child in Majesty, French twelfth century, wood, h. 31″.
The Metropolitan Museum of Art, New York. Gift of J. Pierpont
Morgan, 1916 (16.32.194). Photograph © Metropolitan Museum of Art.

century wood sculpture *Virgin and Child in Majesty* looks decidedly
mature, is this not because he is supposed to represent Divine
Wisdom? Even when depicting adults during the early medieval era,
artists were more concerned to convey the status and rank of their
subjects than individual appearance. Furthermore, not everyone
accepts that the transition to more lifelike depictions of children in
painting and sculpture from the twelfth century onwards reveals an
artistic 'discovery of childhood'. Some historians argue persuasively
that this was more a matter of Renaissance artists rediscovering and
imitating Greek and Roman models than taking a new interest in the
children around them. In short, Ariès appears to think that 'the artist
paints what everyone sees', ignoring all the complex questions about
the way reality is mediated in art.[7]

Secondly, critics of Ariès note his extreme 'present centredness'.
By this they mean that he looked for evidence of the twentieth-
century conception of childhood in medieval Europe, failed to find
it, and then jumped to the conclusion that the period had no awareness of this stage of life at all. In the words of the historian Doris

Desclais Berkvam, this leaves open the question of whether there might not have existed in the Middle Ages 'a consciousness of childhood so unlike our own that we do not recognize it'.[8] In the interim, to take the third line of criticism, historians have had no hesitation in judging the Ariès thesis on the complete absence of any consciousness of childhood in medieval civilization to be overdrawn. They have been quick to show various ways in which there was at least some recognition of the 'particular nature' of childhood.[9] Medieval law codes contained a few concessions to the minority status of children. For example, they usually protected the inheritance rights of orphans, and sometimes required the consent of children to a marriage. The ordinances of Aethelstan, a West Saxon king during the early tenth century, laid down that any thief over 12 years of age who stole goods worth more than 12 pence should be executed. However, Aethelstan later added that he thought it 'cruel to put to death such young people and for such slight offences as he has learnt is the practice everywhere'. He therefore declared that thieves under the age of 15 should not be slain, unless they tried to defend themselves or escape.[10] The regime in the monasteries for oblates, children bound to the religious life by the vows of their parents, was slightly less rigorous than for adult monks. A ninth-century commentary on the Rule of St Benedict allowed the *infantes* more frequent meals than the *maiores*, extra sleep and some time to play in a meadow (even if it was only a meagre one hour per week or per month).[11] Similarly, general works on medicine from the Middle Ages include a section on paediatrics, almost invariably a matter of copying the twenty-three chapters on infant care from the *Gynecology* of Soranus of Ephesus (98–177).[12]

An even more powerful riposte to Ariès's conclusion that an awareness of childhood was lacking during the medieval period comes from the inheritance of Graeco-Roman discourse on the subject. Medieval Latin adopted the Hippocratic tradition of dividing childhood into three stages: *infantia* from birth to age 7; *pueritia* from age 7 to 12 for girls and 7 to 14 for boys; and *adolescentia* from 12 or 14 to 21.[13] The discourse also acted as a medium for Classical thinking on the Ages of Man. Some of the schemes available to scholars gave detailed attention to childhood. A twelfth-century translation of Avicenna's *Canon* subdivided the first stage of life, from birth to age 30, into five parts. There were successively ages when the legs were not fit for walking; for dentition (when the legs were still weak and the gums not yet filled with teeth); for achieving strength and dentition; for producing sperm and facial hair (letting slip a focus on boys); and for the final achievement of bodily strength and full growth.[14] From the thirteenth century, such ideas and the images associated with them including the swaddled baby or the frolicsome child, were widely diffused in the vernacular. They appeared in, among other places, sermons, moral treatises, encyclopaedias, medical handbooks, stained glass windows and house decorations.[15]

There is a risk of exaggerating the impact of such schemes on an awareness of childhood.[16] They were largely academic exercises, owing more to the ingenuity of philosophers in relating the human life cycle to the natural world than to direct observation. Besides the seven ages familiar to us from Jaques's speech in *As You Like It*, three, four and six were also particularly popular. It all depended on whether the author was seeking to draw parallels between the stages of life and, say, the four humours or the seven planets. There was in addition what J. A. Burrow calls a 'confusing instability' in the naming and classification of ages. The classic three stages of childhood were usually too fine for schemes with three or four ages of man: the latter might have a first age running from birth to 14, or from birth to 25 or 30. It is likely that the mass of the peasantry would have had little contact with this type of knowledge. What it did stimulate was a learned tradition of reflecting on the nature of childhood among a literate minority of monks and cultivated laymen.[17]

Now that the dust has settled a little in the debate, it seems unduly simplistic to polarize civilizations in terms of the absence or presence of an awareness of childhood. Following the thinking of David Archard, one might say that the medieval world probably had a concept of childhood, but conceptions of it that were very different from our own.[18] As a historian one must surely acknowledge the role of Ariès in opening up the subject of childhood, profit from his many insights into the past, and move on. A more fruitful approach is to search for these different conceptions of childhood in various periods and places, and to seek to explain them in the light of prevailing material and cultural conditions.

Medieval conceptions of childhood

How, then, did medieval Europe characterize the nature of childhood? There was some recognition of positive qualities, particularly in the very young (adolescents were looked on with some distaste by clerical figures, on account of their licentiousness and 'carnal lust'). A recent French survey proclaims that never has the child been as celebrated as in the Middle Ages. One can quote no lesser personage than Pope Leo the Great preaching in the fifth century that 'Christ loved childhood, mistress of humility, rule of innocence, model of sweetness'. The innocence of children meant that they could have celestial visions, denounce criminals and serve as intermediaries between Heaven and Earth, as in the proverb 'out of the mouth of

babes come words of wisdom'. The cult of the infant Jesus, evident in
Cistercian circles during the twelfth century, provided further occasions to exalt childhood. The Massacre of the Innocents also provided
a powerful image of childhood, in the form of the children slaugh-
tered on the orders of Herod three days after the birth of Christ.
However, it must be said that these were isolated views: in keeping
with the often gloomy view of the human predicament in the Middle
Ages, most commentators among the educated elite preferred to
depict the child as a sinful creature, 'a poor sighing animal'.[19]

Recent authorities on childhood have also suggested that the
Middle Ages understood childhood as a process of development,
rather than a fixed state. In other words, they had some understanding of the dynamics of growth.[20] Such studies have been bedevilled
by accusations of an anachronistic reading of medieval material
through the lens of modern theories on the stages of growth.[21]
However, it is possible to use the medical, didactic and moralizing
literature of the period to demonstrate an awareness of stages in
childhood. Shulamith Shahar, for example, draws attention to an
awareness of turning points around the ages of 2, 7 and adolescence,
and of the characteristics particular to each stage. In similar vein,
focusing on budding saints, Donald Weinstein and Rudolph Bell
document the phases in their growth to perfection during childhood
and adolescence. From the thirteenth century, they argue, female
saints such as Catherine of Siena and Teresa of Avila followed a particular pattern of spirituality. Between the ages of 4 and 7 the girls
grasped what society had in store for them: courtship, marriage and
motherhood. At the same time, they gradually became aware of an
alternative life revolving around perpetual chastity, humility and
charity. There followed a struggle between the world of the flesh,
which might triumph temporarily during adolescence and early adulthood, and that of the spirit.[22]

On the negative side, medieval authors almost invariably preferred
to write about adulthood, and particularly male adulthood, rather
than childhood and adolescence. (Whether the oral culture of the
masses ran along the same lines is of course impossible to determine.)
A survey of histories and chronicles from the early Middle Ages
found them to be 'quite barren' in this area. Another investigation,
this time of English literature, mentioned a thousand-year silence
surrounding children between St Augustine and the Reformation.[23]
There were of course exceptions: one might cite the Middle English
poem *Pearl*, which focuses on the death of a child, and the autobiographical references to childhood in works by Bede and Guibert de
Nogent.[24] None the less, there is no denying that those writing history
in the Middle Ages thought it should be largely a matter of kings,
battles and high politics (a view not unfamiliar even in our own times,
let it be said). Similarly the conventions of hagiography dictated that

a future saint be marked out early in childhood by his or her exceptional maturity. Authors in this genre revelled in detailing the prodi-
gious feats of a *puer senex*, a child who already thought like an old
man. They had St Nicholas displaying his asceticism while still in the
cradle, as he agreed that on Wednesdays and Fridays he would take
the breast only once a day. St Guthlac (evidently anything but a
victim of political correctness) 'did not imitate the impertinence of
children, the extravagant gossip of women, the silly popular stories,
the stupid sayings of peasants, the frivolous and lying chatter of
parties, and the various cries of all sorts of birds, as was the custom
to do at that age'. Bede himself had the young St Cuthbert turned
from a carefree childhood by a mere 3-year-old, 'who began to
upbraid him, with all the solemnity of an old man, for his idleness
and indulgence in games'. Adults reflecting on their own religious
experiences in their turn followed these conventions by emphasizing
maturity. Margareta Ebner, from the later German Middle Ages,
wrote: 'I cannot describe how I lived for the previous twenty years',
that is to say before her mystical experiences began, 'because I did
not take note of myself then'.[25]

Medieval sources were often vague when it came to estimating
ages, and caught by the ambiguities surrounding language in this area.
In the same way as 'boy' used to be applied to an adult slave in
the United States, or *garçon* to a mature server in a French café, so
words for 'child', such as *puer, kneht, fante, vaslet* or *enfes*, often
drifted to indicate dependence or servility. Hence they too might
apply to adults as well as to young people. Early writers also played
fast and loose with any precise form of classification by age. Typically,
the ninth-century monk Magister Hildemar was happy to apply the
term *infans* to a 15-year-old as well as to a 3-year-old.[26] We conclude
that childhood (and adolescence) during the Middle Ages were not
so much ignored as loosely defined and sometimes disdained. The
medievalist Doris Desclais Berkvam sums up the peculiarity of
medieval childhood as its 'unstructured and unspecified' character,
encompassing 'the time and space of youth regardless of where, or
how long, this youth takes place'. The historian James A. Schultz,
perhaps generalizing rather too easily from his source material,
asserts that medieval society in Germany viewed childhood as an 'age
of deficiency' and children merely as 'imperfect adults'.[27]

This limited interest in childhood for its own sake can best be
understood in the context of social conditions in a pre-industrial
society. Ariès was surely correct to depict medieval children being
inserted gradually into the world of adults from an early age, helping
their parents, working as a servant or taking on an apprenticeship.
He was by no means the first scholar to note that the distance in
behaviour between children and adults was less evident in the past
than in the present.[28] With hindsight, what we would perceive as

childhood and adolescence meshed progressively and almost imperceptibly into adulthood. This does not mean that people in this type of 'primitive' society were unaware of different stages of development among the young. There was an obvious grading of the responsibilities with which young people could be entrusted: from odd jobs around the household to shepherding and eventually a formal apprenticeship or work out in the fields. They also played their own games, rather than joining in adult contests.[29] None the less, childhood and adolescence did appear less distinct and special at this early period. The element of choice and experimentation which makes these stages of life so critical for the individual today was also far less in evidence. There were different paths for the young to follow, even in the sixth century. Pierre Riché highlights the contrasts between 'the pupil leaving the charge of the Roman grammarian, the lector attached to a cathedral church, the Barbarian raised in the entourage of his chief, and the monk offered to his monastery as an infant'.[30] However, young people themselves had little say in these matters. Most of them were more or less obliged to follow in the footsteps of their parents, with their occupation and station in life clearly mapped out before them. Childhood in Germany during the early Middle Ages was, for the historian Jean-Pierre Cuvillier, an 'apprenticeship in the conduct of a caste'.[31] One generation therefore shaded unobtrusively into the next. Finally, with most people in a village or neighbourhood undergoing similar experiences as farmers or craftsmen, they were hardly encouraged to engage in debates on the nature of childhood. In this way, social conditions in the villages and small towns encouraged a particular idea of childhood, and it in turn reinforced them. To pursue the issue further, however, one needs to proceed beyond the rather static view of medieval Europe presented so far.

2

The Quest for a Turning Point

When looking for long-term changes in conceptions of childhood, it was once again Philippe Ariès and his *Centuries of Childhood* that first set the agenda for historians. His main concern, of course, was to document the emergence during the early modern period of a *sentiment de l'enfance*: an ambiguous phrase which conveyed both an awareness of childhood and a feeling for it. Ironically, few researchers in the field were at all impressed by his account. He outlined a twofold set of changes between the fifteenth and the seventeenth centuries. At the outset, mothers and nannies launched the new idea by treating children as a source of amusement and relaxation, delighting in their 'sweetness, simplicity and drollery'. He argued, not very convincingly, that 'children's little antics must always have seemed touching to mothers, nannies and cradle-rockers, but their reactions formed part of the huge domain of unexpressed feelings'. Adrian Wilson observes that since Ariès confined his researches to printed sources, the feelings were bound to remain 'unexpressed' until the invention of the printing press.[1] More significantly for Ariès, from the seventeenth century onwards, reformers replaced this coddling of children with 'psychological interest and moral solicitude'. A small band of lawyers, priests and moralists came to recognize the innocence and weakness of childhood, and managed to impose a long childhood among the middle classes. There was, in other words, a shift in the cultural sphere, attributable to the growing influence of Christianity and a new interest in education. Ariès rounded off his account by arguing that the heightened concern for education gradually transformed the whole of society during the nineteenth and twentieth centuries, notably in encouraging a new and spiritual function for the family.[2]

The response from other historians was to balk at accepting change on such a broad scale. They have generally preferred the safer (if less exhilarating) ground of the monograph, aiming to produce a more nuanced picture across the nations, the various social groups and the conventional periods of history. However, this has not prevented many of them proposing an alternative 'discovery of childhood', either before, during or after the seventeenth century. They follow Ariès in the reassuring scenario of an increasingly 'serious and realistic' concept of childhood emerging, whether from the early medieval period or the late nineteenth century.[3] This is all very well, in so far as they have drawn attention to key periods, organizations and thinkers in the history of childhood. Yet the whole notion of a definitive discovery of the particular nature of childhood is open to question. It assumes childhood to be a timeless category 'waiting in the wings of history to be discovered'.[4] This of course rules out the more recent strategy of considering childhood as a social construct that will vary in different periods and places. Moreover, the notion that 'innocence' and 'weakness' are fundamental truths about childhood rather than one such construct is deeply suspect. It would surely now be more illuminating to think in terms of an ebbing and flowing of interest in the young over the long term, and of competing conceptions of childhood in any given society. So, we should ask, when were the important turning points, and how did they relate to changing material and cultural conditions?

'Discoveries' during the Middle Ages

A few notable attempts to upstage Ariès located significant changes in the medieval or even early medieval periods. Pierre Riché, writing during the 1960s, argued that between the sixth and the eighth centuries the monastic system 'rediscovered the nature of the child and all of its richness'.[5] At first sight this appears a highly implausible line of argument. Circumstances during this particular period were hardly encouraging for any such development. Most of the population lived a miserable, hand-to-mouth existence, threatened by plague, famine or invasion by outsiders. The historian Jacques Le Goff has asserted that the 'utilitarian Middle Ages' had no time to display pity or wonder towards children, and so barely even noticed them.[6] The monasteries, however, to which Riché draws our attention, managed to stand out as a taper of light in the general gloom. They also had direct experience of raising and educating children. The custom of parents handing over a child to the Church meant that the majority of recruits to the monasteries were young oblates.[7] It became possible for the odd monastic teacher in various parts of Europe to challenge the generally low opinion of childhood inherited from the Romans and the early Church Fathers. St Columban, in the late sixth century, noted that in some respects a boy could be a superior monk to an adult, because 'he does not persist in anger; he does not bear a grudge; he takes no delight in the beauty of women; and he expresses what he truly believes'. Another illustrious monk, Bede, repeated the same formula in the eighth century, to support his exceptionally favourable view of the child. He claimed to know 'many children endowed with wisdom', and suggested that they were good to teach, faithfully absorbing what was taught to them.[8]

In the period around the twelfth century and its 'renaissance', the trickle of historians opposing Ariès becomes a flood. They talk in terms of 'a truly critical phase in the history of childhood', 'changes in the Christian concept of children', or, more cautiously in the case of Roland Carron, a discovery of the child during the thirteenth century, 'perhaps only for a while'.[9] In the background was a series of upheavals in the social and economic spheres. An 'agrarian revolution' running from the tenth to the thirteenth centuries brought some improvements in techniques of cultivation, forest clearances and the settlement of waste land. Population in Europe more than doubled between the mid-tenth and mid-fourteenth centuries, from an estimated 22.6 million to 54.4 million. The securing of the Mediterranean from foreign raiders encouraged trade to flourish on an unprecedented scale. And, most importantly for our purposes, from as early as the tenth century towns began to recover from their torpor, above all in northern Italy, Flanders, the Low Countries and France. Western Europe remained a predominantly agrarian economy, with a relatively fixed social order. Even so, a society which was once composed largely of priests, warriors and peasants came to include 'such numerous and varied types' as merchants, lawyers, accountants, clerks and artisans.[10] In the urban environment, young people had some scope for choosing a career, and parents sometimes had to confront a childhood different from their own.[11] An Abelard or a St Bernard, for example, had some choice over whether to become a knight, a monk or a secular clerk. Thus Abelard, the son of a knight, wrote that 'I was so carried away by my love of learning that I renounced the glory of a soldier's life, made over my inheritance and rights of the eldest son to my brothers, and withdrew from the court of Mars in order to kneel at the feet of Minerva [goddess of learning].'[12]

The historian David Herlihy has argued that the result was an increased social and psychological investment in children. More resources were devoted to their education and health, and more thought given to child-rearing and teaching methods. Herlihy also notes a new sympathy towards childhood, evident in the devotion to the Child Jesus. The idealization of a 'sweet and sacred childhood', he suggests, might be interpreted as a reaction to the strains and stresses of urban life.[13] The 'renaissance' of the twelfth century also brought new learning. French cities in particular harboured a growth of humanism and an interest in the individual. The injunction 'know yourself' encouraged reflection on human motivation and various forays into autobiography, such as those by Peter Abelard and Guibert of Nogent. No less importantly, broader career choices and debates on the true nature of knighthood or the ideal monastic life provoked a questioning of established authority.[14] Within the rarefied atmosphere of 'urbane and intelligent society', the cultural ambience was surely favourable to a re-evaluation of childhood.

The contribution of the early modern period

Childhood was once again 'discovered' during the sixteenth and seventeenth centuries, if certain historians are to be believed. C. John Somerville contends that 'sustained interest in children in England began with the Puritans, who were the first to puzzle over their nature and their place in society'. Puritans did not necessarily have a high opinion of infants, the more zealous brethren asserting that they were born as 'filthy bundles of original sin', or 'young vipers'. However, according to Somerville, Puritanism as a reform movement eager to win over the younger generation was propelled into taking an interest in their position.[15] Catholic reformers across the Channel in France had a similarly low opinion of children, being no less vehement in denouncing them as feeble and guilty of original sin.[16] Yet the seventeenth-century Jansenists at Port-Royal and other educators argued that children were worthy of attention; that one should dedicate one's life to their instruction; and that each individual needed to be understood and helped.[17] Max Okenfuss asserts unequivocally that 'childhood was discovered in Russia in the 1690's', taking as evidence the series of Slavic primers produced by Karion Istomin (*c*.1640–1717) in Moscow. With their vivid use of illustrations to teach grammar and religion, these primers revealed an awareness that the perceptions of a child differed from those of adults. Okenfuss follows Ariès in attributing this 'discovery' to a new-found interest in education, the school serving to set apart childhood from later stages in life.[18] If some historians look to the cultural sphere to explain the renewed interest in children at this period, others have highlighted the impact of economic change. They argue that the period between the fifteenth and the eighteenth centuries saw the emergence of capitalism in western Europe. Parents in the middling strata of society then had an incentive to ensure that children did not fritter their inheritances, and that their male offspring at least had the skills required for success in commerce or the professions.[19]

The eighteenth century: Locke, Rousseau and the early Romantics

Ariès barely strayed beyond the early modern era in his book, which is curious, given that eighteenth-century thinkers came closer than any of their predecessors to our contemporary notions of childhood. They confidently asserted that children are important in their own right, rather than being merely imperfect adults. The historian Margaret Ezell made a case for John Locke and his *Some Thoughts Concerning Education* (1693) as one of the most important influences in changing attitudes towards childhood in the eighteenth century.[20] Locke's book was certainly popular, running through more than a dozen editions before mid-century, and being translated into French, German, Italian, Dutch and Swedish. It also did much to boost the image of the child as a *tabula rasa*, admitting in its final paragraph that it had considered the Gentleman's son for whom it was written 'only as white Paper, or Wax, to be moulded and fashioned as one pleases'.[21] Whether this image can be taken as the opening salvo in the long campaign by the Enlightenment thinkers of the eighteenth century to eradicate what was left of the doctrine of original sin is a moot point. Given the Lockean view that education can make a 'great Difference in Mankind', there is some logic to suggesting that he saw the child as being born neither good or bad. However, W. M. Spellman counters that Locke had by no means shaken off the gloomy perspective offered by the old notion of 'Christian depravity'. The message of *Some Thoughts* was that learning involved a long struggle to teach the child 'to get a Mastery over his Inclinations', and 'submit his Appetite to Reason'. Unfortunately, according to Spellman, Locke always took it for granted that the great unwashed would refuse to live up to their God-given nature as rational beings, and so were doomed to infinite misery.[22]

The book did at least encourage a sympathetic attitude to children (among the favoured few) that was rare in earlier periods. It called for the tutor to observe closely the 'change of Temper' in his pupils, to help them enjoy their studies. It also accepted that he could not expect the same 'Carriage, Seriousness, or Application' from young children as from older ones: 'They must be permitted . . . the foolish and childish Actions suitable to their Years.' In the final analysis Locke by no means escaped a negative conception of childhood. This followed from his desire to develop the capacity to reason in children from an early age, 'even from their very Cradles'. With their characteristic inadvertency, carelessness and gaiety, children needed help: they were 'as weak People under a natural Infirmity'.[23]

The outstanding figure in the reconstruction of childhood during the eighteenth century must therefore be Jean-Jacques Rousseau. He it was, in the words of Peter Coveney, who most forcefully opposed the Christian tradition of original sin with the cult of original innocence in the child.[24] Although his ideas were not always new, he mesmerized readers of his *Emile* with a whole series of paradoxes and provocations. The work oozes radicalism – for the male Emile if not for his mate Sophie – starting with the famous line that 'everything is good as it leaves the hands of the Author of things, everything degenerates in the hands of man'. The child is therefore born innocent, but risks being stifled by 'prejudices, authority, necessity, example, all the social institutions in which we find ourselves submerged'.[25] Rousseau organized the book around a series of stages during childhood. These included an Age of Instinct, during the first three years of life; an Age of Sensations, between 4 and 12; and an Age of Ideas, around puberty. He scorned Locke's advice to reason with children, on the grounds that this faculty would not be fully developed until the early teens. He countered that nature wants children to be children before being adults. Childhood 'has its own ways of seeing, thinking, and feeling', and in particular its own form of reason: a 'sensitive' or 'puerile' reason, as opposed to the 'intellectual' or 'human' reason of the adult. The very young were not to be burdened with distinguishing good from evil.[26] As innocents, they could be left to respond to nature, and then they would do nothing but good. They might cause damage, but not with the intention of doing harm. They could then learn lessons from things rather than from men, having to do without the furniture or windows that they had broken, for example. 'Respect childhood', he admonished, and 'leave nature to act for a long time before you get involved with acting in its place.'[27]

The Romantic conception of childhood, which first appeared during the late eighteenth and early nineteenth centuries, added a subtle twist to the Rousseauist notion of innocence at this stage of life. Rousseau had not anticipated that children would become virtuous during the first twelve years of their lives, merely that a 'negative education' would shelter them from vice. The Romantics, by contrast, depicted children as 'creatures of deeper wisdom, finer aesthetic sensitivity, and a more profound awareness of enduring moral truths', to quote the literary historian David Grylls.[28] The Enlightenment view of childhood as a time for education, and particularly education for boys, yielded to the notion of childhood as a

Joshua Reynolds, *The Age of Innocence*, c.1788.
Plymouth City Museums and Art Gallery (Plympton St. Maurice
Collection)

lost realm that was none the less fundamental to the creation of the
adult self. The upshot was a redefinition of the relationship between
adults and children: it was now the child who could educate the edu-
cator.[29] Bronson Alcott (1799–1888), the educational innovator and
father of the author Louisa May, proclaimed after spending time with
his daughters that 'Childhood hath *Saved* me!'[30]

Artists and writers have left us with numerous vivid images of
Roussueauist and Romantic conceptions of the child. Late in the
eighteenth century, English portrait painters such as Sir Joshua
Reynolds and Thomas Gainsborough broke away from the tradition
of depicting royal and aristocratic children in ways that indicated
future wealth and status rather than immaturity. These artists reflected the increasing separation of the worlds of adulthood and
childhood in the bodies of their subjects, contrasting the innocence
of the child with the experience of the adult. In *The Age of Innocence*
(*c.*1788), Reynolds made his intentions explicit, portraying his great-
niece Offy as a beautiful but demure infant. As Anne Higonnet points

Thomas Lawrence, *Portrait of Mrs John Angerstein and her son John Julius William*, 1799.
Musée d'art et d'histoire, Geneva, photo Maurice Aeschimann.

out, he evidently revelled in her large eyes, creamy flesh and little, dimpled hands, but had her fully covered in a shapeless white dress. Sir Thomas Lawrence followed a similar path with his *Portrait of Mrs John Angerstein and her Son John Julius William* (1799), in which a magnificently sensual mother stands beside her rather dreamy son. Similarly, in the United States, after about 1750 family portraits became less concerned to display children as adults-in-the-making, accepting instead their playfulness and immaturity.[31]

On the literary side, Romantic poets played their part in the 'invention' of childhood innocence. Victor Hugo proclaimed that 'Christopher Columbus only discovered America. I discovered the child!'[32]

William Wordsworth's *Ode. Intimations of Immortality from Recollections of Childhood* (1807) was arguably as powerful an influence on nineteenth-century ideas of childhood as Freud has been on present-day ones. The lines that we are born 'trailing clouds of glory', and that 'Heaven lies about us in our infancy!' were repeatedly quoted, plagiarized and adapted by later writers.[33] What stands out in the poem is the sense of loss of the visionary qualities of the child, 'Nature's Priest', as the years go by:

> Full soon thy Soul shall have her earthly freight,
> And custom lie upon thee with a weight,
> Heavy as frost, and deep almost as life!

The German Romantics produced an equally exalted view of the child. Jean Paul Richter suggested in his *Levana* (1807), a tract on education, that children were 'messengers from paradise', and that 'a single child on earth would appear to us as a strange, angelic, supernatural creature'.[34]

The Romantic view of childhood was far from sweeping all before it. For a start, the older tradition of tainting children with original sin died hard. It was even given a boost in England from the late eighteenth century onwards by the rise of the Evangelical movement. The intensely moralistic Mrs Sherwood wrote in a familiar vein that 'All children are by nature evil, and while they have none but the natural evil principle to guide them, pious and prudent parents must check their naughty passions in any way they have in their power.'[35] Furthermore, the emphasis on childhood innocence had little relevance to the lives of the majority of young people, still being immersed in the world of adults at an early age. The new ideas resonated most powerfully in middle-class circles, where the interest in domesticity and education was particularly developed. They also served as a powerful antidote to the strains and stresses of the French and the industrial revolutions. As Coveney suggested, in the Machine Age the child could readily symbolize Imagination and Sensibility.[36]

Towards a long childhood and adolescence, c.1900

Finally, a number of authorities have plumped for the late nineteenth- and early twentieth-century period as significant in the construction of modern childhood. Viviana Zelizer famously asserted that between the 1870s and the 1930s there emerged in America the economically 'worthless' but emotionally 'priceless' child. By the middle of the nineteenth century, she suggested, the notion of an economically worthless child had already been adopted by the urban middle classes. However, working-class families continued to rely on wages from their children until child labour legislation and compulsory education 'destroyed the class lag'. To encourage the withdrawal of children from the workplace, American reformers promoted a 'sacralization' of childhood. As one of them put it in 1905, to profit from the work of children was to 'touch profanely a sacred thing'. The outcome was a massive increase in the sentimental value of children in both working-class and middle-class circles.[37] Carolyn Steedman has detected a similar 'reconceptualization of childhood' in Britain at the same period. She focuses on the efforts of the social-ist intellectual Margaret McMillan to deploy a new and politicized version of the Romantic child. McMillan modified the original image of innocence and death to one that allowed her to explore the mys-teries of growth and decay. In this way she could highlight the thwarted development of children from the unskilled labouring poor. Her Marigold (of 1911–12) was an evocation of Goethe's Mignon, a strange, deformed child with the same potential to reclaim the sensi-bility of the adults around her.[38]

The years around 1900 were also notable for the 'discovery' of adolescence.[39] The American psychologist G. Stanley Hall was by no means the first thinker to centre a distinct stage of life on puberty. However his massive, two-volume work, *Adolescence* (1904) did much to popularize the concept – surprisingly, in a way, since its grue-somely pedantic style is almost a caricature of 'academic' writing. Hall based his approach to adolescence on the law of recapitulation.[40] In his version, the individual retraces the development of the human race, from animal origins to civilization. Between the ages of 8 and 12, the child represents 'some remote, perhaps pigmoid stage of human evolution'. Adolescence brings a 'new birth', and a transitional stage between childlike savagery and maturity. 'Development is . . . suggestive of some ancient period of storm and stress when old moorings were broken and a higher level attained.'[41] Needless to say, as in the case of childhood, historians have debated how far an awareness of 'adolescence' can be traced back to early modern or even to medieval Europe.[42] Revisionists have cited a number of institutions, nearly all of them male, that fulfilled in the past at least some of the functions – mainly violence and mayhem – that we now attribute to adolescence. These include packs of twelfth-century aristocratic youths in France, apprentice boys in early modern English towns, and the *abbayes*, *capitanages*, *Königreichen*, and similar organizations that were found among youth in much of sixteenth-century Europe.[43] No less importantly, social scientists have noted that adolescence is as much a cultural construct as childhood.[44] Hall thought of 'storm and stress' as a universal characteristic of this stage of life, physiologically determined by the onset of puberty. He thereby ignored the possibility that it might reflect more his own social and cultural environment, and the peculiar pressures facing young people in the modern West. Nevertheless, Hall's thinking did encourage the notion of an extended period of transition between infancy and adulthood. Following his recapitulatory principle, he hoped that children would be indulged in their savagery, their 'tribal, predatory, hunting, fishing, fighting, roving, idle, playing proclivities', adding plaintively, 'if only a proper environment could be provided'. Likewise, he envisaged a long spell of adolescence, from 14 years of age until the mid-twenties, which should give full rein to the contradictory impulses towards enthusiasm and lethargy, euphoria and gloom, selfishness and altruism, and so on, which he perceived at this age.[45]

The heightened interest in defining a prolonged period of childhood and adolescence from the late nineteenth century can partly be explained by the fact that young people were being increasingly segregated from adults at this point, notably in age-graded schools. There was, however, a more sinister backdrop to these discussions: a widespread anxiety over the future. The nineteenth century was self-consciously an age of progress, and yet many people were disturbed by the forces unleashed by the new industrial civilization around them. In the atmosphere of heightened competition towards the end of the century, the older powers in Europe feared being overtaken by new rivals, notably the Germans, Russians, Americans and Japanese. French elites were particularly exercised by the problem of a declining birth rate, or 'depopulation', in the face of a rampant population across the Rhine. Ironically, the Germans soon faced a similar crisis among conservative and religious groups once their birth rate began to decline during the 1890s.[46] The British meanwhile began to feel insecure about their industrial and military prowess, as 'national efficiency' became the order of the day. The Boer War was a deeply humiliating experience for them, as a supposedly invincible imperial power struggled to overcome what was perceived as a rag-tag bunch of farmers. Baden-Powell, founder of the Boy Scouts, worried that the British would go the way of the young Romans and lose their Empire by being 'wishy washy slackers without any go or patriotism in them'.[47]

There was also a more generalized unease in the West over the physical and moral condition of populations living in an advanced, but 'fatigued and sensual', civilization. Historians have explored in some depth the adoption of medical terminology to describe the 'degeneration' of national stock. The press played upon such fears with sensational accounts of crimes by youthful street gangs, symbolized during the 1900s by the menacing figure of the London hooligan or the Parisian *apache*.[48] G. Stanley Hall worried that America, as an 'unhistoric land', was particularly at risk: 'never has youth been exposed to such dangers of both perversion and arrest as in our own land and day'. He pointed in particular to the 'increasing urban life with its temptations, prematurities, sedentary occupations, and passive stimuli'.[49] One obvious way to turn the tide was to look to the health, education and moral welfare of the rising generation: 'the child of today holds the key to the kingdom of the morrow', as a British journal put it in 1910.[50] This was the era of institutions such as the Child Study movement and organized youth movements like the Scouts and the German *Wandervogel*.

It would be satisfying to end by arguing that the wheel has turned full circle since medieval times with the 'disappearance' of childhood during the late twentieth century. Neil Postman followed Ariès in assuming that the idea of childhood is a relatively modern invention, and then attempted to update him (in 1982) by observing that 'Everywhere one looks, it may be seen that the behaviour, language, attitudes, and desires – even the physical appearance – of adults and children are becoming increasingly indistinguishable.' He even cited the rush of publications in the field of childhood history as evidence, on the grounds that historians move in when a social artefact becomes obsolete![51] With even a little hindsight, Postman emerges as a shrewd enough observer of contemporary developments in age relations, notably challenges to the assumption of innocence and vulnerability among children, but his 'disappearance' looks as exaggerated as the 'discovery' posited by Ariès.[52] A more plausible approach is surely to retain in the forefront the protean forms of childhood as a social construct.

Conclusion

Various historians doubtless risk a somewhat overblown claim to the 'discovery' of childhood, in a bid to dramatize the significance of their findings. Any long-run survey of this area is likely to make a mockery of attempts to limit the emergence of key insights to one period. The cultural history of childhood has its turning points, but it also meanders over the centuries: a child might be thought of as depraved in the early twentieth century as well as in the early Middle Ages. On the one hand, then, the long-term shift to a pluralistic urban society favoured the gradual emergence of a prolonged version of childhood and adolescence. The middle classes, whether in twelfth-century Italy or Britain during the Industrial Revolution, accepted the need for an extensive education and a certain segregation of young people from the world of adults. On the other hand, cultural influences such as Christianity and the Enlightenment promoted series of debates that took a cyclical rather than a linear form. It remains as our final task to pull together the themes hinted so far.

3

Some Themes in the Cultural History of Childhood

Running like a red thread through the historical literature is the contradictory nature of ideas and emotions concerning childhood. It is striking how often the words *ambivalence* and *ambiguity* appear in relation to widely different periods in history. This is perhaps hardly surprising if one assumes that societies are likely to harbour competing conceptions of childhood. A number of dichotomous images emerge from the debates on childhood hinted at in the previous chapters, as people thought about the 'extent, nature and significance of childhood'.[1] Did children come into the world innocent, or with the stain of original sin upon them? Were children like a blank sheet at birth, or did they arrive with a number of innate characteristics already in place? Should they experience a 'short' or a 'long' childhood: in other words, should they be cosseted in their families or launched into the world of adults? And, on a rather different tack, was the main focus on age or gender relations: on children or on boys and girls? One can readily identify extremist stances on these issues, and shifts back and forth along the spectrum at different periods of history. Yet many commentators fall somewhere in between the extremes. It is easy to waver between thinking of infants as little angels and little devils, or to feel obliged to protect a child and to fear being exhausted by it.

Depravity/innocence

The trouble started with Adam and Eve: to quote the psalm, 'Behold, I was shapen in iniquity; and in sin did my mother conceive me'.

The Christian doctrine of original sin did not in fact emerge until St Augustine (354–430) became embroiled in the Pelagian heresy during the early fourth century. He concluded that the taint of sin was passed down from generation to generation by the act of creation. In his *Confessions* he reflected that in the sight of God 'no man is free from sin, not even a child who has lived only one day on earth'. The only way by which original sin could be remitted was through the sacrament of baptism. As the literary historian Robert Pattison observes, the Augustinian position 'brought down upon the child the great weight of Christian dogma'.[2] The child was now seen as a wilful creature and, in this respect, no different from an adult. Infants who were unfortunate enough to die unbaptized would therefore be consigned to the flames of hell. Augustine was not entirely unsympathetic to children: he objected to the custom of 'hitting an innocent child with the fist if he runs between two people walking together'.[3] Even so, his firm line on infants being born in sin generally prevailed until the twelfth century over the opposing one of infant innocence.

It also reappeared in a new form when Luther and other Protestants of the Reformation reasserted the importance of original sin. A German sermon dating from the 1520s contended that infant hearts craved after 'adultery, fornication, impure desires, lewdness, idol worship, belief in magic, hostility, quarrelling, passion, anger, strife, dissension, factiousness, hatred, murder, drunkenness, gluttony' and more. Luther himself proved an 'elusive witness' on the nature of the young. On the one hand, he asserted that original sin was as deep-seated in the child as in the adult. On the other, he accepted the innocence of children during the first five or six years of their lives: 'God's little fools' as he affectionately called them.[4] English and American Puritans resolved the issue by asserting that children were assuredly born with evil in their hearts, yet might be likened to the familiar image of 'narrow mouth'd vessels', which were 'ready to receive good or evil drop by drop', or to young twigs which could be bent the right or wrong way. The eighteenth-century Presbyterian Samuel Davies, writing in Virginia, wondered whether his son was an 'embryo-angel' or an 'infant fiend'.[5] The Jansenists, sometimes described as the Catholic Puritans, were no less vehement in condemning the corruption of children than their Protestant counterparts. From their stronghold at Port-Royal one of them thundered that 'the effects of lusting after flesh, which are not extinguished in us until death, are all the more violent in them [children] because their reason is more feeble and they have as yet no experience of the world'. Paradoxically, though, their very weakness made children model Christians, since they were incapable of putting into practice their evil plans, or of resisting the efforts of those responsible for them. The faith that the infant placed in his parents provided an excellent example for adults in their relationship with God.[6]

The belief in the original innocence of children was equally rooted in the Christian tradition. Jesus Christ himself was quoted by St Matthew as saying 'Verily I say unto you, Except ye be converted, and become as little children, ye shall not enter into the Kingdom of Heaven.' Odd voices were to be heard from the monasteries in praise of childhood during the early Middle Ages. At this point opinions were particularly polarized on whether children were channels of diabolical or divine influence. The historian Janet Nelson draws attention to the way stories of the conversion of future saints during their early years highlighted the ambiguity in the Church's attitude to childhood. The underlying conception of childhood, she observes, oscillated between two extremes as children's behaviour was taken to reveal either good or bad supernatural power.[7] The first major assault on the Augustinian position had to await the twelfth century, when Peter Abelard and Peter Lombard denied that unbaptized infants went to hell. St Thomas Aquinas (in the thirteenth century) settled on a special *limbus puerorum* for the souls of infants, where they were spared the flames but deprived of the Beatific Vision. What childhood had in its favour for the medieval churchman was its supposed ignorance of sexual lust. With his weak 'sexual movements', Bartholomew the Englishman wrote about 1230, the child (*puer*) is named after the purity (*puritas*) of his natural innocence.[8]

Protestants no less than Catholics could take this line: Philip Greven found that in America during the seventeenth and eighteenth centuries fiercely 'evangelical' parents were complemented by 'moderates', who believed wholeheartedly in the innocence of their offspring.[9] Indeed, the association of childhood with innocence became deeply embedded within Western culture, particularly after the Romantics had made their mark in the nineteenth century. Yet it was one thing to proclaim the angelic nature of childhood in a poem, quite another to create well-rounded characters in a novel, or deal with street urchins who were far from innocent. Charles Dickens may occasionally have lapsed into sentimentality when describing children, as in *The Old Curiosity Shop* (Oscar Wilde is supposed to have quipped that one must have a heart of stone to read the death of Little Nell without laughing) and *David Copperfield*. But, as Peter Coveney has observed, in the strongest Dickensian depictions of childhood there is a powerful mingling of pathos and idealization with the squalid. The sentimental atmosphere surrounding the Victorian child would in any case be dissipated by the appearance of Freud's theories concerning the human personality.[10]

Nature/nurture

If medieval writers paid scant attention to children, this was partly because they did not always share our modern view that the early years of life are critical for character formation. Doris Desclais Berkvam uses texts from twelfth- and thirteenth-century France to show that moralists from this period felt that the nurturing of a child would only be effective if it was in harmony with its nature, this latter determined by class and gender rather than individual circumstances. Should a noble boy happen to be adopted by peasants or merchants, his true *nature* would out, as he inevitably reacted against an unsuitable environment or *norreture*. Thus in *Tristan de Nanteuil* Doon reveals his noble lineage by spending far beyond the means of the poor foresters who are raising him, and by killing his foster-brother. Surprisingly to us, the author treats all this as entirely acceptable, heroic even, for a budding knight. Conversely, Middle High German texts assume that a base character like Judas, brought up to be a noble, is bound to turn out badly. Who can argue with the comment from the narrator that 'anyone who takes a leopard skin and sews it over a donkey, expecting it to jump like a leopard, is no smarter than a very young child'? To the medieval mind, according to Berkvam, the nature one is born with is the most important influence on life, the raw material without which the finest nurturing will be wasted. It suited the hereditary aristocracy all too well to promote this line on lineage. They were even willing to believe that a youth would respond almost instantly to instruction in his true calling, as Parzival became an accomplished knight relatively late in life after a few words of instruction from Gurnemanz.[11] Yet this heavy stress on nature did not go entirely unchallenged. The later Middle Ages at least were familiar with the notion of the child as soft wax, which could be moulded in various ways, or as a tender branch which needed to be trained in the right direction. Educators identified childhood as the period in life when people were most receptive to teaching, and hence stressed the importance of providing good examples for the young to follow.[12]

The balance of nature versus nurture gradually shifted towards the latter from the Renaissance onwards. The middling and upper classes in particular began to pay more attention to the nurturing of the young, and the detailed advice on child-rearing and education provided by moralists. The idea that 'the hand that rocks the cradle shapes the destiny of society' became received wisdom. John Locke made the stirring assertion that 'of all the Men we meet with, Nine Parts of Ten are what they are, Good or Evil, useful or not, by their

Education'.[13] At the same time, he made some concession to hereditary influences by noting the need to prescribe remedies for the
'various Tempers, different Inclinations and particular Defaults, that
are to be found in Children'.[14] During the Enlightenment period,
there were high hopes that various 'wild' children found alone in the
forests would throw some light on this issue. In the event, notably
with the so-called Wild Boy of the Aveyron, the failure of such
children even to acquire a spoken language was disappointing for
those with a Lockean faith in the powers of education.[15]

Various scientific developments during the late nineteenth and
early twentieth centuries brought a formidable reaction against the
environmentalist strain in social thought. To put it crudely, scientists
denied that the child entered the world as a blank sheet, and began
to ask what was in its genes. Their assertion of the hereditary nature
of intelligence had important implications for the question of who
should have access to education at various levels. In 1906 Karl
Pearson spelt out the fundamental premise, standing Locke on his
head by observing that 'the influence of environment is nowhere
more than one-fifth that of heredity, and quite possibly not one-tenth
of it.'[16] American psychologists made the early running in this area.
They latched on to the tests of mental ability among children devised
in Paris by Alfred Binet (1857–1911), but used them for purposes he
had never envisaged. In 1905 Binet published his tests to identify
pupils performing so poorly at school that they needed some form of
special education. The American versions had far more ambitious
aims. They assumed that the test scores measured an 'innate intelligence'. It followed in their thinking that all children could be sorted
on a single scale by an IQ test, educated according to their inheritance, and later directed into jobs appropriate to their biology. These
American pioneers further assumed that there existed significant differences in general intelligence between various races. Lewis Terman
wrote that 'border-line' deficiency (an IQ in the 70–80 range) was
'very common among Spanish-Indian and Mexican families of the
Southwest and also among negroes'. He therefore envisaged that
children from these racial groups be segregated into special classes,
where they would not have to 'master abstractions', and be turned
into 'efficient workers'.[17]

In England Cyril Burt was thinking along similar lines, though it
was the supposed differences in average intelligence between social
classes rather than races that concerned him. Finding (from a very
small sample of forty-three cases) that boys from upper-class
families in Oxford performed better in his tests than those with a
lower-middle-class background, he concluded in 1909 that parental
intelligence may be inherited. Later in his career he argued that an
elaborate education would be wasted on most of the population, since
it could never develop much in the way of intelligence. His main pri-

ority was to identify and nurture through the education system that 'small handful of individuals who are endowed by nature with outstanding gifts of ability and character'.[18] The most recent tendency in this debate, let it be noted, is to stress the interaction between nature and nurture, rather than to prioritize one over the other.

Independence/dependence

Humans are born helpless, and when they become independent, with a household of their own, they are deemed to have left childhood and youth behind them. Some never achieve full independence, as in the case of slaves and servants, and so suffer the indignity of being thought of partly as a 'child' for the whole of their lives. Conversely, older children become less and less dependent on their families, leading to a certain ambiguity in their position.

As late as the nineteenth century, the majority of children in the West were encouraged to begin supporting themselves at an early stage. The age of 7 was an informal turning point when the offspring of peasants and craftsmen were generally expected to start helping their parents with little tasks around the home, the farm or the workshop. By their early teens they were likely to be working beside adults or established in an apprenticeship. They might well have left home by this stage, to become a servant or an apprentice of some sort.[19] This is not to say they were treated as miniature adults, but they were expected to grow up fast. How fast was a matter of uncertainty, as divergences in the age of majority indicate. Jerome Kroll found that the legal definition of minor in the Middle Ages varied considerably 'across time, nations, classes within nations, and for various purposes'.[20] From the twelfth century onwards, as medieval pedagogy began to pay attention to the training of laymen, various authorities stressed the importance of learning a trade early in life. Thomas Aquinas noted that 'to the extent that something is difficult, so much the more must a man grow accustomed to it from childhood'.[21] Medieval thinkers reflected this view of the child as an adult-in-the-making by favouring child prodigies above all others. The Puritans of colonial America also expected a great deal from children. Fearing that they might die at any moment, they taught them to read as early as possible so that they could study the Bible.[22] There is too the question of how early young people began to have a sex life in the past. It may be that low rates of illegitimacy during the seventeenth and eighteenth centuries provide evidence of 'sexual austerity' outside marriage. Alternatively, and in our view more persuasively, Jean-Louis Flandrin argues in the French case that youthful libido found various outlets short of full intercourse. Young people could indulge in homosexuality, masturbation and intimate courting customs such as peasant 'bundling'.[23]

Since the sixteenth and seventeenth centuries, the 'middle-class' desire has been to isolate children, and later adolescents, from the world of adults. Young people have been increasingly 'infantilized' by efforts to keep them out of the workplace, to repress their sexuality and to prolong their education in schools and colleges. The child, as a weak and vulnerable being, was to be constantly supervised, detached from the temptations of the world and subject to rigorous discipline. Young males, for example, were thought to need a series of demanding exercises and detailed rules to regulate their conduct: hence the learning of languages was considered particularly suitable for them.[24] However, this eventually led to tensions between a Romantic-inspired vision of children as charming and helpless, and the realities of life for young people.

It was one thing for a Rousseau or a G. Stanley Hall to recommend that the young remain continent until their twenties, quite another to prevent them masturbating or experimenting with the opposite sex. From the late sixteenth century onwards, particularly in Protestant areas such as Britain, Holland and north Germany, a number of voices threatened those indulging in 'onanism' with all sorts of debilitating diseases and insanity. The very title of the famous *Onania, or the Heinous Sin of Self-Pollution, and All Its Frightful Consequences, in Both Sexes, Considered. With Spiritual and Physical Advice for Those Who Have Already Injur'd Themselves by This Abominable Practice* (1716) gives an indication of the opprobrium involved. There were even sad letters to eighteenth-century medical experts like Tissot in Lausanne in which the writers reported symptoms and diseases which they attributed to years of masturbating. None the less, the desperate nature of some of the proposed remedies suggests that moralists were aware they were fighting a losing battle. In France, during the 1840s, the scientist F. V. Raspail wanted all school children to wear drawers impregnated with camphor; a Dr Demeaux hoped to shame masturbators with regular nude inspections in the schools.[25] Middle-class reformers in Victorian England struggled in similar fashion with the contradiction between their notion of the sexual innocence of children and the hard-nosed choices forced on young prostitutes.[26] By the turn of the twentieth century, Freud and several others had come to admit the reality of child sexuality.[27] Efforts to prevent children earning a wage also clashed with peasant and working-class notions of early independence. These tensions came to a head in many countries during the nineteenth and early twentieth centuries, as governments attempted to impose the new model by means of factory legislation and compulsory schooling. With hindsight, as Arlene Skolnick observes, it may be that developmental psychologists have consistently underestimated the capacities of children, and the resemblance between the minds of children and those of adults.[28]

Age/sex

How did people in the past combine their perception of age (a child or adolescent as opposed to an adult) with that of sex (a male as opposed to a female)? In other words, did they have a sexless (or androgynous) child figure in mind, as opposed to a boy or a girl? During the Middle Ages, when they used the word 'child' in written sources, they often appear to have had a boy in mind. In the Occitan literature of southern France during the twelfth and thirteenth centuries, Linda Paterson found girls to be 'virtually invisible'. Middle High German texts paid some attention to them, but in general male lives were more varied and interesting. Ariès noted that the first attempts to distinguish children from adults by means of costume during the seventeenth century concerned boys: the dress of girls remained close to that of a woman. Boys, he suggested, 'were the first specialized children'.[29]

The coming of the Romantic movement during the late eighteenth century overturned the prevailing mode in literary sources of concentrating on the rearing of young males from the elite. There was even a tendency for the stock character in Victorian fiction of the child redeemer, who reconciles estranged members of families or helps adults to see the errors of their ways, to be thought of as a girl. One thinks of Sissy Jupe, Little Nell or Florence Dombey in the work of Dickens.[30] Advice on the dress, diet and exercise appropriate for children and infants in Victorian England minimized sex differences. As Deborah Gorham makes clear, however, parents were relaxed about this because they were more certain than we are today about innate differences between males and females. By playing together, it was hoped that 'the girl's weakness [would be] strengthened, and the boy's roughness softened'.[31] The ideal of 'manliness' for the middle classes during the early nineteenth century has also been characterized as 'androgynous', in contradistinction to the 'masculine' version that held sway in the late nineteenth century.[32] The programme of 'godliness and good learning' developed in the English public schools during the 1820s and 1830s by influential figures such as Thomas Arnold at Rugby was heavily laced with conventionally 'feminine' virtues. Tom Brown, eponymous hero of the novel by Thomas Hughes, was, for all his prowess on the games field, not afraid to kneel down and say his prayers in front of the other boys.[33] For a while, then, the child was conceived in some circles as an androgynous figure. Goethe's Mignon was a precursor, the strange young acrobat who bemused the observer Wilhelm Meister following a brief encounter on the stairs at an inn:

> A little short silk waistcoat with slit Spanish-style sleeves and long close-fitting trousers with puffs looked very well on the child . . . He looked at the figure in astonishment and could not make up his mind whether he should declare it to be a boy or a girl.[34]

James Kincaid goes as far as to argue that the 'perfect erotic child' of twentieth-century American culture is an androgynous figure, short-haired, active and even aggressive when nominally female, and long-haired, soft-featured and passive when nominally male.[35]

Conclusion

Most societies in the West divide the human life span into a series of 'ages', each with its particular characteristics, rather than seeing it as a single trajectory. Such schema take some fairly obvious biological feature of the age in question and graft on to it a series of more general qualities. Thus the infant in Shakespeare's seven ages of man, 'mewling and puking in the nurse's arms', might be an Augustinian sinner, out to dominate those around it, or a Romantic innocent, as yet uncorrupted by civilization. This chapter has argued that a repertoire of themes has been used to construct and reconstruct images of the child and the adolescent in the West. This of course is to deny that any one period, be it the sixth or the sixteenth centuries, has managed to discover some supposed timeless qualities associated with childhood – least of all 'innocence' and dependence. The cultural influences on the construction of childhood have been many and varied, with inputs from Classical antiquity, the barbarian invaders, humanism, and above all Christianity. Over the long term, one can certainly discern a growing interest in discussing childhood and adolescence, which has been linked here to various pressures emerging in the process of economic development. One can also see a more positive image of the child coming to the fore, as the emphasis on original sin declined gradually from the eighteenth century onwards. These developments would influence, and in turn be influenced by, child-rearing methods, child labour, maternal welfare measures and education.

PART II

Growing up: Relations with Parents and Peers

Parents have received a bad press in much of the historical literature. Lloyd deMause went further than most in a ringing denunciation of child-rearing in the past:

> The history of childhood is a nightmare from which we have only recently begun to awaken. The further back in history one goes, the lower the level of child care, and the more likely children are to be killed, abandoned, beaten, terrorized and sexually abused.

For his critics, deMause had in effect written little more than a history of child abuse. He was, however, in good company during the 1970s. Lawrence Stone asserted that during the sixteenth and seventeenth centuries children in England were 'neglected, brutally treated, and even killed'. Edward Shorter contrasted the indifference of mothers to the development and happiness of infants in traditional society with the 'good mothering' of the modern period. Elisabeth Badinter in her turn wrote that maternal love is 'uncertain, fragile and imperfect', with the result that devotion to children ebbed and flowed down the centuries. These authors generally consider the eighteenth century to have been an important turning point, as might be expected from the momentous changes in ideas about childhood at this period. DeMause, for example, talks in terms of 'the great transition in parent–child relations' during the eighteenth century – though he doubted whether even in the middle of the twentieth century most parents had the emotional maturity necessary to see children as persons separate from themselves.[1]

More recent studies of parent–child relationships have generally taken a more tolerant line on past practices.[2] Steven Ozment deflated earlier claims by observing that 'surely the hubris of an age reaches a certain peak when it accuses another age of being incapable of loving its children properly.'[3] Historians have attempted to distinguish more carefully between practices considered in the best interests of the children at the time, even though they might be considered wrong-headed today (swaddling, for example), and others, such as child murder, condemned outright in the past as in the present. The general drift of the revisionists' argument is that continuities in parenting are more in evidence than any dramatic turning points. Examples of cruel and abusive parents can be found in any age, they suggest, but the vast majority always felt affection for their offspring, and did the best they could for them. Linda Pollock, for example, denied that children were neglected or systematically ill-treated in the past because of an alleged inability to appreciate the needs of the young. Her bold counter-assertion, based on British and American material, was that there were 'very few changes in parental care and child life from the 16th to the 19th century in the home'.[4] This is all very well, notably in the efforts to understand what parents were trying to achieve, but the danger is surely of underestimating the influence of conflicting ideas about childhood. The logic for parents who considered infants as evil little creatures was to 'break the will' of their offspring, while those who thought children basically innocent were more likely to allow some spontaneity. There remains the problem of finding evidence to settle what appear to be two plausible but contradictory cases which of course is not easily overcome. None the less, an interesting agenda for debate now exists, which we will explore in the following four chapters.

4

Parent–Child Relations:
The First Stages

The desire for children

To begin at the beginning: were children wanted? The answer from historians is that married couples at all periods generally did hope to have children, but not too many of them. There was no shortage of warnings to would-be parents of what was in store for them. The fourteenth-century French poet Eustache Deschamps wrote with evident relish, 'Happy is he who has no children, for babies mean nothing but crying and stench; they give only trouble and anxiety.' Medieval Christianity was ambivalent when confronting procreation. Its highest ideal was clearly the ascetic one of renouncing marriage and family life – one that its priests, monks and nuns were required to follow. To help them prepare for this burden, an early English text, the *Hali Meidenhad*, railed against marriage, and 'that loathsome act, that beastly copulation, that shameless coition, that foulness of stinking ordure and uncomely deed'.[1] The Gnostic version of Christianity and its successors took this position to its logical extreme and considered all sexual activity to be inherently evil. There was even a pleasing vision, expressed by a Cathar in the Pyrenean village of Montaillou around the turn of the fourteenth century, of all God's creatures gathered together in heaven, once they had agreed to remain barren. Certainly, more orthodox Catholic churchmen during the Middle Ages liked to stress the distractions to study and good works caused by having noisy, dirty children in the house. John Chrysostom advised women contemplating marriage to ponder the dangers of childbirth, the risk of sterility or an excessively large number of children, and the feeling of responsibility for all the misfortunes of a family. At the same time, the Church recognized that most people would not wish to choose the rigours of a celibate life. Although it never hid its preference for chastity, it also valued marriage and children born in wedlock. Sermons on this topic during the central Middle Ages consistently stressed the essential goodness of marriage, the begetting of children and the sacramental character of marriage. Alanus ab Insulis preached,

> How great is the worth of marriage, which had its beginning in paradise, which removes the evil of incontinence, which embraces within itself a heavenly sacrament, which preserves the faith of the marriage bed, which maintains between the husband and wife an undivided life together, which preserves children from dishonour, which preserves carnal intercourse from guilt!

In short, people could follow the biblical injunction to 'grow and multiply' with the encouragement of their priests.[2]

How the mass of the population in medieval times responded to such a climate of ideas is difficult to determine. It may be that the jaundiced view of sexuality espoused by the early Church Fathers, and their association of original sin with sexual sin, haunted some unfortunate men and women to the extent that they became impotent or frigid. On the whole, though, medievalists are inclined to assert that most people were content to leave chastity to priests, monks and nuns (or, in the case of Cathars, to the 'perfects'). They assume that couples were eager to have children, or at least dreaded the prospect of being childless even more. A homily delivered in Montaillou makes the Devil say, 'You will have children. And you will rejoice more for one child, when you have one, than for all the peace you now enjoy in Paradise.'[3] Some of the names given to children also indicate that children were counted as a blessing: the 'gifts from God' found in Tuscany, such as Diomildiedi and Deodato, or their French equivalents, Dieudonné and Amédée ('loved by God').[4]

Much of the evidence cited by historians comes in the form of the huge repertoire of medical and magical measures available throughout Europe to promote fertility. Certain foods were recommended (with no great subtlety in the symbolism, let it be said): men, for example, were to concentrate on anything which would heat them up, notably chestnuts, carrots, leeks and asparagus. Women meanwhile could take potions made from a variety of substances, mandrake being a particular favourite, or a suppository of laudanum. Advice to Anglo-Saxon women eager to conceive included finding a bone in a hart's heart or belly and tying it to her arm. People at all levels of medieval society invoked holy relics to ward off sterility, such as the girdle of the Virgin, or the foreskin of Jesus Christ (there was a choice of at least fourteen in the West), and visited sacred springs, fountains, stones and groves. The parents of the fourteenth-century St Nicholas of Tolentino had their prayers for a son answered when an angel appeared in a dream and commanded them to go the shrine of St Nicholas of Bari.[5] In Tuscany, the custom was to give married women little figures of the Christ child, the so called *bambini*, as fertility devices. Couples were counselled to follow certain rules in the sexual act. They were to adopt the missionary position during intercourse, and the woman was to rest for a while afterwards while the sperm came to life. Following Galen and the 'two-seed' theory of procreation, they also had to ensure that both the man and the woman came to orgasm. A further set of rituals was designed to help couples conceive either a boy or a girl – usually the former. Boys were more likely to be conceived in the morning, girls in the evening. Drinking thistle juice was good for the womb, and for the conception of a male; so too were the sexual organs of a hare, when dried, powdered and dissolved in wine. Once pregnant, mothers-to-be were advised to pay attention to their diet, Bartholomew the Englishman recommending in his *De proprietatibus rerum* (1230) that they avoid heavy meals and too much salt. They could also invoke the help of the Virgin Mary or a special saint: the latter varied between regions, but St Leonard and St Margaret were particularly favoured. Medievalists are surely right to suggest that these findings cast doubt on easy assumptions about widespread indifference to children during the Middle Ages.[6]

From the twelfth century onwards, there were signs that the Catholic Church was softening its line on procreation. The historian Doris Desclais Berkvam points to a growing devotion among Catholics to the Virgin Mary, the mother of Christ, and speculates that this may have encouraged a more positive view of maternity. None the less, old ideas continued to flourish among the ecclesiastical hierarchy: in 1563, for example, the Council of Trent affirmed the superiority of virginity to marriage, and clerical celibacy to clerical marriage. Catholic humanists like Erasmus and Protestant reformers were more forthright in their celebration of the joys of marriage and domesticity. Martin Luther proclaimed the production and raising of children a central responsibility of all Christians. The Puritans of sixteenth- and seventeenth-century England and New England took all this to heart, being second to none in promoting married love.[7] It is perhaps not surprising that Linda Pollock, using British and American autobiographies and diaries from the early modern and modern periods, found that most people rejoiced at the birth of a child. She did unearth the odd character who resented his children, notably the novelist Evelyn Waugh. Otherwise, reactions to a birth ranged from a dry recording of the event to an emotional welcome, the vast majority of both men and women veering towards 'delight and pleasure'.

Among the Americans, for example, William Byrd (1674–1744) noted in his diary humble thanks to God 'for so great a blessing' on the birth of a son, while Bronson Alcott (1799–1888) recorded that 'Joy, gratitude, hope, and affection, were all mingled in our feeling' when his first child, a daughter, was born.[8] As in the medieval period, there was a variety of possible motives for having children: they might seal the bond of love between a man and a woman, assure the family succession, provide pleasurable company, and hold out the prospect of security in old age and infirmity.[9]

Measures to control fertility

Not all births were welcome, however, even within marriage. Poorer families always struggled to feed the extra mouths that appeared, and mothers often felt worn out by repeated childbearing. Hester Thrale (1741–1821) wrote in her diary: 'this is a horrible Business indeed: five little Girls too, & breeding again, & Fool enough to be proud of it! Oh Idiot! What should I want more Children for?'[10] Since antiquity, societies, or groups within society, have had various mechanisms to control their fertility. Breeding at levels close to what is biologically possible has been the exception rather than the rule in the West. In the first place, social customs could influence the proportions of women of childbearing age who were married. An oft-cited paper by the demographer John Hajnal has noted that west of a line running from St Petersburg to Trieste a distinctive 'European marriage pattern' prevailed. It was characterized by a high age at marriage (generally over 24 for women) and a high proportion of people who never married at all (at least 10 or even 15 per cent of women).[11] This means that by the eighteenth century the western part of Europe had experienced some kind of 'Malthusian' revolution, from early and universal marriage to a system which encouraged women to delay marriage for at least ten years after they had reached puberty. With illegitimacy rare until the later part of the century, the effect was to prevent women conceiving for approximately one-third of their childbearing years.

Societies also had ways to alter levels of marital fertility. Even within the fifteen or so years during which married women in western Europe were able to bear children, there were a number of constraints on fertility in medieval and early modern Europe. Canon law required couples to avoid intercourse at various times including Sundays, Wednesdays and Fridays, and during Lent, Advent, Easter and Pentecost – though most of the peasantry were probably blissfully unaware of such taboos, or wilfully ignored them. An extended period of lactation tended to space out pregnancies, and so too did undernourishment. It is possible that during the Middle Ages couples in certain milieux were already attempting some form of birth control. In fifteenth-century Tuscany, to take one of the rare cases that has come to light, David Herlihy has found some indirect evidence of contraceptive practices. The records show an earlier decline in the fertility of married women in Florence compared to those in the surrounding countryside: around the age of 35 about half of the urban wives appeared barren, as opposed to less than one-third in the countryside. Within the town, wives of the wealthy merchant elite showed no sign of any controls on fertility, while those from middle-class and poor households did. Herlihy concludes that 'families with limited resources wanted limited numbers of babies, and somehow achieved that goal'.[12] By the late Middle Ages scientific and medical treatises were making known a whole repertoire of recipes which claimed to aid contraception and abortion, including the pessaries and suppositories passed down from Roman and Greek sources, and the potions preferred by the Germans and the Celts. In Montaillou, during a seduction, the priest Pierre Clergue produced what his mistress Béatrice de Planissoles described as a 'herb wrapped up in a piece of linen' on a cord: probably a magic amulet, or possibly a pessary.[13] It may be that, beyond the educated elite, women in particular were passing down the generations the detailed knowledge required to administer herbal contraceptives and abortifacients. As John M. Riddle wrote recently, the effectiveness of these herbs depended on knowing harvest times, methods of preparation, the amount to be taken and the proper time to do so. However, a more plausible conclusion must surely be that these early contraceptive measures were very hit-and-miss affairs.[14] Meanwhile, during the early fourteenth century, theologians in various parts of western Europe were complaining of the sexual practices which allowed sex to be indulged in for pleasure rather than procreation, such as sodomy and coitus interruptus.[15] Many of these techniques may have been largely deployed outside marriage, as in the case of Pierre Clergue and Béatrice, but a lack of evidence means one can only speculate.

The early modern period brought more efforts in some circles to prevent births, as opposed to merely postponing or spacing them. However, a general decline in fertility would have to await the late nineteenth century in western Europe and the United States, and the early twentieth-century period in eastern Europe. The reasons for the shift in marital fertility are not entirely clear. One possibility is that middle-class parents were finding that they had a better chance of meeting heightened expectations on child rearing and education with a smaller family. Workers meanwhile were being pushed in a similar direction by reduced opportunities for child labour, the appearance of factory legislation and compulsory education. German workers mentioned improving their own position as well as that of their children. A master mechanic from Berlin informed a researcher in 1916: 'We want to get ahead, and our daughter should have things better than my wife and sisters did'; while a wagon builder felt that 'Nowadays a person can't educate more than two children properly'.[16] None the less, considerable variations between regions, ethnic groups and social classes continued during the nineteenth century. In France, regions such as Brittany, the north, and the Lyonnais were conspicuous for high fertility, while in Germany, it was peripheral areas such as parts of the Rhineland, Württemberg, Bavaria and West Prussia that stood out from the other states and provinces. Catholics tended to have higher levels of fertility than Protestants and especially Jews, if the German case during the late nineteenth and early twentieth century is anything to go by. And if, say, civil servants and people in the liberal professions had a tendency to limit births, coal-mining areas were well known for their large families, a consequence of limited opportunities for women's work outside the home.[17] In the long term, then, there was the paradox that when parents began to consider children important they had fewer of them.

Delivering the baby

Childbirth was a trying time for women: the historian Mireille Laget talked in terms of their 'ancestral dread' of the ordeal.[18] The least fortunate mothers at all periods bore their infants alone: servant girls desperately trying to conceal their condition, or peasant women caught by surprise in the fields. Russian women seem to have had a particular concern to protect their privacy, sometimes retiring alone to a separate room even when a midwife was available.[19] Most mothers managed their delivery at home in the company of other women. In fact, childbirth remained something of a female mystery until the eighteenth century, although husbands might be involved in an isolated farmstead, or during a difficult birth. The twelfth-century poet Chrétien de Troyes even had the King of England deliver a baby on his own, to the evident discomfort of his wife:

> Mais de çou est moult esmarie
> Que de feme n'a point d'aïe,
> Dont ele grant mestier eust,
> Qui mix d'ome aidier li seüst,
> Mais tant estoient de gent loing
> Que nule feme a cest besoing
> N'i peüst mie a tans venir;

But she was very upset
Not to have the help of a woman,
Of which she was greatly in need,
Because she could have assisted her better than a man,
However, they were so far away from any other human being
That no woman for this task
Could arrive in time to help her.[20]

Husbands were expected to be on hand, but they were generally not welcome in the birthing chamber itself. Physicians, however, were sometimes called to attend a birth. There are, for example, various references to their presence in fifteenth-century Florence, perhaps a reflection of the precocious development of the profession in the city. Everywhere, though, physicians and surgeons appear as a last resort, brought in only when either the mother or the baby was in dire peril. Specialized 'men midwives' appeared in the eighteenth century, distinguished by their willingness to use forceps and other instruments to help with a difficult birth. However, they were largely confined to Britain and its American colonies, and even in these countries they made little impact beyond the towns and a wealthy elite. Educated physicians also began to attend births in upper- and middle-class homes as a matter of routine in these two countries from the late eighteenth century onwards, undermining the role of midwives and other women in these circles. Meanwhile, ethnic immigrant communities, poor whites and blacks in America, and the urban and rural poor in England, remained faithful to traditional procedures.[21] For the most part, then, the baby came into the world at the hands of female relatives and friends of the mother, and, most importantly, a 'good mother'. This was an older woman, almost invariably married and with children herself, who had revealed some competence at delivering babies.[22] In nineteenth-century Russia this *povitukha* was well versed in the rituals and prayers valued by village women, but was also prepared to help with household chores for two or three days around the birth. For this reason, peasants obviously turned to her rather than to the new medically trained midwives.[23]

Professional midwives have in fact been traced as far back as the thirteenth century in certain towns. Some European states made particular efforts to regulate and license midwives during the early modern period, notably in Germany and the Netherlands. Many of the women had undergone some form of training, such as an extended apprenticeship, but they readily shaded into the ranks of the 'good mothers'. Otherwise, initiatives to improve the education of women in the arts of midwifery would have to await the eighteenth century, most famously with the doughty campaign by Madame Du Coudray in France.[24] By the early twentieth century, Britain and

America were conspicuous for their lag behind continental Europe in the training and regulation of midwives. Their custom of relying more on doctors than midwives had its drawbacks: physicians might ensure a faster and safer delivery, but they were also under pressure to 'perform' their art, with the attendant risk of excessive intervention. The medical historian Irvine Loudon has recently noted the impressive record of maternal care in a number of western European and Scandinavian countries during the twentieth century, which he attributes to their emphasis on home deliveries by trained midwives.[25]

It follows that the village women relying on traditional lore were perfectly capable of managing a normal birth. Their policy of letting nature take its course had much to recommend it. However, they were poorly equipped to cope with the small minority of cases when complications arose. Peter Boaistuau described in graphic detail what happened in the sixteenth century when midwives failed and 'Chirurgians, Mediciners, and Barbars' had to 'dismember the children and pull them out by pieces', and sometimes 'to open the poor innocent mother alive, and put iron tools in her body, yea to murder her, for to have her fruit'. Not surprisingly under these conditions, it was common in the Christian tradition to stress the redemptive quality of labour pains for women, and to link man's bloody and painful entrance into this world with the 'image and figure of sin'.[26] By the eighteenth century medical opinion was becoming increasingly critical of many customary practices, yet the popular culture did act consistently to try to preserve the lives of mother and child.[27] The women prepared the chamber where the birth would take place with much care. In a wealthy household they could drape it with white silk, stoke up a good fire and lay in all the sheets, bandages and cloths that would be required. The poor had to make do as best they could, in the main room within the house or, if necessary, in a stable, barn or (in Russia) bath house, but they too would provide warmth and some rudimentary material for a bath, cleaning up, and so on. Peasant women closed windows and sealed crevices to keep out unwelcome draughts – and evil spirits. For medical opinion this eventually became known as the 'suffocation method'. In nineteenth-century Alsace, however, the populace still believed that at the moment of birth the devil, witches and the 'people of the waters' would try to steal the soul of the baby.[28] Mothers liked to have amulets in place during the birth to add further protection, notably the 'eagle-stone' still found in all European countries during the nineteenth century, and to follow the supposedly correct posture for limbs, hands and fingers. All of these could be traced back to antiquity. Archaeological evidence from Anglo-Saxon burial sites, for example, reveals that graves for mothers and babies included little boxes that may have contained herbs and charms.[29] Finally, after a successful birth, midwives massaged the belly of the mother, rubbed in unguents, brewed special drinks and recited prayers to ease the delivery.

The well-known encyclopaedia produced by Bartholomew the Englishman in the thirteenth century laid out a routine for the baby once it was born. The midwife was to cut and knot the umbilical cord, wash the baby in warm water and check its reflexes and its bones. Bartholomew also advised rubbing the body, especially of a boy, since the lad would need toughening up for his work later in life – gender influences appeared from the very beginning.[30] Some interventions were vigorous in the extreme: midwives occasionally resorted to household bellows to start a baby's breathing, and they habitually attempted to reshape bodies to remedy defects, whilst in Russia the custom was to plunge the newly born into a cold bath immediately after a warm one, possibly to 'temper' the body. A traveller in the mid-eighteenth century reported that Muscovites 'wash their new-born infants in cold water, and roll them upon ice, and amongst snow'.[31] Louise Bourgeois, midwife to the future Louis XIII of France, resuscitated the child with the common custom of blowing a mouthful of wine into him or her. Other rituals rested heavily on symbolism. Mothers in nineteenth-century France, for example, often kept the umbilical cord of a son, symbol of her close relationship with him in the womb, as a good-luck charm to help him escape military service. While midwives were sometimes accused by the medical profession of indifference to the fate of an apparently dead or dying infant, for the historian Jacques Gélis this was probably more a matter of weary resignation, brought on by a long experience of frequent deaths.[32]

Baptism

The baptism ceremony

To be baptized was to be cleansed of original sin and all the impurities associated with birth, and at the same time to be admitted to the Christian community. Catholics were anxious that the ceremony should take place as quickly as possible, since they believed that children who died before baptism went to hell, or, from the fourteenth century, into limbo – an intermediary position between heaven and hell. The first thing a visitor to hell in a medieval French romance noted was the children:

> Des petitez, des alaitanz,
> Cels que as meres toli mort,
> Braient et crïent, plorent fort

Tiny ones, nurselings, all those whom death carried off from their mothers. They howl, scream and cry loudly.[33]

Parents in Renaissance Florence left evidence of their beliefs in the *ricordanze* (account books): thus Bartolomeo Valori wrote that his little daughter, born two months premature, had lived long enough to be baptized and then gone to heaven.[34] The Catholic Church was even prepared to allow members of the laity to baptize a newly born infant at home, if it looked likely to die before a priest arrived. The person merely had to pour some clean water over it and recite in Latin or in the vernacular the words 'I baptize you in the name of the Father, the Son and the Holy Ghost'.[35] For the stillborn, from the fourteenth century onwards, there were special chapels which were usually dedicated to the Virgin Mary. Parents laid out the little bodies on the altar, in the hope that the child would show some sign of life. At the least pretext, an emission of fluid, say, or a spasm of some sort, the priest rushed forward and performed the baptism. Those present then attempted to revive the corpse, by warming it and ringing a peal of bells. Such efforts almost invariably failed, needless to say, but at least the parents could feel that they had saved the soul of their child. These sanctuaries survived until the eighteenth century in Switzerland, Germany and France.[36] The official baptism in a church usually occurred on the day of the birth or the one following, except in the case of noble or wealthy bourgeois families, where a little more time might be needed to assemble kin and prepare elaborate ceremonies. Between birth and baptism, according to traditional lore, the baby remained vulnerable to the forces of evil. Fortunately various rituals were on hand to protect it. Parents never took an infant out of the house at this point; midwives drew a pentagram on the threshold to try to keep out the evil spirits; and families might leave certain objects around, such as a knife in Lorraine, or a pair of the father's breeches in Thuringia, to ward off any that managed to penetrate the house. Best of all, family and neighbours rubbed the new-born child with salt, important for many forms of exorcism, and watched over it with a lighted candle always burning alongside.[37] Protestants, it should be added, were divided on the issue of whether baptism was essential for salvation. The upshot was that they were normally prepared to wait until the Sunday following the birth, or even later, for baptism, but Anglicans in England, and Lutherans in German cities such as Nuremberg and Frankfurt, were prepared to sanction emergency baptisms by midwives.[38]

The Catholic baptism ceremony fell into two distinct parts. To begin with, the priest met the baptismal party at the church door for the ritual exorcism. One of the godparents or the midwife usually carried the baby, for the mother had no role to play in the ceremony. The Church continued and adapted a Jewish tradition by banning women who had given birth from holy places for forty days. The priest blessed the baby, put a little salt on its tongue and drove out any demons. The party then went into the church for the second phase of the ceremony: the baptism itself. Originally babies were completely immersed in the font, but at some point in the Middle Ages the custom shifted to pouring a little water over their heads. (In Russia, it might be noted, a few die-hards in the Orthodox Church continued to immerse children in cold water during the nineteenth century – sometimes killing them in the process.[39]) Infants also received a chris- tening gown or bonnet, the chrisom, named after the holy oil used to anoint them. For the populace, this garment would protect the child by means of its magical powers. To lose it was an ominous sign of mortal danger. After the ceremony, the godfather might throw almonds, hazelnuts or little coins to the assembled children of the parish, signifying that the newly born had paid his or her admission to the world of the living. Finally, the party celebrated the event with a feast.[40]

Choosing godparents

Baptism was an important turning point for the child in providing it with a set of godparents and a name. In principle, godparents were to oversee the spiritual life of the child, teaching it the Creed and the Lord's Prayer, and providing general moral guidance. They were also to provide assistance whenever necessary, as the little gifts they brought to the baptism indicated. By a judicious choice of god- parents, parents sought to strengthen their own standing among kin, friends and patrons or employers, and to help the child become estab- lished in such networks. They therefore had some tendency to seek godparents slightly higher up the social scale than themselves – though it was also possible for the wealthy to use the institution as a form of patronage. Indeed, until the Council of Trent insisted on lim- iting Roman Catholics to choosing one godparent, or one of each sex, parents often followed the aristocratic practice of naming several. The Florentine Matteo di Giovanni Corsini, for example, had eleven godfathers for his first child.[41] Baptismal sponsorship might also be used to secure political alliances. Eighth-century popes, for example, sought *compaternitas* with the Carolingians to tighten links with the Frankish dynasty.[42] The custom among Italians was to choose god- parents among friends in their neighbourhood, while the French generally preferred to resort to members of their own family. How relations between children and their godparents turned out in prac- tice is difficult to determine. It is likely that spiritual kin set out to provide the child with friendship rather than a religious education.[43]

In northern Europe and North America the Protestant influence
undermined 'coparenthood' from the sixteenth century onwards. In
Catholic Europe, however, various obligations remained, such as
taking in an orphaned godchild. Pierre-Jakez Hélias indicated that in
his Breton village about 1900 being a godparent was neither an empty
nor a gratuitous honour, since orphans were still being offered food
and refuge, for a while at least, with a godfather or a godmother.[44]
Godparents were also involved in many cases with giving a name to
the child.

Naming the child

People in the Middle Ages may have invested first names with even
more importance than we do today. To quote from Leon Battista
Alberti, writing in Florence during the 1430s, 'Beautiful and mag-
nificent names . . . somehow add lustre to our virtues and our dignity,
and make them still more splendid and admirable.'[45] By the twelfth
century, aristocratic families were trying to ensure that the eldest son
was named after his father or his grandfather. Lower down the social
scale, godparents in England and France often gave children their
own names: a practice recommended by instruction manuals for
priests. Among a group of tradesmen in late fifteenth-century York,
required to prove that they were English rather than Scottish,
baptismal records revealed that 65 per cent of godsons had the
same name as their godfathers. Italian parents, by contrast, jealously
guarded the right to choose names themselves.[46] The range available
fluctuated over time, though in different ways across Europe. In the
Forez region of France, for example, parents made use of 258 first
names during the fourteenth century, compared to only sixty-five
during the thirteenth. In Tuscany, conversely, the stock of names
declined radically between 1219 and 1427. In the latter case, parents
at the outset could choose names with a variety of meanings, including references to the nonsensical (Mezovillano, or 'half a peasant',
for example), pilgrimages, cities, saints, chivalric culture (Roland and
Oliver), physical and moral qualities, flowers and the family. The
custom of naming a baby after a saint first became common in the
Mediterranean area during the twelfth century, and gradually spread
to the north. Thirteen of the fifteen most popular names for boys in
Florentine Tuscany came from saints (Antonio, Giovanni, Piero, and
so on), and fifteen of the seventeen among girls (led by Caterina,
Antonia and Giovanna). By the late Middle Ages, according to David
Herlihy, the name had become a lecture for the young. It could simultaneously link them to an ancestor, evoke a legendary past (as in the
case of Sebastian, the Roman soldier who became a Christian martyr)

and augur a successful future. Each name had its own particular resonance: the massively popular Giovanni or Giovanna (as Jean and Jeanne, or John and Joan) summoned a powerful protector in the form of John the Baptist.[47] Protestants reacted against 'popish' names, some of the more devout preferring to delve into the Old Testament to find the Ebenezers and Ichabods, or into the Geneva Bible of 1560 for the Thankfuls, Accepteds and Safe-on-Highs. However, old habits died hard throughout the modern period, and traditional names continued to predominate. A trawl through the census lists of London's Three Colts Lane, Bethnal Green, for 1871 revealed a short list dominated by such familiar Christian names as Emma, Sarah, Catherine, William, Charles and Thomas.[48] Meanwhile the Catholic Reformation mounted its own campaign, encouraging a limited list of saints' names led by Mary, Anne, Catherine, John, Francis and Joseph – though naturally preferences varied by region and class. Again, as the historian François Lebrun noted, names had both a religious and a magical charge to them, seeking protection for the child by a saint and by an ancestor.[49] The nineteenth century brought some new fashions in France, such as Eugénie and Julie for girls, and Victor and Edmé for boys, but the old names remained preponderant.[50]

An epitaph

On the eve of the First World War, baptism remained the norm for children in the West, though it was perhaps more of a formality than it had been in the past for many people. In a heavily politicized environment, notably that created by tensions between the Catholic Church and the Republic in France after 1870, a section of the population might embrace a civil baptism. Others of course did not consider it worth bothering with the ceremony at all. Yet they were the exceptions: if over a third of all babies were not baptized in any religion in Paris in 1908, the corresponding figure in Marseilles was a mere 4 per cent. Similarly, figures for England during the years 1902–14 reveal that Anglican baptisms accounted for around two-thirds of live births, and baptisms by Catholics and Nonconformists probably took up most of the rest. In the East End of London, many working-class families left their children unbaptized, or treated the ceremony more as a source of health and good luck than religious initiation. Godparents were named, but not taken seriously.[51] The old rules for choosing names were also falling into disuse in the West, as parents preferred to make their own choices. Hence the custom of giving the same name to more than one sibling, which followed from naming children after godparents, was long gone by this late period.

Welcoming the child into the community?

After the trials and tribulations of childbirth, parents were ready to celebrate a successful delivery. Women from the village or neighbourhood came to visit the mother and admire the new baby. In a wealthy family this was an elaborate ceremony, displaying the sumptuous furnishings of the bed chamber and the fine clothes of the mother. Relatives also gave gifts to the mother and child. Among the merchant elite in Florence, for example, they liked to present silver cups with the coats of arms of the two families.[52] Some children were more welcome than others, it must be said. The first-born were always received with particular gratitude, since they proved that the couple was fertile. The first son was also considered a great blessing: Ralph Josselin opened his diary in 1641 with the words 'I was borne to the great joy of Father and mother being much desired as being their third child, and, as it pleased God, their only sonne.'[53] Folklore in the West had ways of registering delight at the birth of a boy, and disappointment at that of a girl. In nineteenth-century Brittany the arrival of a son was greeted by three strokes of a large bell, a daughter by two on a small bell. In the Marche, also in France, mothers were rewarded for producing a son with a slice of bread dipped in warm, sweetened wine; a daughter entitled them only to some salted milk broth. Girls were commonly thought of as the product of sexual relations corrupted by sickness, debauchery or a broken taboo.[54] Parents readily confessed their feelings, Mary Hatton, for example, writing to her brother in 1676 that 'Though a son would have been more welcome I am confident, both to your Lordship and all your relations, yet I am very well assured you was very glad to have a daughter.' The problem perceived with daughters in an agrarian society was they were likely to leave home early, and take a dowry with them. There was a Russian saying, 'Feed a son and do well by yourself; feed a daughter and you provide for other people.' However, many parents did express contentment when they bore a girl, and not necessarily because they had sons already. In early nineteenth-century Massachusetts, Leverett Saltonstall wrote to his father: 'It is with much happiness that I inform you that at five o'clock this morning we were blessed with a daughter, – a fine, healthy child.'[55]

Legitimate children would also be more welcome than illegitimate ones in many societies, though this was by no means invariably the case. During the Middle Ages a good deal depended on the social status of the parties involved. Until at least the twelfth century, young male nobles frequently fathered the children of non-noble concubines before moving on to marriage. A powerful ruler like Charlemagne could also have many concubines beside a wife. William the

Conqueror, Duke of Normandy, was the son of such a union by his father Robert. These 'bastards' were accepted into families without animosity (the word itself had not yet taken on a pejorative meaning), enjoying a similar position to legitimate children. They were able to inherit property, for example, and take clerical orders. The exception was the fruit of an adulterous relationship, where a married woman (as opposed to a concubine) had an affair. Given the assumption that during intercourse the woman was merely a passive receptacle for blood passed from the male, the outcome of such a relationship was thought to be a corruption of the male lineage by an outsider. A more hostile attitude to illegitimate children in general appeared very gradually, accelerating in the wake of a campaign by Pope Gregory VII (in office 1073–85) to clamp down on those produced by the clergy. As early as the ninth century, Alfred the Great, King of Wessex from 871 to 899, comes across in Asser's *Life* as married with five legitimate children, whereas it is possible that he had at least one illegitimate son. By the thirteenth century, in all parts of France, bastards were becoming increasingly isolated, being denied inheritance rights and brought up by their mothers alone. A study of fourteenth-century Ghent suggests that they were still valued as much as legitimate offspring, though the author detects 'a certain reserve' towards them.[56]

Illegitimacy became a comparatively rare phenomenon during the early modern period in Europe and colonial America: a figure of 2 per cent of all births can be cited as a benchmark for rural areas in sixteenth-century France.[57] The shame and expense for young, single people producing a child varied according to circumstances, but as a rule it was burdensome. Besides hostility from the churches for transgressing moral codes, in northern Europe and North America in particular they faced measures from secular authorities to ensure that they (rather than the public purse) shouldered the financial burdens of child-rearing. During the seventeenth and eighteenth centuries, for example, as the American colonies followed the lead taken by the Elizabethan Poor Law, they passed laws to make bastardy a civil offence as well as a sin.[58] The attitude of ordinary people in the neighbourhood to illegitimacy also came into play. In the Wildberg District of Württemberg a dense network of officials, Pietist pastors, church elders and 'public-spirited' citizens conspired to make life difficult for the parents of illegitimate children. During the sixteenth century, they could be refused citizenship by a community, and single women who became pregnant were regularly thrown out of the principal town.[59] In southern Europe, where female honour was at a particular premium, it was the families of unmarried women which reacted vigorously to a pregnancy. In parts of Corsica, for example, even in the nineteenth century fathers and brothers would threaten to kill a seducer who refused the responsibilities of marriage.[60]

Illegitimacy ratios increased dramatically during the eighteenth and early nineteenth centuries, though not all regions were affected. In England, in the wake of the agricultural and industrial revolutions, the historian John Gillis has contrasted the divergent attitudes to illegitimacy in the arable areas of the south and east with those prevailing in the more pastoral and industrialized rural areas of the north and west. In the former, where the agrarian proletariat had no hope of providing property or employment for its children, parents expected the young to leave home early. A pregnancy therefore almost invariably led to pressure on the wayward couple for a cover-up marriage. In the latter, rural industrialization made parents more dependent on the labour of their children, causing their reactions to an illegitimate birth to be more relaxed. In the weaving village of Culceth, in Lancashire, for example, young women might have a few children before they married and left home. The Basque country provides a further example of a region where little shame was attached to producing an illegitimate child, attributable in this case to the slow penetration of post-Tridentine Catholicism.[61] One group of women, who feature prominently in statistics on illegitimacy in a number of countries, and for whom an unwanted child was an unmitigated disaster, consisted of servants. Their position was by custom incompatible with marriage. Yet they were vulnerable to exploitation from their employers, and (like other women workers in a big city) they risked deception when their partners were either unwilling or unable 'to do the decent thing' and marry them when they became pregnant.[62]

Coping with death

'A pregnant woman has one foot in the grave' according to a proverb from Gascony.[63] Childbirth was indeed perceived as a perilous time for the baby as well as the mother until the nineteenth and twentieth centuries. Sadly, the numerous precautions taken to protect them sometimes failed to save their lives. Mothers may in fact have succumbed less often than was once thought. 'Best' estimates for England indicate a maternal mortality rate of 16 per thousand births during the late seventeenth century, which fell to just over 10 during the first half of the eighteenth century, and to between 5 and 6 in the early nineteenth century. Other samples, covering the period between the late seventeenth and late nineteenth centuries, show rates of 11.8 per thousand births in the Vexin region of Normandy, 10.9 per cent in the town of Rouen, and 6.1 per cent among the Mormons of Utah. Yet Judith Walzer Leavitt is surely right to argue that even today the emotional impact of childbirth for women is beyond its actual danger.[64] When such deaths did occur, they invariably left the father in difficult circumstances, and the newly born infant with a limited chance of survival. Widowers tended to remarry quickly, which probably reflects more their desperate need for a partner than a shallow emotional commitment to marriage.

However, it was the baby who was more likely to die prematurely. Death took a heavy toll on the very young in traditional societies: infant mortality rates (the number of deaths during the first year of life per thousand live births) were generally in the range of 150 to 300 in the West. In Russia they were still close to 250 during the early twentieth century: the period when infant mortality began its final and very belated decline in most Western countries.[65] At first sight it therefore seems reasonable to follow Ariès in thinking that parents would be reluctant to become attached to their fragile and ephemeral offspring. He cites Montaigne (1533–92), who admitted to having 'lost two or three children in their infancy, not without regret, but without great sorrow'. Such indifference to the fate of young children continued until the seventeenth century, he thought, and even until the nineteenth century 'in the depths of the country'. The historian Lawrence Stone took a similar line, arguing that, since so many infants died in the early sixteenth century, they could only be regarded as expendable. More recent authorities have doubted whether parents were quite so callous during the medieval and early modern periods, whilst not denying that it is difficult to know how ordinary people felt on the matter in the past.[66]

In the first place, most historians accept that the death of a newly born baby was always less distressing for parents than that of a child with whom they had experienced several years of bonding. In 1769 William Ronald attempted to console the Virginian James Parker on the loss of a son with the thought that it was his younger rather than his older boy, for 'the heart can be but a little affected with their loss in comparison with what we feel when deprived of those whose infant prattle and dawning reason ... has deeply impressed their image in our breasts.'[67] Secondly, historians note that one can as easily find examples of 'searing grief' at the death of an infant as of indifference. Medieval representations of parents in mourning for their children frequently depict them 'weeping, crying out, imploring'. Martin Luther wrote during the sixteenth century, after the death of his daughter Elizabeth at eight months: 'I so lamented her death that I was exquisitely sick, my heart rendered soft and weak; never had I thought that a father's heart could be so broken for his children's sake.'[68] This ambivalence in the evidence doubtless reflects a diversity of reactions to infant deaths at all periods. At the same time, it may point to a tension between private grief and public stoicism among devout Christians. Moralists during the Middle Ages advised restraint: if the birth of a child was a gift from God, so too was its death, and it was not for mere mortals to question divine judgement. Luther himself criticized his eldest son for 'childlike weakness' in grieving inconsolably for a dead sister. The Virginian William Byrd followed the traditional line of thought in 1710, noting in his diary after the death of his six-month-old son: 'God gives and God takes away; blessed be the name of God.' Preachers at Protestant funerals liked to assure parents that they would be reunited with their children in heaven. Hence, in the words of the historian David Cressy, the Puritan vicar Ralph Josselin could be 'disciplined but distraught' when burying his son in 1648. Josselin was confident that the soul and the body of the deceased would arise to enjoy God, and that 'these mine eyes shall see it'.[69] Thirdly, looking over the long run, one can discern certain periods when sensitivity to infant mortality came to the fore. The late Middle Ages was arguably one such, with its numerous representations of the massacre of the innocents and infants risking death (as in the Judgement of Solomon). The eighteenth century has claims to being another, the historian Jean-Louis Flandrin, for example, linking the first stirrings of birth control in France to concerns over high infant mortality. Henk van Setten also highlights the Romantic era for its increased attention to comforting parents who had lost a child. He notes a 'sudden explosion of literature about dead children' in the Netherlands during the early nineteenth century, by poets, preachers and even by friends, relatives and the parents themselves.[70] In sum, to follow a recent French survey of childhood in the Middle Ages, using a quote from Montaigne to propose that the death of an infant would not upset the family goes too far. Rather, responses to infant deaths show the extent to which childhood was valued.[71] In more recent periods, parents have left ample evidence of their grief, some of it almost unbearable to read. We end with the words of the American Elizabeth Prentiss after she had lost both her 3-year-old son Edward and her baby in 1852:

> Here I sit with empty hands. I have had the little coffin in my arms, but my baby's face could not be seen, so rudely had death marred it. Empty hands, empty hands, a worn-out exhausted body, and unutterable longings to flee from a world that has had for me so many sharp experiences. God help me, my baby, my baby! God help me, my little lost Eddy![72]

Conclusion

Bringing children into the world was a risky venture for couples, until modern medicine made its impact from the late nineteenth century onwards, but ultimately it proved a satisfying one for most of them.

Those who married expected to have children, until the eighteenth century at the very earliest, and were distressed if this was not possible. The newly born were generally welcomed as a gift from God, and considerable efforts were made to ensure they remained alive. Parents could hardly avoid a fatalistic attitude to the deaths of so many of their offspring, but only after they had tried everything else. Yet this brings us to a paradox, noted recently by Louis Haas in Renaissance Florence: after lavishing care and attention on the birth and baptism of their child, many parents immediately sent them away to an uncertain future with a wet-nurse.[73] How can this be explained?

5

Caring for Infants?

A persuasive case can be made to show that the alleged indifference
to childhood in the medieval and early modern periods resulted in a
callous approach to child-rearing. Infants under 2 years of age in
particular were thought to suffer appalling neglect, with parents considering it unwise to invest much time or trouble in a 'poor sighing
animal'[1] who was all too likely to die young. Infant mortality rates
did after all remain high in the West until the late nineteenth and
early twentieth centuries. Symptoms of this negligence included
leaving babies to stew in their own excrement for hours, the resort
to 'mercenary' wet-nurses and the large-scale abandonment of children. Edward Shorter famously accused mothers of failing the 'sacrifice test', meaning they did not put the life and happiness of
their infant above everything else. Only when the more enlightened
views on childhood in the eighteenth century came to the fore, he
asserted, did middle- and upper-class parents begin to adopt more
'modern' approaches to childcare. Certainly, there was no shortage
of testimony from moralists and physicians on the lack of interest
among parents for their youngest children.[2] Yet it may be that
some historians have sided a little too hastily with Enlightenment
reformers in denigrating traditional child-rearing practices. These can
be written off as the result of ignorance and superstition. A more sympathetic view suggests that peasants in the past were acutely aware
of the dangers facing their children, and made great efforts to counter
them, even though the rationale behind their actions was very
different from our own. Françoise Loux describes traditional remedies as a combination of common sense and 'psychosomatic medicine before its time'. They were arguably as effective as anything

that the medical profession could offer before the late nineteenth century.[3]

The wet-nursing business

Mother or nurse?

At first sight, nothing would appear more heartless than to snatch a new-born babe from its mother and send it off to a wet-nurse. Such a practice flew in the face of advice from the majority of physicians and theologians down the centuries. During the thirteenth century, Bartholomew the Englishman asserted that: 'the infant raised on his mother's milk is more praiseworthy than one raised on the milk of another'. On the one hand, he and his contemporaries believed that breast milk was a form of blood, and that the mother 'naturally' passed on her qualities to her child by this medium. On the other, Bartholomew was impressed by the emotional bond that developed between mother and child at the breast, as she 'very much loves her infant, embraces, kisses, and lovingly nurses and feeds it'. The popular medieval image of the *Virgo lactans*, Mary nursing the infant Jesus, provided a powerful visual image to reinforce the message.[4] During the sixteenth century, the influential *Rosengarten* by Eucharius Rösslin was no less decisive in preferring maternal breastfeeding to wet-nursing, on the very practical grounds that the infant was healthier and happier with it.[5] Protestant writers in Europe and North America were notable for their fervent exhortations to mothers on this matter. Some drew on the scriptures to argue that it was God's will that they should suckle their young; others turned to nature, the English Puritan Henry Smith noting that every beast and bird was nourished by its mother. This latter line, felicitously labelled the 'Fierce Jungle Beasts' argument by Nancy Senior, was also common in Germany and France: Scévolle de Sainte-Marthe complained in 1629 that even bears in the Alps, tigresses and all wild beasts in general took their young to the breast. The seventeenth-century Dutch writer Jacob Cats even composed a hymn to the maternal breast, which began: 'Employ O young wife, your precious gifts / Give the noble suck to refresh your little fruit'.[6] There was, in short, a weighty tradition in place long before Rousseau and his contemporaries in the Enlightenment made their famous plea for 'maternal solicitude'.[7] Yet in many parts of Europe, wealthy families routinely turned to wet-nurses: women paid to suckle a child from another family.

The scale of wet-nursing

A study of wet-nursing in Florence indicates that the custom was well entrenched among the middle class by the middle of the fourteenth century. Over one-third of the infants in the sample had parents who were outside the wealthy ruling elite, including skilled craftsmen, small merchants or landholders, and notaries.[8] However, not for the first time, Florence emerges as something of an exception: the general picture during the medieval and early modern periods was of wet-nurses being confined to a narrow circle of aristocratic and wealthy bourgeois families.[9] A final, spectacular flourish for wet-nursing emerged during the eighteenth and nineteenth centuries, as it took on a whole new scale in a number of cities. This was particularly the case in France, where a combination of rapid urbanization and gradual industrialization arguably produced an exceptionally favourable set of conditions for the practice to flourish. In 1780, the lieutenant-general of police in Paris estimated that only one in thirty of the 21,000 babies born each year in Paris was nursed by its mother. The rest, he reported, went out to wet-nurses in the suburbs and the surrounding countryside.[10] By this period, in Lyons as in Paris, the very wealthy had been joined by large contingents of artisans, shop-keepers and even servants. Parents of a sample of 2,000 infants who died with wet-nurses in villages near Lyons during the 1760s included nobles, merchants, shoemakers, tailors and domestic servants. The coming of the railways in the nineteenth century also meant that the cities could send infants to more distant locations, such as the Morvan in the case of Paris.[11]

A critique of wet-nursing

The case against wet-nursing was formidable.[12] Contemporaries accused mothers of refusing to breastfeed because they were more concerned about their figures and the social round than the welfare of their children. 'Fine ladies', according to a Lutheran pastor in Hamburg in 1660, wanted wet-nurses so that they could 'remain smooth and beautiful and sleep the night through'.[13] Critics also pilloried fathers for selfishness, with the allegation that they sent away infants so that they would not have to abstain from sexual relations with their wives for an extended period – intercourse during lactation was thought to spoil the milk. As for the nurses, they supposedly acted as true mercenaries, treating their tiny charges as a commodity like any other. According to their detractors, they deceived parents in their reports on the condition of the nurselings, offered milk to their own children first, and supplemented their overstretched milk supplies with animal milk or with 'pap' made from flour or bread-crumbs and water. A police report of 1777 described the pathetic sight of a nurseling in a hovel near Lyons, alone and 'garrotted in a filthy cradle, uttering a series of piercing cries, gulping down his tears, and having for nourishment nothing more than a cup of sour wine and a buckwheat cake'.[14] Above all, the wet-nurses allegedly deprived infants of the care and attention they needed. As James Bruce Ross observes, it is hard to see how an overworked countrywoman could have been able to find time to do anything more than the minimum. A study of infant mortality in the suburbs of eighteenth-century Paris noted the seasonal peak to the deaths during the summer months: precisely those when peasant women were most occupied in the fields. In eighteenth-century England, John Stedman complained bitterly of his four wet-nurses:

> The first of these bitches was turn'd off for having nearly suffocated me in bed; she having sleep'd upon me till I was smother'd, and with skill and difficulty restored to life. The second had let me fall from her arms on the stones till my head was almost fractured, & I lay several hours in convulsions. The third carried me under a moulder'd old brick wall, which fell in a heap of rubbish just the moment we had passed by it, while the fourth proved to be a thief, and deprived me even of my very baby clothes.[15]

Historians have added some more modern concerns, criticizing parents for not visiting their children, and noting the emotional costs to the child of changing nurses, as frequently happened when, say, a nurse became pregnant or was discovered to be negligent.[16] To clinch the case for the prosecution, so to speak, there was the appalling 'mas-sacre of the innocents' in the villages. The historian George Sussman suggested three levels of infant mortality among those born in French cities during the eighteenth century. The lowest (and rarest) rate stood at 180 to 200 per thousand live births, for those breastfed at home by their mothers. A medium range of 250 to 400 per thousand occurred among those put out to nurse in the countryside. Finally, there was a catastrophic 650 to 900 per thousand striking foundlings, also placed in rural areas, though with pitifully limited resources.[17] These esti-mates should be treated with caution, for there were significant local variations. Most authorities, none the less, agree that babies were more likely to die with a wet-nurse than with their mother.

Some mitigating circumstances

Such a critical approach to those involved in the wet-nursing busi-ness has not gone unchallenged. The most important point to bear in mind is that a wet-nurse was often the safest alternative to maternal breastfeeding until the 'Pasteurian' revolution of the late nineteenth century. This was particularly the case in warm, temperate zones or in the Mediterranean regions, where milk and other foodstuffs quickly became sour or contaminated.[18] Popular prejudice against animal milk, based on the assumption that infants inherited the traits of those who fed them, perhaps had its uses in the end. The Tuscan merchant Paolo da Certaldo warned in the middle of the fourteenth century that a baby fed on the milk of a cow, sheep or ass 'always looks stupid and vacant and not right in the head'.[19] Mothers may have believed that peasant women were stronger than they themselves were, and that the countryside was a healthier place than the city. Some of them certainly were forced to hire a nurse, when they proved unable to breastfeed themselves as through ill heath or some more specific problem with their milk supply.[20] The very wealthy probably took for granted the privilege of handing over childcare responsibilities to someone else without much reflection. It was, indeed, a symbol of gentility.[21] For many others further down the social scale, however, the need to balance the conflicting pressures of work and family meant that hard choices had to be made on nursing. Wives were considered essential in helping to run a small workshop or business. In the case of the often hard-pressed silk weavers of eighteenth-century Milan and Lyons, or families running a café or a shop, the presence of wives was required all day long. The historian Rudolf Dekker points out that hiring a wet-nurse in the Netherlands at this same period was an expensive option, far more costly than the alternative of feeding an infant pap. He concludes that sending the child off was generally 'an act of love' by parents.[22] Quantitative evidence indicates that wet-nurses for their part generally only hired out their services when they had weaned their own children.[23] Moreover, if some people had bitter memories of suffering at the hands of their wet-nurses, others retained fond memories of them. During the fourteenth century in Florence the father of Giovanni Morelli remembered his *balia* as 'the most awful bestial woman that ever was', but Jeanne-Marie Philipon (the future Mme Roland during the French Revolution) maintained a close relationship with her nurse even after she had returned home. Memoirs written by children from noble families in Imperial Russia remembered the serfs who nursed them as loving and attentive – doubtless the poor women were in no position to be anything else.[24] A higher death rate among infants sent out to wet-nurse than among those remaining with their mothers might be expected. The delay while babies made the perilous journey out into the countryside must have weakened them. Many foundlings put out to nurse by hospitals were also in poor physical condition from the start, notably those inheriting syphilis from mothers who were prostitutes. Indeed, the sad plight of these poor children risks distorting our view of wet-nursing as a whole.

What counted under these various circumstances was the capacity to find and retain a good wet-nurse. Parents sought a woman who would be kind to their child, in good health and likely to produce untainted milk. Once again, the belief that infants inherited the temperament and passions of whoever was nursing them added a moral dimension: hence the old saying in England that 'He sukt evil from the dug'.[25] Indeed, advice to parents on selecting a nurse hardly changed down the centuries, as authors routinely copied passages going back to Greek and Roman authors, especially the physician Soranus of Ephesus (96–138). The Venetian Francesco de Barberino, whose fourteenth-century work was influential in Renaissance Italy, recommended that the *balia* should be:

> Between twenty-five and thirty-five years, as much like the mother as possible, and let her have good colour and a strong neck and strong chest and ample flesh, firm and flat rather than lean, but by no means too much so, her breath not bad, her teeth clean.[26]

Certain beliefs proved remarkably resilient: redheads were thought to be unsuitable because of their hot temper, and large breasts unmanageable for the nurseling. There was even a little 'nail test' mentioned by Soranus in the second century AD for the breast milk that ran down the centuries. The parent was advised to place a drop on a fingernail, and ensure that it spread gently, rather than running off immediately or thickening like honey.[27]

The wealthy could afford to have a nurse living in with them, or located near to their homes. This made it easy to supervise the nurse, and to maintain contact with the children. Christiane Klapisch-Zuber alleges that during the Renaissance Florentine parents were more inclined to keep a boy at home for nursing than a girl. This is entirely plausible, though whether her sample of infants is representative enough and large enough to warrant such a conclusion is open to question. She also observes that Florentines paid little attention to the moral qualities of their nurses, flying in the face of their advice books. 'Girls who had been seduced, "bestial" Tartar slave women, or mothers who had abandoned their children all made good nurses if their milk was "young" and abundant.'[28] Plantation owners in the southern colonies in America were another group who defied conventional wisdom in the eighteenth century, shocking outsiders by using resident slave women to suckle their progeny. The less affluent in Western countries had to venture further afield to find a nurse. Women in outlying areas charged less, but transporting the baby to them was hazardous, and the detection of abuses more difficult. Even so, there were signs that these parents made efforts to secure the welfare of their babies, by placing them with relatives or business contacts.[29] Worst placed of all were the charitable institutions seeking to find places for their orphans and foundlings. They had to use the very cheapest nurses, and often burdened them with more than one infant.

The end of the wet-nursing business

The wet-nursing business proved remarkably resilient in both Europe and the United States, surviving in places until the middle of the twentieth century. Various charitable societies attempted to counter it by promoting maternal breastfeeding among the poor, notably the Sociétés de Charité Maternelle founded in the major French cities under the First Empire. Local and national governments in their turn took steps to regulate it from the eighteenth century onwards.[30] Paris founded a Bureau of Wet Nurses in 1769 to try to bring some order to the business. It guaranteed payments to the nurses, for example, and sued parents who defaulted on their payments. Defeat in the Franco-Prussian War precipitated the passing of the Loi Roussel in 1874. This law extended Parisian regulations to the whole of France, most importantly insisting on medical supervision for both nurses and infants. The Italian Government went no further in 1918 than to provide medical inspections of wet-nurses with a view to curbing syphilis.[31] A number of forces were at work to make the custom redundant. The renewed interest in childhood discussed earlier must be an essential backdrop to the effort to preserve infant lives threatened by lax feeding procedures. The availability of sterilized milk and feeding bottles in the late nineteenth century was also a precondition for wholesale change. For historian George Sussman, however, the most significant influence was the movement of young married women out of the work force during the early twentieth century.[32] Before then, the conclusion must be that it was 'a necessity, but not a very attractive one', for mothers who were unable to breastfeed and for those whose constant presence was thought to be essential in a workshop or small business.[33] Doubtless many of these mothers would have failed Shorter's 'sacrifice test', as would their more favoured counterparts in the 'leisured classes'. Yet it is surely naive to think that mothers will invariably be willing to give up involvement in, say, politics, work outside the home or charitable activities to concentrate exclusively on their children. There may have been periods when upper-class mothers were keen to raise a child *à la Jean-Jacques*, as happened briefly in the late eighteenth century, or when married women were largely excluded from the labour force, as in

the early twentieth century. At others, by contrast, the need to con-
tribute to the family economy has been more pressing for some, or
even to cut a figure in 'society'.

Food, clothing and hygiene

Traditional practice

All the brouhaha surrounding the final years of wet-nursing risks distorting our overall perspective on infant feeding practices. The consensus among historians is that most mothers in the past breastfed
their own children. Wet-nursing was after all confined to the larger,
older cities of the West, and correspondingly rare in villages, small
towns and the new industrial centres of the nineteenth century. In the
latter, women tended to work outside the home in a factory for a few
years only before they married and had children. They might well
take up part-time employment at home afterwards, but a seamstress,
for example, had more opportunity to combine paid work and mothering than the wife of an artisan or a shopkeeper. Wet-nursing was
also far less in evidence in Germany, Holland, America and perhaps
England than in France and Italy. Data on the extent of breastfeeding in the past are not easy to come by until the early twentieth
century. A sample assembled from the reports of medical officers of
health in twenty-one English local authorities over the period
1894–1912 revealed that approximately three-quarters of all infants
were breastfed, with a further 12 per cent partially fed at the breast,
and only 14 per cent fed solely by artificial methods. Others indicated
that about 85 per cent of mothers in the southern United States
breastfed their own children, while in the city of New York, in 1908,
65 per cent of mothers were still breastfeeding infants aged nine
months.[34] Certain regions of Europe do provide an exception to the
general rule, by harbouring a tradition of feeding infants by hand
rather than by the breast. This was notably the case in parts of
Germany, Switzerland, Russia, Sweden, Finland and Iceland. Official
surveys in Germany during the early twentieth century revealed startling contrasts between neighbouring regions, with infants from the
northern and western sections of Bavaria and Baden, and from
Hessen, usually being breastfed, whilst the majority from southern
and eastern Bavaria were fed artificially. Statistics from the children's
hospital in Munich suggested that during the 1880s no less than
86.4 per cent of children had never been breastfed. In central Europe
the infants were raised from birth on 'meal pap', a mixture of cows'
or sheep's milk and barley flour; in Scandinavia the custom was
to provide animal milk alone. The German evidence, as in many

developing countries today, suggests a strong association between breastfeeding and low infant mortality. However, Valerie Fildes notes that hand feeding did not necessarily harm the infants, perhaps because the cool climate of some of these northern or mountainous regions provided a favourable environment for it.[35]

The traditional custom was to wait a few days before putting babies to the breast, it being thought that the first milk was a 'bad' substance. New-born infants were given a range of substitutes such as milk from another woman or a purge of sugared wine. The benefits of colostrum were not generally recognized until the French surgeon François Mauriceau turned the tide in the late seventeenth century. Nurselings were customarily fed on demand at all levels of society. The German physician Friedrich Hoffmann reported in the 1740s that 'for the most part the breast is given in the first months every two hours; after three or four months, six or seven times a day; and at length only twice or thrice a day'.[36] Such a generous regime was probably confined to mothers from wealthy backgrounds: peasant women, burdened with a heavy work routine, must have been obliged to leave infants for long spells without a feed. Slave mothers in the American South had to manage with the occasional session nursing their babies, rather begrudgingly conceded by plantation owners, between long hours working in the fields.[37] Where necessary, breast milk could be supplemented with other foods such as the many variants of 'pap' or, less commonly, 'panada' (usually based on broth and breadcrumbs). By their fifth week, infants in Russian peasant families were expected to digest pieces of bread and gruel made from barley or buckwheat.[38] Curiously, a recent survey by Valerie Fildes concludes that these infant foods became less nutritious between the sixteenth and the eighteenth centuries, as fewer eggs, dairy and meat products were used in the recipes.[39]

Weaning was an important rite of passage, which varied considerably according to such considerations as the wealth of the parents (especially when paying a nurse), the health of the mother, the sex and size of the infant, and local customs. It generally occurred somewhere between six months and two years. Evidence from ninth-century France suggests that boys were weaned around the age of 2, girls at 1. Similarly, the doctor Laurent Joubert indicated in 1608 that girls might be weaned six months before boys, though other studies have revealed more equality between the sexes in the length of time allowed for breastfeeding. A future king of France in the seventeenth century had over two years at the breast; peasant children in nineteenth-century Bavaria would be lucky to manage six months. The long-run trend was towards earlier weaning. In a sample of (mainly middle-class) British children, the median age shifted from eighteen months in the early sixteenth century to seven in the late eighteenth century. The latter anticipates the pattern in an urbanized society, where reliable artificial foods are available.[40] The experience of weaning for children could also be unpleasant. An ancient custom, which has left traces down to the twentieth century, was to precipitate an abrupt end to breastfeeding by smearing the nipples with a bitter substance. Hermann von Weinsberg (1518–97) claimed that when his mother felt she was running out of milk she painted her breast black. Alice Foley, born in 1891, recalled that in the Lancashire town of Bolton: 'Poor mothers daubed their breasts with soot to discourage suckling, and dim memories remain of spasmodic howls of rage produced by the offer of those coal-black nipples.'[41]

Providing infants with sufficient nourishment was the overriding problem for parents among the 'lower orders' until the nineteenth century. Keeping them warm was a further challenge. For the first month or so of their lives, in Europe and America, children were tightly bound with strips of cloth over their swaddling clothes, the techniques used varying according to region. In Italy, the custom was to bind them closely like an Egyptian mummy, whilst in France, Germany and England, mothers simply crossed the band two or three times around the body. Everywhere the babies were wrapped with their arms held straight at their side and their legs extended together, with additional support to hold the head steady. At a later stage the arms and head were left free, until, after a few months, they were ready for the little coat worn by both boys and girls. Medical opinion gradually became hostile to swaddling during the seventeenth and eighteenth centuries. Critics argued that it restricted the freedom of young limbs, risked constricting the breathing of the child, and left it wrapped in its own urine and faeces for long periods. They also felt that hanging a swaddled child from a nail for long spells was the height of negligence. Rousseau, for example, was scathing: in *Emile* (1762) he asserted that: 'The countries where children are swaddled teem with hunchbacks, cripples, men with stunted or withered limbs, men suffering from rickets, men misshapen in every way.'[42] Yet observers were bound to recognize that, besides keeping infants warm, swaddling made them easy to carry, and helped protect them from being bitten by domestic animals – pigs in particular. Peasants believed that these bands, together with tightly fitting cribs, helped the child develop strong bones and an upright posture. They also felt that it helped distinguish the child from an animal, by preventing it from crawling on all fours. Swaddling was a complex and time-consuming task, especially if done three, four or even seven times a day after feeding, but perhaps also a satisfying one. The midwife Jane Sharp advised in 1671 that one should handle the child 'very tenderly and wash the body with warm wine, then when it is dry roll it up with soft cloths and lay it into the cradle'.[43] The custom gradually died out from the eighteenth century under the weight of criticism from educated opinion, though it lingered into the twentieth century in remote country areas.[44] Pierre-Jakez Hélias recorded that in Brittany on the eve of the First World War he spent hours every day alone and tightly swaddled in his crib, while his parents and his grandfather were out working.[45]

Parents were not particularly concerned with cleanliness for much of the past, nor indeed were physicians, until the eighteenth century. Medieval authors recommended frequent bathing, but it is doubtful whether their advice was followed much beyond a narrow circle of wealthy town dwellers.[46] Dirt in fact played a protective and symbolic role in popular lore. Mothers believed that it was better to dry nappies than to wash them, because of the healing powers of urine. They also thought that a layer of dirt on the head preserved the fontanel. In the Haut-Vivarais, to take one example from many, people thought that washing a child's head would make it simple-minded, and that cutting its nails and hair before a year and a day was up would cause it to be, respectively, mute and a thief.[47] They were in no hurry to start toilet training either. Once again, however bizarre such beliefs and practices may seem from a present-day per-spective, they do show a consistent effort to enhance the health and happiness of the child rather than parental negligence.[48]

The scientific approach to child-rearing

Traditionally mothers learned how to raise their children from other women: a mother, a midwife, relatives and friends. Knowledge on childcare passed down the generations without being questioned – accompanied by a certain resignation in the face of its shortcomings, evident in frequent infant deaths. All this was to change during the eighteenth and nineteenth centuries. Parents came under an increas-ing barrage of advice from doctors and others eager to pontificate on child-rearing. The old female lore was contemptuously dismissed by educated opinion. The rationalist spirit of the Enlightenment was incompatible with many of its beliefs, leading to calls for lighter diets, looser clothing, and so on. During the early nineteenth century, according to Sylvia Hoffert, the weight of expectation concerning child welfare meant that in the urban north of America the joys of motherhood were already beginning to be undermined by feelings of 'anxiety, guilt, frustration, and fear'.[49] More intrusive in the end was the offensive from an increasingly confident medical profession during the 1880s and 1890s. Armed with Pasteur's discovery of the germ theory of disease, and hence with knowledge of asepsis and anti-sepsis, doctors could at last come up with a coherent and effective set of recommendations for mothers. These included boiling cow's milk (the process now known as pasteurization), sterilizing feeding equip-ment and washing hands before feeding. The new-found confidence was reflected in the tone of baby-rearing manuals. In 1870 French mothers could still find advice from 'a good old fellow with long experience', who was prepared through uncertainty to admit to several possible courses of action, and to let nature be a guide. A few years later choices were out, medical science had taken over from nature, and the doctor was definitely giving orders. In America the popular *Care and Feeding of Children* (1894) by the paediatrician Luther Emmett Holt started out as a training manual for nurses.

The advantages of taking advice from doctors were soon apparent, in the form of a sharp decline in infant mortality and healthier children. Unfortunately, that was not the end of the story. Some commentators have linked efforts to diffuse scientific methods of child-rearing to a broader project: bringing order to an anarchic working class. The sociologist Luc Boltanski cited a French manual for young housewives, *La Jeune Ménagère* (1904) of Mme Sevrette, which contrasted the ways of two working-class mothers. The 'good' one, steeped in the ways of 'la puériculture moderne', had to teach the bad one to feed her infant milk rather than heavy soups, to wash its head rather than to leave the scabs on it, and generally to organize her time more carefully. To ensure that the 'good' prevailed over the 'bad', Boltanski argued, working-class girls were compelled to take lessons in hygiene, child-rearing, cooking and other household tasks in the primary schools. Such an overtly class-based interpretation of events may not convince now. All the same, the programme on offer from medical experts at this period left little to maternal intuition. The mother was presented with rules on regular feeding times, bathing procedures, sleep patterns and early toilet training. Her role was increasingly to be a professional mother, as the cult of domesticity discouraged her from working outside the home. She was not without support in this sphere, for besides all the child-rearing manuals and school lessons, there were charitable organizations to help. In France she had the Sociétés Protectrices de l'Enfance; in England Infant Health Societies and Schools for Mothers. From the Child Study Movement she had a mass of information on 'milestones': when the baby should reach certain heights and weight, begin crawling, utter its first words, and so on. In this climate it was all too easy to feel inadequate as a mother. This may have rubbed off on to children: more remained alive, but there was talk in this *fin-de-siècle* period of an increase in the number of 'neurotic children'.[50]

Infanticide and child murder

The parent–child relationship could of course break down completely, most dramatically in cases where parents killed or abandoned their infants. On the surface, infanticide appears exceedingly rare during the medieval and early modern periods, for few cases ever came before the courts.[51] In England, Barbara Kellum notes that they were conspicuously absent from a selection of Coroners' Rolls between 1265 and 1413. Barbara Hanawalt came across no more than two examples among a sample of 4,000 homicides in the late medieval era. R. W. Malcolmson in his turn reported that they were 'never very numerous' during the eighteenth century. Most historians, however, see these isolated examples as merely the tip of the iceberg. They are bound to admit that the real incidence of the crime is unknowable, but they sometimes speculate that the crime was 'widespread' or 'woefully common'.[52] Occasional pieces of evidence give a hint that this was the case. The *polyptyque* of Saint-Germain-des-Prés, drawn up during the early ninth century for fiscal purposes, reveals that the population on the abbey's lands exhibited a marked imbalance of the sexes in favour of males. The historian Emily Coleman suggests that this may indicate a willingness, on the smaller farms in particular, to kill off unwanted daughters at birth. More grisly signs of the crime came to light in the Breton town of Rennes during the 1720s, when workmen on a building site opened a drain and chanced upon the tiny skeletons of over eighty babies.[53] The 1860s brought an 'infanticide scare' in England. Official statistics, even though thought still to be under-representing murders of infants, suggest that the physicians raising the issue had a point. Of the 5,314 cases of homicide recorded by the Registrar General between 1863 and 1887, 3,355 concerned a child under 1 year of age. This meant that infants were more likely to be murdered than any other age group. Moreover, their 63 per cent of the total can be compared to the equivalent figure of only 6.1 per cent a century later in 1977.[54] One can make three points with some confidence in what is a generally rather murky area.

Firstly, the law in the West was slow to recognize the killing of a new-born baby as a crime, and certainly to equate it with an adult homicide. Several earlier civilizations had openly practised infanticide, and the legal codes of various Germanic tribes continued the tradition. Among the Anglo-Saxons, the Frisian Law permitted mothers to expose a baby before it had been fed at the breast, although it was the grandmother who had the final say in the matter. In tenth-century Iceland, fathers could choose whether to accept or reject a new-born baby. In normal circumstances the custom was to sprinkle it with water and gave it a name, symbolizing its acceptance into society. Killing a child after it had undergone this ceremony was a serious crime. However, in the case of an illegitimate child, a deformed one, or one which a poor family felt unable to support, fathers had the right to order that it be killed or exposed rather than sprinkled. The introduction of Christian practice into law in 1000 did not entirely eliminate the custom: as a concession to the poor, they were allowed to expose children as before. In Norway the Christian influence was even slower to make an impact, suggesting that infanticide continued throughout the Middle Ages. Elsewhere the law codes could be harsh, with a seventh-century Spanish law, for example, punishing infanticide with death or blinding.[55] During the High Middle Ages, secular authorities were usually content to leave such cases to the Church courts, reserving for themselves only the most scandalous cases. The occasional unwed mother caught disposing of an unwanted infant could come to a gruesome end, buried alive, burnt or drowned according to French and German law codes. Otherwise, societies treated infanticide as a sin rather than as a crime. The ecclesiastical authorities concentrated on suffocation by 'overlaying', warning parents on the dangers of taking a baby into bed with them. The Church courts could do no more than impose a penance on guilty parties. In fourteenth- and fifteenth-century Florence, couples absolved of the sin of suffocation usually had to pay money to a charity and stand in front of the parish church on a Sunday wailing their repentance. Elsewhere, they often faced a year on bread and water. During the late fifteenth and sixteenth centuries, the imperial and royal legal systems in Europe once more turned their attention to infanticide. Their concern was the unwed mother: a series of draconian measures put the onus on her to prove her innocence if a bastard child died following a concealed birth. A French law of 1556 attempted to make secret confinements difficult by obliging unmarried women or widows to declare any pregnancy they might have to a magistrate. The death penalty loomed for a woman who ignored this procedure and was 'reputed to have murdered her child'. The English act of 1624, stipulated that an offending 'lewd mother' should 'suffer death as in the case of murder except such mother can make proof by one witness at the least that the child (whose death by her intended to be concealed) was born dead'.[56]

The second point to note is that historians suspect that married couples were able to dispose of unwanted children with relative impunity – and without having to resort to the infanticide characteristic of early Western civilizations. The essential backdrop here was the combination of high mortality rates and rudimentary forensic medicine. The first autopsies, for example, were not undertaken until the seventeenth century. Parents had several options open to them. They could engineer an 'accident'. It was after all very difficult for anyone to discover what lay behind an 'overlaying', a drowning, a scalding or a burning to death. They could opt for a strategy of deliberate neglect: what the Bavarians called 'live and let die' (*himmeln lassen*). This might involve feeding an infant indigestible food, poisoning it with laudanum or leaving an illness untreated. They could also send out a baby to a wet-nurse, though how far this was a matter of negligence as opposed to necessity remains an open question, as we have already noted.[57] Why would parents be prepared to commit such an apparently 'unnatural' or irrational act? The obvious explanation is poverty, many of the infanticides right up until the late nineteenth century being in effect late abortions. Beyond that, Barbara Kellum draws attention to the number of mothers in late medieval England who were pardoned for their murder on the grounds of insanity. She links this finding to the common perception of the infant as something evil, especially if it was unbaptized. Ominously for some infants, perhaps, people believed that the new-born babe risked being carried off by fairies and replaced with a changeling – and that the way to be rid of the intruder was to place it close to a fire so that it would disappear up the chimney.[58]

Finally, starting in the sixteenth century, infanticide came to be seen primarily as a matter of unwed mothers disposing of their illegitimate offspring. Whether this in any way reflected their share of the crime is unknowable. It may be that the hostile disposition of the law and of the population at large pushed them somewhat unfairly into the limelight. They certainly featured prominently in the judicial records. An investigation into sixty cases of infanticide that came before the courts in early seventeenth-century England revealed that fifty-three of the accused were described as spinsters, six as widows and only one as a married woman. Its author, Keith Wrightson, estimates that around 2 per cent of bastard children were killed at birth in rural Essex. Similarly, 70 per cent of those prosecuted for infanticide in Massachusetts between 1680 and 1780 were unmarried.[59] By the nineteenth century, the wholesale murder of illegitimate infants in the cities was perceived to be a public scandal. In London, the odd lurid court case exposed lethal versions of 'baby farming', whereby unscrupulous operators agreed to dispose of an infant for a substantial sum of money.[60] The context here was the risk of shame and immiseration for single mothers – though, as we have already noted, some were more vulnerable than others. Those in Mediterranean countries were in a particularly difficult position, because of acute sensitivity to the 'honour' of women in the local culture. They were likely to be thrown out of the parental home and reduced to destitution for disgracing their families. In northern Europe, it was servant girls who were most likely to be prosecuted. For them a good 'character' was all-important: if found to be pregnant, they faced instant dismissal from their job, followed by the same poor prospects of a marriage partner.[61] The atmosphere for single women may have been more oppressive in the villages and small towns than in the cities. The historian Mark Jackson notes that in northern England during the eighteenth century few women from large towns such as Leeds and Newcastle were prosecuted for child murder. Most came from smaller communities, where neighbours were acutely sensitive to any changes in the appearance or behaviour of an unmarried woman, and where the body of a child could more easily be traced back to its mother. Similarly in France, Richard Lalou found that 80 per cent of those accused of infanticide between 1825 and 1910 came from rural areas.[62] The evidence from nineteenth-century Bavaria, however, does rather point in the other direction. There farmers valued the work of a good farm servant above everything else, to the extent that they would welcome back a woman convicted of infanticide once she had served her sentence.[63]

During the late nineteenth and early twentieth centuries rather less was heard about infanticide. Some of the pressures behind it began to ease, as living standards rose and birth rates declined. There was in addition a general improvement in infant mortality rates, linked to a growing interest in maternity and childcare. In Britain there was even an Infant Protection Society from 1870, following various 'baby-farming' scandals during the 1860s, and Infant Life Protection Acts in 1872 and 1897. It might be added that societies in the West had already begun to treat women committing the crime with more compassion by this period. Many people came to see them as victims of poverty, intolerance and male seduction rather than as 'Monsters of Inhumanity'. From the eighteenth century onwards, juries and judges in various parts of Europe and North America became reluctant to convict when the death penalty was involved. Lawmakers responded by making it possible to hand out more lenient punishments (and, it must be said, to secure more convictions). In 1774 the commonwealth of Massachusetts created the offence of concealment of the death of a bastard child, punishing it by a fine of not more than 100 dollars or by imprisonment for not more than one year.[64] The English followed suit in 1803 by repealing the 1624 statute, again ending the tendency to make concealment of the death of an illegitimate infant a capital offence. Henceforth, in cases where the prosecution for murder was unable to prove that a child had been born alive, the woman might still receive a sentence of up to two years in prison for concealing the birth. In France a law of 1832 gave juries the right to grant extenuating circumstances to those they convicted. The upshot was that the customary death sentence for infanticide could be replaced with five years of hard labour. By the twentieth century, mothers who killed their children were generally considered in need of psychiatric help rather than punishment.[65]

The abandonment of infants

Infanticide would probably have been more common in the past had it not often been relatively easy to abandon a child. The scale of abandonment in certain towns was simply staggering, particularly during the late eighteenth and early nineteenth centuries. The practice had a long history by then, of course: in early medieval Europe, as in Rome, children were exposed on the streets, sold by their parents, bound to a religious house or given up to the wealthy as servants. Cassiodorus, a sixth-century observer in southern Italy, described peasants selling their children at a fair in matter-of-fact tones, assuming that the young people would be better off working in the town than in the fields. The aristocratic families who donated sons and above all daughters to a monastery were arguably attempting a humane form of abandonment.[66] They were indeed accused of off-loading their feebler members on to the Church. A new abbot, arriving at his house in the diocese of Arras in 1161, was shocked by the sad state of his flock: 'some were lame, some were crippled, some were one-eyed, some were cross-eyed, some blind, and even some missing a limb appeared among them; and almost all of these were of noble stock.'[67] A first indication of the proportion of children likely to be abandoned comes from fifteenth-century Florence, where the famous Ospedale degli Innocenti was taking somewhere between a tenth and a twentieth of all baptisms in the city.[68] Such figures may appear grim, but they pale before those registered in the modern period. In Paris, during the early nineteenth century, the equivalent of approximately one-fifth of all babies born in the city were abandoned; in St Petersburg, during the 1830s and 1840s, it was between a third and a half; and in Milan, up until the 1860s, between 30 and 40 per cent.[69] Most were abandoned at a very tender age. In seventeenth- and eighteenth-century Languedoc, for example, the majority were aged between birth and three months; children abandoned over 2 years of age were exceptional, or, in rural areas, unknown.[70] As in medieval times, the adults involved were not necessarily poor. The occasional doctor, lawyer, artist, military officer and noble, for example, turned up as a father in the records of the Hôpital des Enfants-Trouvés in eighteenth-century Paris – and was surely open to the common accusation of 'debauchery', rejecting the outcome of an illicit liaison, perhaps.[71] The chances of a baby surviving the ordeal of abandonment were slim, even when it was being cared for by a foundling hospital. Indeed, August Ludwig Schlözer, a hostile commentator in eighteenth-century Germany, described foundling hospitals as 'death-camps for infants and morals'. These institutions were forced by tight budgets to rely on the poorest-quality nurses, and sometimes to expect them to feed two, three, or even four babies at a time. During the 1620s, the clerk of the London parish of St Botolph without Aldgate quivered at the thought of the conditions in which local nurses existed: 'hee that loveth his dogg would not put it in such a place to be brought upp'.[72] Johann Ludwig von Hess estimated that

22 per cent of foundlings and orphans sent out from Hamburg to wet-nurse in the countryside during the late eighteenth century died in infancy. With some justification, he considered such a proportion 'not too great'. At the same period, 46 per cent of abandoned children in Reims would not survive their first year, nor would 92 per cent of their counterparts in Rouen. During the mid-nineteenth century, infant mortality rates hovered between 58 and 72 per cent for foundlings sent out from Moscow to peasant foster homes, and between 69 and 79 per cent for those from St Petersburg.[73]

To understand what lay behind this apparent failure to honour parental responsibilities, three key points need to be borne in mind. Firstly, those abandoning a child could reasonably expect that someone else would adopt it. As James Boswell has noted, the English word 'exposed', which is often used interchangeably with 'abandoned', is misleading, in so far as it brings to mind death through heat or cold, rather than the 'putting out' explicit in other languages.[74] Parents almost invariably left their child in a place where it would be readily found, in the doorway of a wealthy household, for example, at a market, or, more commonly, in the porch of a church.[75] Increasingly during the early modern period, specialized institutions were established for the children, so that fewer and fewer 'foundlings' were in fact discovered on the streets. The great foundling hospitals and their notorious 'wheels' or turning cradles (known as *tours* in France, *ruote* in Italy, and *rodas* in Portugal), which allowed people to abandon a child anonymously, were particularly associated with Catholic Europe. They began during the late Middle Ages with the foundation of a number of institutions in Italy, Spain and Portugal. They were developed further during the eighteenth and nineteenth centuries, with France, Russia and the Habsburg Empire also involved this time, partly as a way of discouraging infanticide. By the nineteenth century, it was customary (though not entirely accurate) to compare the so-called 'Catholic' system for protecting illegitimate children with the 'Protestant' one.[76] The latter, most typically associated with Britain and the German states, permitted the authorities to investigate the paternity of a child and expected kin to support it.[77] The former, which included Orthodox Russia as well as many Catholic countries, prohibited the establishment of paternity, provided some support for unwed mothers and funded places for illegitimate children in foundling homes. Whether the 'Catholic' system met a pressing need or merely exacerbated the problem it set out to solve was a matter of fierce debate among contemporaries. The whole apparatus did eventually collapse under the weight of numbers during the late nineteenth and early twentieth centuries. None the less, what concerns us here is that the large-scale abandonment of infants was made possible in Catholic Europe by the policy of

providing institutional care for foundlings. (Conversely, it was discouraged most of the time in 'Protestant' Europe and America by a
very different policy from Church and state authorities.)[78]

The second point to bear in mind is the desperate situation faced
by certain sections of the population attempting to raise a child. This
is not to assert that all those abandoning children will inspire our
sympathy. There were always families prepared to sacrifice an incon-
venient child: one that was deformed, a stepchild, the product of an
adulterous relationship, or even one that interfered with inheritance
plans. Occasional signs of child abuse emerge, as in the case of the
baby girl delivered to the hospital in Florence during the 1450s who
'had been beaten in several places on the head and in the face so that
her nose was squashed to the sides of her mouth'. There is also evidence that, in some societies, parents abandoned girls more readily
than boys. In early fifteenth-century Florence, for example, 61.2 per
cent of foundlings admitted to the asylums were girls; and in
eighteenth-century St Petersburg, approximately eighty boys entered
the Foundling Home for every 100 girls.[79] At the same time, a number
of studies have revealed the close links between poverty and abandonment. During the medieval era, abandonment probably acted in
part as an informal mechanism to transfer children from poor families to wealthy or childless ones.[80] Subsequently, with the foundling
hospitals, it acted in part as a safety valve for these same families with
too many mouths to feed, and for single mothers struggling to support
a child. The notes left pinned to abandoned children gave some
insight into the plight of the parents. One from early eighteenth-
century London was from 'unhapy parents which is not abell to
privide for it', another mentioned 'my husband being dead & the
times is severe hard & having had much sickness this half year'.[81]
Statistical evidence from the seventeenth and eighteenth centuries in
particular indicates close links between surges in the abandonment
of children and periods of economic crisis. In the Norman town of
Caen, for example, a rise in the price of wheat would soon be followed by an increase in the number of abandonments. In Russia, the
soldatki were prominent as abandoning mothers during the early
nineteenth century: that is to say, the wives and daughters of men
drafted into lifetime military service.[82] The most tangible sign of the
poverty driving many mothers to part from a child was the miserable
state in which the babies turned up at the foundling homes: sad little
bundles sparsely clad in old and filthy pieces of clothing.

Single mothers had to cope with the particular problem of the
shame associated with their condition. Indeed, for some of them
hostile attitudes within the local community might be more in evidence than material difficulties. In seventeenth-century England,
according to the historian Ruth McClure, everyone took for granted
that a foundling was a bastard, and that a bastard meant disgrace.[83]

However it was in Mediterranean Europe that social attitudes bore down most heavily on illegitimacy, making it almost impossible at all levels of society to raise a child outside marriage. David Kertzer has recently argued that in eighteenth- and nineteenth-century Italy the 'engine that drove the abandonment of illegitimate children' was an obsession with female honour. Any unmarried woman who compromised her sexual purity with a pregnancy would find herself under pressure to keep her condition secret and to dispose of the infant anonymously.[84] The foundling hospitals were often designed to cope with precisely this eventuality. Even in a rare English venture into such institutions, the London Foundling Hospital, the aim by Victorian times had become one of rescuing working women of 'irreproachable character' who had 'yielded to artful and long-continued seduction, and an express promise of marriage', to quote from an official report of 1847.[85] The proportions of illegitimate and legitimate children in the foundling hospitals in fact varied considerably according to period and place. The reasons for this included differing attitudes to bastardy, fluctuations in economic conditions and the particular admissions policy of each institution. In fifteenth-century Florence, only one of the first hundred infants admitted to the Innocenti hospital appears to have been legitimate, but by the nineteenth century over half were in this category. In Paris, only 5 per cent of foundlings at the beginning of the nineteenth century were legitimate, 15 per cent at the end. And in Portugal, during the 1860s, the percentage of legitimate foundlings ranged from 30.4 in the south-eastern district of Evora to 96.5 in the central one of Castelo Branco.[86]

Finally, parents often made it clear that they hoped to reclaim their children at a later date, when their circumstances had improved. Parents frequently slipped little forms of identification into the babies' clothing, such as ribbons, medals or playing cards, not to mention the plaintive notes hoping for a brighter future.[87] They may even have believed that their offspring would have a better chance of survival with the foundling hospital than at home, apparently unaware of the lethal conditions in the hospitals and among the hard-pressed wet-nurses. The foundling hospitals did after all enjoy considerable prestige, and by the nineteenth century, the mortality rate in some was declining. Hence there arose the paradox of mothers 'abandoning through love'.[88] Of course, most were to be denied any such happy ending, by their own continuing difficulties, and by the premature death of the child. Some of the hospitals, in any case, had a policy of discouraging parents from reclaiming their children. There was a somewhat utopian belief in the background that the institution could raise the child more successfully than the unfortunate parents. (Russian enthusiasts in the eighteenth century saw the foundlings as the *tabula rasa* beloved of the theorists on childhood.[89]) In eighteenth-century Oporto, the percentage of foundlings reclaimed from the Casa da Roda varied from 3 to 15 per cent according to the year. By the nineteenth century, however, Volker Hunecke has shown how parents in Milan were subverting the original intention of the foundling hospitals, the support of illegitimate children, by treating the institutions as a source of free nursing for their legitimate off-spring. This they could manage because of the exceptional willingness of the Pia Casa hospital to return children on request. He cites, admittedly as an extreme case, the handloom weaver Maria G., who managed to produce twenty-two children in twenty-eight years, and had all but the last nursed by the hospital.[90] In these circumstances one is entitled to suggest that infants were being 'temporarily entrusted' to a charitable institution by parents rather than abandoned.[91]

Conclusion

The historical literature has homed in on certain features of early childhood, such as infanticide, mass abandonment and mercenary wet-nursing, at the expense of daily routines in peasant and artisan households. This is entirely understandable, given the dramatic nature of the story to be told, and the extensive documentation left by insti-tutions such as foundling hospitals and courts of justice. It is also only right and proper that we be made aware of the huge gap that exists between the present and the past in these areas, and so this chapter has explored them in some depth. Yet it is worth reiterating that most children were spared such traumas. Mercifully, their stories were more banal. The inclination in this chapter has been to depict parents struggling in difficult circumstances to preserve the fragile lives of their young, rather than neglecting them. It has noted the impact of wealth and poverty on the raising of infants, and also a raft of cultural influences, notably attitudes to gender, to illegitimacy and to physical deformities. One might also keep in mind the first signs that a child could shape its own destiny. Until the late nineteenth century, and a wave of concern with strict feeding times, infants had some control over when they were breastfed. In some cases they had the possibility of exploiting competition between mothers and nurses for their affections. And, more generally, Bronson Alcott during the 1830s was surely neither the first nor the last parent to feel 'a bit uneasy' when confronted by the loud protests of a baby being forced to do something against its will.[92]

6

Parent–Child Relations during the Second Phase of Childhood

Historians have long been aware of the varied approaches to child-rearing among parents. They have classified these in a number of ways, taking into account above all religious and social influences. Bogna W. Lorence, for example, contrasted the indifference of many upper-class parents in eighteenth-century Europe to the intrusiveness of certain middle-class parents, motivated by religious zeal to 'totally mold and supervise their children'. She also indicated a third group, a small minority stressing the mutuality of parent–child relations. Similarly, in the seventeenth- and eighteenth-century American context, Philip Greven constructed another tripartite system revolving around 'evangelical', 'moderate' and 'genteel' temperaments.[1] Part of the explanation for these differing strategies lies with the varying conceptions of childhood among the population. It was logical for parents who believed in the innate sinfulness of children to adopt the 'intrusive' or 'evangelical' mode. At the other extreme, those who preferred to see children as naturally innocent were prepared to work with rather than against children's natural inclinations.

It is not easy to remain dispassionate when confronting the regimes imposed on children in the past. The more moderate ones are bound to appear preferable to most people now that belief in original sin at birth is rare. Indeed the 'intrusive' or 'evangelical' type of parent, setting out deliberately to break the will of their offspring, appears rather sinister. The more fervent Protestants usually emerge as the villains of the piece (though there were plenty of Catholics who were equally ruthless). To quote from a famous letter written by

Susanna Wesley to her son John in 1732, 'In order to form the minds of children, the first thing to be done is to conquer their will and bring them to an obedient temper.'[2] Child-rearing then risks becoming a grim story of cold and formal relationships between parents and children, rigid rules, harsh punishments and heavy-handed moralizing. Recently, though, historians have attempted to present a more sympathetic view of 'puritan' parents following a close investigation of both theory and practice.

Relations with mothers and other carers

Maternal (and paternal) love for children

After weaning, children moved into a second phase of childhood, which by common convention lasted until about the age of 7: the age of reason. At this point they were mainly in the hands of women, such as nurses, governesses, grandmothers, aunts, sisters, and above all mothers. The nature of maternal love during the medieval era remains something of a mystery, given that the sources available, almost entirely written by men, largely ignore the subject. Appropriately enough, one study of motherhood describes the Middle Ages as the 'time of silence'.[3] On the one hand, this very silence may be taken as evidence that there was little scope for expressing affection for children at this early period. On the other, it does not rule out such a sentiment either, and the occasional literary reference, such as the 'maternal tenderness and joy' mentioned by Boccaccio (1313–75), hints at the possibility of a warmer relationship with children. The few examples of mother–child relations which can be documented are drawn exclusively from royal and aristocratic circles, and in the final analysis they are equivocal. Queen Eleanor of Aquitaine (1122?–1204) emerges as too preoccupied with public responsibilities to have much time for child-rearing, while her ancestor Queen Margaret of Scotland (reigned c.1070–93) left evidence of a close and loving relationship with her offspring.[4]

Certainly there has been a common notion in the more recent past that mothers should provide love and affection for young children, while fathers should remain in the background as figures of authority – though neither necessarily chose to follow their allotted roles.[5] Some mothers undoubtedly continued to be indifferent to the fate of their offspring, an attitude often linked to sections of the European aristocracy. Children in this milieu were routinely handed over to a nurse or a governess, not always happily. Mme de Montglat, responsible for the offspring of Henri IV in seventeenth-century France, was described as a 'violent and unkind' woman. During the nineteenth century Russian nobles often remembered their governesses as arbitrary and punitive characters.[6] The French statesman Talleyrand (1754–1838) spent his early years separated from both his father and his mother on the outskirts of Paris, claiming that they had rarely set eyes on him by the time he went away to college at the age of 8.

At the other end of the social scale, mothers from the labouring classes struggled with difficult material circumstances, which may have strained relationships with their sons and daughters. Children were a potential nuisance for women who had a heavy routine of work on a farm or a workshop, not to mention a tight budget to manage. Many peasant and working-class autobiographies from the nineteenth century recall with some resentment the lack of physical warmth in their relationship with their mother. At the same time, they generally recognized that she was trying to look after them as best she could. Adelheid Popp, born near Vienna in 1869, claimed that she had been deprived of a childhood guided by motherly love. 'In spite of this', she went on to observe, 'I had a good, self-sacrificing mother, who allowed herself no time for rest and quiet, always driven by necessity and her own desire to bring up her children honestly and to guard them from hunger.'[7] Similarly, gruelling days working in the fields left slave mothers in the American South with little time or energy for their children. Jennie Webb informed a researcher, 'All my childhood life, I can never remember seeing my pa or ma gwine to wuk or coming in from wuk in de daylight, as dey went to de fiel's fo' day an' wukked till after dark. It wuz wuk, wuk, all de time.'[8] In addition, these slave mothers faced the peculiarly debilitating circumstances of plantation life for close family relationships: rivalry from the all-powerful masters and mistresses for the affections of their children, and the constant threat of separation through being sold on to different owners. Frederick Douglass provides an illustrious example of a slave who was separated from his mother during his infancy. He met her only four or five times in his life, before her death when he was about 7. On these occasions she managed to sneak in to see him at night.[9] Yet, if some were either unwilling or unable to do much for their children, most slave mothers made every effort to love and protect them as best they could.[10]

Puritan parents in Britain and colonial America have a reputation for remaining aloof from their young. Thomas Cobbett did after all assert in 1656 that wise parents would keep a 'due distance' between their children and themselves, on the grounds that 'fondness and familiarity breeds and causeth contempt and irreverence in children'.[11] Besides the possible fear of becoming attached to a fragile being likely to die young, common to all social strata during the seventeenth century, Puritans had to cope with the natural repulsiveness of supposedly depraved and ungodly infants. The English Puritan Mrs Housman (1680?–1735) tried to convince her young daughter of her 'Sin and Misery, by Nature and Practice'.[12] A number of historians have found parent–child relations in this type of middle-class milieu emotionally arid.[13] Others have interpreted the same material to reveal a deep-seated parental affection for children among such Puritan luminaries as Thomas Shepherd and Cotton Mather. David Leverenz has recently argued that the Puritans insisted on the need for love to permeate all acts of authority. They expected mothers if anything to be too loving with young children. Thus *The Child-Bearer's Cabinet* (1652) by William Gouge recommended that between the ages of 3 and 7 children 'be educated gently and kindly', suggesting that their original sin would still be tolerated at this stage.[14] It can even be argued that a Susanna Wesley might display a steely determination to break the will of her progeny, but that she also provided them with a caring and supportive environment. American evangelicals often recalled with some fondness the prominent role of their mothers in shaping their piety and character. Increase Mather, from Massachusetts, recorded that his mother was a 'Holy praying woman' with a particular love for him, and that 'her affection caused her to be the more earnest in prayer to God for me day and night'.[15]

As for those mothers (and fathers) who attempted a more affectionate and child-orientated approach, the historian Lawrence Stone argued that they first appeared among the English landed and professional classes during the late seventeenth century, before spreading to the Continent and to other classes. In America, Philip Greven located his 'genteel' mode of child-rearing among a newly emerging American gentry during the seventeenth and eighteenth centuries, notable for the intensity of love and affection between members of the family. A study of family life on the plantations of eighteenth-century Virginia and Maryland confirms this view, with strong evidence of parental tenderness towards young children. Well-to-do parents in these Chesapeake colonies, free from the Puritan obsession with infant sinfulness, mixed easily with their young. During the 1790s in Maryland the wife of Thomas Gilpin recorded that he spent hours playing with his children, cultivating 'a freedom and sociability with his Tender offspring In order to Unite Filial Obedience with affection'. There is always the risk of underestimating parental interest lower down the social scale.[16] None the less, it certainly helped to have the material security, and support from servants in handling the demands of the young, current in this milieu.[17]

The role of fathers and other relatives

Other relatives were often available to help mothers with their children, even when they did not live in some form of extended family.

Grandparents were rarely mentioned during the Middle Ages, presumably because few of them lived long enough to make their mark, but they crop up regularly in the sources after that. John Wesley even warned parents of the danger that indulgent grandparents living with them would undo their own good work. Interestingly, he remarked that his own mother, the formidable Susanna, 'could never govern one grand-child'.[18] In early modern England, gentlewomen were accustomed to send children to stay with their own parents for extended visits. Otherwise, there are many examples in auto-biographical sources to reveal the support provided for hard-pressed parents on small farms or businesses. Lucy Larcom, born about 1825 in Massachusetts, remembered her grandfather, a jovial French veteran of the Napoleonic Wars, and various 'aunts' from the neighbourhood. More significantly, Antoine Sylvère began his life staying with his maternal grandparents in the Auvergne during the 1880s, while his mother went off to Lyons as a wet-nurse, and returned to them when his brother was born.[19] Slaves in the Old South were particularly inclined to rally round to prop up fragile families. They extended the network of blood relatives by adopting additional aunts, uncles and cousins, and looking after parentless children.[20]

One should not ignore the role of fathers in the care of young children either. Certainly military or business affairs kept many of them away from home for long periods. The historian Randolph Trumbach draws attention to the way a keen sense of hierarchy distanced fathers in the eighteenth-century British aristocracy from their children, and above all their daughters. In nineteenth-century working-class autobiographies the drunken and abusive father became something of a stock character. Robert Roberts's father in Salford had the reputation of being a 'royal boozer'. A. S. Jasper from Hoxton (in East London) wrote that the main object in life of his father 'was to be continually drunk'. Long hours and low wages also took their toll, as fathers were too tired or depressed to pay much attention to children. The ideology of the male breadwinner encouraged men to leave child care largely in the hands of women.[21] Yet many fathers did take a close interest in the way their children were developing, and all of them might have to step in at any time if their wife was ill. Tender domestic scenes, including fathers feeding and singing to their infants, occasionally appear in Dutch art of the seventeenth century. Lucy Larcom recalled from nineteenth-century New England that her father was not a demonstrative man, but that when clinging to him about the age of 2 she realized that he 'really loved me as I loved him'. Medieval pictures sometimes show slightly older children following their father around, watching him chop wood, for example, or scaring birds as he sows seed. Even a heavy drinker like the father of Alice Foley, in Bolton about 1900, swung between bouts of ill-temper and happier moods, when he would amuse his children with tales from Irish folk-lore and passages from Shakespeare (a legacy from his time as a scene-shifter in the local theatre).[22]

Besides these adults, parents in the labouring classes regularly called upon their children to look after younger brothers and sisters. The oldest child, according to a recent study of medieval childhood, was by definition a replacement mother or father.[23] To a considerable extent, children raised each other. Whether this generated resentment between siblings or bonds of affection doubtless varied between families. There was always the risk that underlying tensions over inheritances and dowries might sour relations, or that personalities would clash. Emilie Carlès, raised in the Alps on the eve of the First World War, respected her older brother but grated with her older sister: 'the character of a pig'.[24] In general, older children seem to have approached their task with some relish. 'Little mothers' on the streets of nineteenth-century London proudly held and soothed babies while young lads kept an eye on infants in the middle of games of cricket. On the other side of the Atlantic, slave children between the ages of 8 and 12 affectionately 'nursed' those younger than themselves during the working day.[25]

In the very long-term perspective it is worth remembering that for most people in the West, right up until the nineteenth century, the family fulfilled many functions. It had to provide for the subsistence of its members, plus their education, vocational training, health, entertainment and old age. Parents understandably might find themselves impatient of their children's demand for attention on many occasions. One thinks of the young peasant 'Toinou' (Antoine Sylvère, b. 1888) in the Auvergne, reassessing his relations with his parents after his mother affected indifference to him as he howled under a table. Instead of consoling him she remained absorbed in peeling vegetables, making him realize that grown-ups were 'utilities' which would only intervene when it suited them. Henceforth, he decided to separate his affairs completely from those of his parents.[26] However, the slow emergence of the child-centred family was not necessarily an unmixed blessing for the young. Recent experience suggests that when the role of the family shrinks to providing emotional security for the individual, relationships often become overheated. Far from being a 'last refuge of love and decency', to adopt the terminology of Christopher Lasch, the family all too often descends into generating hostility between parents and children.[27] In other words, there may have been considerable compensation for children in the past through the solid links they established with parents and other relatives as producers, educators, storytellers, nurses, and so on.

Early training: hygiene, walking and talking

One of the first tasks facing parents and nurses was toilet training. Modern authors have often expressed surprise at the relaxed attitudes in this area until the late nineteenth century. For the majority of the population, living in the countryside, a mess on a beaten earth floor was easily cleared up with the help of some ashes. Moreover, with young children going without any form of underwear beneath their gowns, there was no problem with soiled clothing. Even in more bourgeois circles, it often passed without comment in diaries, or was treated lightly. During the 1680s a Dutch authority counselled parents to avoid frightening infants during the process, and (a most exceptional approach) to treat bed-wetting as merely a passing phase.[28] Perhaps the key was the very different approach to hygiene before the nineteenth-century discovery of germs: as David Hunt reminded us, even the corridors of the royal palace in seventeenth-century Paris reeked from 'a thousand ordures' where courtiers had relieved themselves.[29] John Locke gave a hint of the more intrusive regime to come in *Some Thoughts Concerning Education* (1693), by recommending that children be 'set upon the stool' every morning after breakfast.[30]

Parents might prove more anxious when teaching their children to walk, not surprisingly, given the large numbers of people who ended up lame or rickety. They discouraged infants from crawling on all fours, partly for the practical reason that floors were cold and damp, and partly for its association in their minds with animal rather than human behaviour. In medieval society, artists never represented an infant in this position. Experts did make a point of warning that it was dangerous to try to force a child to walk before it was naturally ready. Bartholomew the Englishman advised waiting until at least the age of 1, and trying the earliest steps on a smooth, soft surface, to avoid one leg becoming longer than the other. Even so, parents attached leading strings to clothes and used little frames to encourage children to remain upright as soon as possible. Medieval iconography also showed the familiar scene of a child being encouraged to walk towards the outstretched arms of its mother. To protect the head at this stage, infants sometimes wore little padded caps. If the worst came to the worst, and the child was slow to take its first steps, there were various saints to help, or springs dedicated to the god Mercury.[31]

Medieval authorities linked learning to talk with the onset of teething: infants by definition were those who could not speak because they had no teeth. Teething was therefore a further time of anxiety for parents, given that it affected the child's ability to speak properly in later life as well as its health in the short term. Popular medicine was on hand to help with teething rings, amulets and the recommendation, which survived into the twentieth century, to rub the gums with salt and honey. Parents also provided babies with rattles to bite on, some made of wolves' teeth, in the hope that the child's own would be as white and strong. Bartholomew the Englishman felt that nurses should teach the child its first few words early on by pronouncing them as if she had a stammer: words like *mama*, *papa* and *babeu* were particularly suitable.[32] Mothers and nurses could also turn to a whole repertoire of verses to help them teach their children to talk, as well as to soothe and amuse them.

At the very beginning, they would sing lullabies as they rocked the baby's cradle. Most of these revolved around pastoral scenes (helped by the way 'sheep' conveniently rhymes with 'sleep' in German and English) or versions of the calming word 'lulla', such as this from the pen of an Anglo-Irish friar in 1315:

> Lollai, lollai, litil child,
> Whi wepistou so sore?

Others, curiously enough, dwelt on the harsh realities of life. A German example, presumably from the time of the Thirty Years War in the seventeenth century, urged the child to pray because Count Oxenstierna and his Swedish army would be coming in the morning:

> Bet' Kinder, bet',
> Morge kommt der Schwed'.
> Morge kommt der Oxestern,
> Der wird die Kinder bete lern.
>
> Pray, children, pray.
> The Swede will be here in the morning,
> Oxenstierna will be here in the morning
> And he'll teach the children to pray.

In similar fashion, Spanish infants were caressed with warnings of a Moorish lady spreading sleep, and English ones with warnings that Bonaparte might pass their way. Russian lullabies made a compelling association between cats and sleep, one hoping that grey cats would bring drowsiness. For a slightly later stage in early childhood, mothers had rhymes to accompany games such as a knee-ride or counting fingers and toes. While British and American children had 'this little pig went to market', their counterparts in Poitou recited 'La petite fontaine – où les oiseaux vont boire – celui-ci l'a pris – celui-ci l'a plumé – celui-ci l'a fait rôtir – celui-ci l'a mangé – et le petit n'a rien eu, rien eu! [The little fountain – where the birds go to drink – this one caught it – this one plucked it – this one roasted it – this one ate it – and the little one had nothing, had nothing!]. More obviously educational in intent were the rhyming alphabets used at home and in the schools: 'B,A, BA mon père me bat; B,I, BI, à coups de béquille; B,O, BO, à coups de sabots; B,U, i n'me battra plus'. (An English version might be: 'B,E, BE my father beats me; B,U, BU he beats me with a shoe; B,I, BI the beating makes me cry; B,A, BA he won't beat me today.') In Britain and America mothers could also sing or recite from a broad repertoire of the verses known from the early nineteenth century as nursery rhymes or Mother Goose's songs.[33]

Folklore collections give the impression of a rich cultural heritage for children in all languages. What they cannot convey is a sense of how often mothers, nurses and other adults made use of it. In other words, were children immersed in their language by nursery rhymes almost from birth? One can only speculate. Some sources give the impression of a lively atmosphere for the infant. In Lille and the Departement of the Nord in France, for example, the P'tit Quinquin, a lullaby written by Desrousseaux in the nineteenth century, became something of a 'national anthem' for the region. Yet there may be a risk of romanticizing life in a peasant or working-class family. A selection of autobiographies covering working-class households in Vienna around 1900 indicated that the use of language was reduced to the bare essentials.[34] It should be added that children themselves happily played with language in rhymes, riddles, tongue-twisters, counting-out formulas and the like, independently of adults. Specialists have traced certain of these verses back to antiquity, and noted the close parallels between versions in different languages. While English-speaking children recite 'Humpty Dumpty sat on a wall', Saxon ones have 'Hümpelken-Pümpelken sat op de Bank'. At the same time, Bettina Hürlimann contrasts the tender stories evident in German collections with the nonsense beloved of the English.[35] She draws attention to the dazzling interplay of rhyme and rhythm in an English verse such as

> Simple Simon went a-fishing
> For to catch a whale;
> All the water he had got
> Was in his mother's pail.

Beginning a child's education: toys and books

A child's education began on its mother's knee. She was traditionally responsible for teaching her offspring how to make the sign of the cross, to kneel while praying, and basic prayers such as the Credo and

the Lord's Prayer. During the Middle Ages Italian mothers had a
formidable range of religious pictures to show their babies, and, in
Florence, there is the example of little dolls representing the infant
Jesus for the more pious daughters. Moralists also advised mothers
to contrive lessons from everyday events, making children think of
vegetables thrown into a pot of boiling water as sinners going to hell,
or timing the cooking of a dish by a prayer (a boiled egg needed an
Ave Maria).[36] During the seventeenth century the future Louis XIII
learned moral lessons from his governess, as others would through
their mothers, by repeating various maxims and proverbs. The folktales that passed down the generations may also have helped children as well as adults learn to cope with the world around them.
Members of the educated elite might start to learn to read and write
in a casual way about the age of 4 or 5. During the 1620s, Adam
Martindale, the son of a Lancashire yeoman, learned to read with the
help of an ABC, taught by his older siblings and 'a young man that
came to court my sister'.[37]

From the time of the Renaissance in particular, parents in the
upper and middle ranks of society made every effort to ensure that
the young acquired good manners and all the other conventional
signs of superior breeding. Erasmus, writing on civility in children
during the 1530s, gave detailed descriptions of correct behaviour:
well-bred children would not, *inter alia*, wipe their noses on their
sleeve, hold their mouth agape like a fool, or swear. Mealtimes in
particular were a fertile period for parents to insist on patience and
deference in the very young. In other words, as Norbert Elias put
it, with the new sensibilities of the sixteenth century, children had to
attain in a few years the advanced level of shame and revulsion
that had developed among adults in Western society over several
centuries.[38] For parents who had only the most rudimentary education themselves there were little books available from hawkers, such
as *The Rules of Christian Propriety and Civility, Very Useful for the
Education of Children and for People Who Lack both the Good
Manners of Society and the French Language* from sixteenth-century
France.

Toys and games

Toys and games were a means to encourage the intellectual and
physical development of the young, as well as to amuse them. At all
periods, young people have managed to improvise toys from everyday objects or to make their own. It was, for example, a simple matter
to make a rag doll or a hobby-horse. In the Nivernais region of
France, folklorists reveal that children made themselves little flutes,

rustic carts (bending branches to form wheels), and traps to catch sparrows. The young were also adept at creating their own fantasy worlds: alternatives to the adult world, according to the historian Bernard Mergen, but clearly modelled on that same world.[39] During the seventeenth century, Dr John Dee mentioned in his diary that 'Arthur Dee and Mary Herbert, they being but 3 yere old the eldest, did make as it were a shew of childish marriage, of calling each other husband and wife.'[40] Early examples of toys made by adults have survived from the Middle Ages: rattles, wooden tops spun by a whip or the fingers, dolls, miniature cooking utensils and dinner sets in ceramics or base metals, model boats, lead soldiers, little clay animals, and so on. One might assume that those that survive were for children from well-off families, but young people in poor families were not necessarily deprived of such amusements. Parents and local artisans could presumably make something simple for them. Children played with these in a group, rather than on their own, and often with songs or rhymes to go with them. Take the spinning top. In Rennes, boys drew concentric circles on the ground and placed a 'sleeping' (immobile) top in the inner one. The first player had to try to nudge this top out of the circle with his own, but without either going outside the second circle. Such games called in their various ways on physical strength and co-ordination, a grasp of current technology (with miniature water or wind mills) and basic know-how (carving with a knife). Historians have observed how some of these toys led the child towards the world of adults, with boys soon having the hobby-horse, girls the doll and the dinner set. At the same time, children proved quite capable of subverting such expectations. In antebellum America, for example, many girls preferred vigorous outdoor activities such as skating and sledding to playing with dolls. Towards the end of the century, G. Stanley Hall found three-quarters of the boys he studied playing with dolls, while girls sometimes acted more aggressively with them than parents might have hoped.[41]

Later, in the modern period, the toy industry began to supply young people with innovations such as board games, little sets of tools and jigsaw puzzles, as well as the traditional lines. The French had a long tradition of producing playing cards with information on geographical, historical or classical themes. The earliest board games, an English speciality, certainly trumpeted their educational content, with titles including 'A Journey through Europe' (1759), 'Royal Geographical Amusement' (1774) and 'Arithmetical Pastime' (1798). From the 1760s jigsaw puzzles, another English invention, depicted maps, historical scenes and the like. A Maria Edgeworth might take a rigorous line on the educational value of toys, denouncing dolls, action toys, and squeaky pigs in favour of those requiring imagination or exercise, such as plain pencil and paper, or hoops and tops. None the less, entrepreneurs had spotted a market for a huge range of playthings which would allow parents to divert and stimulate their offspring. By the middle of the nineteenth century, manufacturing centres such as Nuremberg in Germany and the Black Country in England were turning out huge quantities of cheap wooden and metal toys. An American observer, Kate Douglas Wiggin, stressed national differences evident at the Universal Exhibition held in Vienna during the 1890s:

> The French toy represents the versatility of the nation touching every topic, grave or grotesque . . . From Berlin come long trains of artillery, regiments of lead horse and foot on moving tramways . . . The American toys . . . refer the mind and habits of the child to home economy and husbandry and mechanical labour.[42]

Even working-class households might be able to afford some of these goods. George Sturt, the son of a wheelwright in Surrey, recalled playing with marbles, tops and hoops; but also having little carved animals 'clean and whitish from Swiss or Norwegian chiselling'.[43]

Children's books

Parents could give their offspring books, most of which, until the middle of the eighteenth century, came into the category of those which sought to teach children or improve their minds as opposed to children's' books proper, defined by Harvey Darton as those designed primarily to give pleasure.[44] During the early phase 'a pall of dejection' hung ominously over juvenile literature.[45] English-speaking Protestants had the *Token for Children* (1671–2), written by the dissenting preacher James Janeway, which makes its content clear in the subtitle: 'An Exact Account of the Conversion, Holy and Exemplary Lives, and Joyful Deaths, of several young Children'. In nearly all of the examples Janeway insisted on the original sin of children, referring to the 'corruption' or 'miserable condition' of their nature, which could only be redeemed by conversion.[46] *The Divine Songs, Attempted in Easie Language for the Use of Children* (1715) by Isaac Watts, also ubiquitous on both sides of the Atlantic during the eighteenth and nineteenth centuries, was no less preoccupied with punishment and pain.[47] Young Protestants read the Bible from an early age, young Catholics the *Lives of the Saints*: in a *dévot* region such as Brittany, the youngest child able to do so read aloud from this latter work at mealtimes.[48]

It was not all a matter of gloom and doom, however: young people took the initiative in reading other books that came their way. Children in Europe and, to a lesser extent in America, shared the adult taste for chapbooks (in France, the *Bibliothèque bleue*). These were cheaply produced little works that were scorned by the educated minority but devoured by ordinary men and women between the late seventeenth and mid-nineteenth centuries. They covered a wide range of subjects, including the legends, medieval romances and adventure stories which particularly appealed to children. A number of writers recalled reading these during their childhood. The poet Goethe (1749–1832) fondly remembered how when young he would often spend his money on a *Volksbuch*. Although almost illegible, being printed on 'the foulest blotting paper', Goethe considered these books to be a precious remnant of the Middle Ages. He listed as favourites '*Eulenspiegel, The four sons of Aymon, Fair Melusine, Kaiser Octavian, Fortunatus* – the whole bunch, right down to *The Wandering Jew*'.[49] Among the books originally written for adults which young people read with pleasure were Foxe's *Book of Martyrs* (1563), Cervantes's *Don Quixote* (1605), Bunyan's *The Pilgrim's Progress* (1678), *The Thousand and One Nights* (available in French by 1717), Defoe's *Robinson Crusoe* (1719) and Swift's *Gulliver's Travels* (1726). *Robinson Crusoe* was famously seized on by Rousseau as the most suitable work for his Emile, and it spawned a whole list of imitators (known as *Robinsonnades*): Campe's *Robinson der Jüngere* (1779), Saint-Pierre's *Paul et Virginie* (1787), Wyss's *Der Schweizerische Robinson* (1812–13), and so on.[50]

With John Newbery and his *Pretty Little Pocket Book* (1742) entre-preneurial publishers began to open up the market for children's books. Even so, the didactic motive continued to loom large in books and magazines during the late eighteenth and early nineteenth centuries. Rousseau's *Emile* inspired a host of works, such as those produced in France by Mme de Genlis and Arnaud Berquin, and in England by Maria Edgeworth and Thomas Day. Take the case of the boy who got his come-uppance for revelling in the sufferings of fishes caught on his line when he tripped and caught his chin on a meat hook:

> Poor Harry kicked and call'd aloud,
> And screamed and cried and roared,
> While from his wounds the crimson blood
> In dreadful torrents poured.[51]

There was also a potent evangelical strand in the literature, continu-ing the Puritan tradition in England and America. Perhaps the most intense moralist of this group was Mrs Sherwood, an author whose output featured prominently in the Sunday reading of many Angli-can households for much of the nineteenth century. She is now best known for the infamous passage in *The History of the Fairchild Family* (1818) where the parents react to a squabble between brothers by laying on an evening walk to see something 'they will remember as long as they live': the rotting corpse of a man hanged for murdering his brother. (In French and German versions the corpse was removed to take account of 'Continental sensibilities'.) More appetizing fare for children soon appeared, however. German authors in particular mined a rich vein of fairy tales and folk poetry. The brothers Grimm, to take the outstanding example, managed to breath new life into ancient folktales for the benefit of children in *Kinder- und Hausmärchen* (1812–15). They inspired others to explore similar material in their own national cultures, leading to works for young people by Andrew Lang (1844–1912) in Scotland and most famously by Hans Christian Andersen (1805–75) in Denmark. It was, however, the English and Americans who produced the most diverse literature for young people of various ages, including the adventure stories launched by Captain Marryat (1792–1848) and James Fenimore Cooper (1789–1851), the fantasy works of Charles Kingsley and Lewis Carroll during the 1860s, and the school story pioneered in 1857 by Thomas Hughes with *Tom Brown's Schooldays*.[52] Most of these works were aimed at boys, though this did not stop girls enjoying them too. Eventually the market began to consider the interests of girls more seriously, the 'domestic novels' of American authors such as Louisa M. Alcott and Susan Coolidge being outstanding.[53]

By the end of the nineteenth century, the earnest moralizing tone evident during its earlier years had largely disappeared from children's literature. Indeed, authors began to revel in Romantic notions of childhood as a lost self. The association of children with the peaceful haven of a garden was always tempting, as in *The Secret Garden* (1911) of Frances Hodgson Burnett. Children's books continued to be written by adults, of course, and their authors had to keep in mind that they had to appeal to parents as well as the young. Adventure stories, for example, soon gave up any element of preaching, but an author like G. A. Henty promoted the more secular values of courage and resourcefulness. None the less, children could to some degree shape the market for books and periodicals. One can surely discern their influence in the rise of the escapist 'dime novels', 'penny dreadfuls' and *romans à quatre sous*, all so despised by 'respectable' opinion for their supposedly subversive influence on young and old alike. There was in addition the success of rivals to these works, such as the *Boys' Own Paper*, first issued in 1879 by the Religious Tract Society, and its companion magazine the *Girls' Own Paper*.[54]

Some harsh lessons: fear and irony

The ethnologist Arnold Van Gennep asserted that a peculiar feature of education in France was its reliance on fear and irony – though it seems more a feature of child-rearing in peasant societies everywhere. Parents, he suggested, terrified children by tales of the supernatural rather than by blows, at least until education and child psychology made their impact during the nineteenth century.[55] This was certainly one way of responding to a problem faced by peasant families everywhere: keeping youngsters out of danger while adults were busy. Bernard de Gordon, a physician in fourteenth-century Montpellier, described early childhood (*pueritia*) as 'the age of concussion', on the grounds that 'in that age they begin to run and jump and to hit each other'.[56] Children were free to roam around the streets and the countryside for much of the time. The American Lucy Larcom wrote that children in her neighbourhood during the 1830s enjoyed the privilege of 'a little wholesome neglect'. At the same period Olivier Perrin reported that in Brittany once children could walk they were left very much to themselves until the age of 7 or 8.[57] The downside to such liberty was the sad catalogue of accidents afflicting the very young. Not for nothing were godparents charged at baptism with guarding children from fire and water up to the age of 7. Medieval coroners' inquests in England, to take a well-documented case, reveal them drowning in wells and ditches, burning to death and scalding themselves with pots of boiling water.[58] Hard-pressed adults, so the argument goes, therefore threatened their charges with an assortment of sinister creatures: fairies and bogeymen lurking around wells, werewolves running loose at night, and so forth.[59] *Little Red Riding Hood* then becomes a 'warning tale', with its predatory wolf lurking in the forest. In rural Holland parents threatened children with monsters such as 'haantje pik' (a rooster that ate children) or a bogeymen like 'Zwarte Piet'. Isabella de Moerloose, born in 1661 near Ghent, remembered tales of 'the man with a long coat' who tried to kill firstborn children, as a device used by her mother to lure her home on time. In Brittany, Pierre-Jakez Hélias remembered being threatened with the Man with Carrot Fingers, a tall figure in a cloak who liked to play tricks on travellers. Fritz Pauk introduced a handy modern variant from Germany about 1900: 'When we were bad, my aunt would just say, "The Social Democrats are coming!" Then we ran away like rabbits.'[60] As for irony, it was easy to mock children who complained of hunger with 'eat your fist, and keep the other till tomorrow', or, of a cut, with 'that will make a good blood-pudding'. Yet there was always a strain in pedagogical literature that opposed such tactics. During the second half of the nineteenth century, for example, advice manuals directed at middle-class parents in America dismissed such scare tactics as backward. Indeed they specifically counselled mothers not to use threats of old men prowling about to steal children, on the grounds that they might 'embitter the whole existence of her offspring'. The enlightened mother would adopt gentler, but more time-consuming methods of persuasion.[61]

Engraving from *L'Illustration*, 12 December 1874, showing various causes of death among young children. Bibliothèque Nationale de France, Paris.

Breaking the will

The most challenging role for the more 'intrusive' parents, be they Catholic or Protestant, was passing on moral and religious values. For as long as most people believed in the innate depravity of children, the only way they could envisage breaking in such stubborn creatures was by drawing up a tight set of rules and strictly enforcing them. A German manual on disciplining and instructing children, dating from 1519, barked out its orders:

> Sleep neither too little nor too much. Begin each day by blessing it in God's name and saying the Lord's Prayer. Thank God for keeping you through the night and ask his help for the new day. Greet your parents. Comb your hair and wash your face and hands.[62]

Even tiny infants who broke the rules risked fierce retribution. During the 1600s, the future king Louis XIII of France was first whipped by his nurse while only 2 years of age. Susanna Wesley noted in a chilling passage concerning her offspring that 'when turned a year old (and some before) they were taught to fear the rod and to cry softly'.[63]

Whether many parents stayed the course driving out the 'old Adam' in their children must remain a matter of speculation. Some operated in a manner reminiscent of a military campaign. By a certain perverse logic, Mme Acarie in seventeenth-century France consistently forced her children to eat dishes which they disliked, and denied them those they appeared to enjoy. John Locke cited with approval the example of a 'prudent and kind mother' who whipped her infant daughter eight times in one morning to master her stubbornness. Had she stopped at the seventh, he commented, 'she had spoiled the child for ever'. The American Baptist minister Francis Wayland described in some detail his battles with his fifteen-month-old son during the 1830s, on one occasion depriving the boy of food for three days to win an argument over a crust of bread. He reported that: 'Since this event several slight revivals of his former temper have occurred, but they have all been easily subdued' his son had become 'mild and obedient'.[64] The stakes were high for the more pious parents: nothing less than the eternal salvation of their sons and daughters. However, wearing down a child's resistance was a daunting task, being most likely to succeed, according to the historian Philip Greven, in a relatively isolated and self-contained household. Only then could parents control their children without fear of contaminating influences from outside. The constant complaint from moralists during the early modern period that mothers loved to spoil their children may give a hint that the extremes were generally avoided. During the 1530s in Ulm, Conrad Sam sounded a familiar theme, with 'Children today are badly raised; not only do parents permit them their every selfish wish, but they even show them the way to it.' John Locke famously warned parents during the 1690s against 'humouring and cockering' little children.[65] There is no doubting that Puritan parents cared deeply for their families, and feared that their own tenderness and indulgence would interfere with discipline.[66]

There was a widespread custom of 'beating, whipping, abusing and scolding children and holding them in great fear and subjection', as Pierre Charron observed in 1601.[67] As always, those inflicting corporal punishment were convinced that it was for the good of the child. As a medieval French verse put it:

> Myeulx vault chastier sur le cul
> De verges son petit enfant
> Que le voir pendu quant est grant.

> Better to beat your child when small
> Than to see him hanged when grown.

'Better whipt, than Damn'd' was the Puritan version from Cotton Mather, indicating their preoccupation with the hereafter. A survey of the experiences of American children found that during the period 1750–99 every single boy and girl in the sample had been beaten with an instrument, ranging from a hickory stick to a horsewhip. Even during the nineteenth century, when advice manuals were beginning to move away from recommending corporal punishment, approximately three-quarters of the children experienced such punishments. The historian Elizabeth Pleck concludes that the whipping of children by both mothers and fathers was a routine matter which, if it did not occur daily, was far from rare. Slave parents on the plantations had a more earthly justification for their harsh regime: instilling the unwavering self-control necessary to survive the oppressive 'etiquette of race relations'. Richard Wright, born on a plantation in Natchez, Mississippi, in 1908, had painful memories of this tradition during the post-emancipation era. He recalled being beaten with a stick by his mother to the extent that he lost consciousness and spent several days in bed with a fever – though it must be said that he had just burnt down half of the family home.[68]

At the same time, there was an equally long tradition of challenging such brutal treatment of the young. During the eleventh century, St Anselm engaged in famous conversation with an abbot who complained of the boys in his cloister: 'They are bad and incorrigible. We beat them night and day, but they only get worse and worse.' Anselm replied that since the boys felt no love or pity, no good-will or tenderness in the attitude to them, they 'believe that all your actions proceed from hatred and malice against them'. He pointed out the advantages of kindness in upbringing, suggesting to the abbot that, like a goldsmith who moulds his leaf with gentle, careful, pressure rather than with blows, he should form the boys' characters by cheerful encouragement and loving forbearance.[69] Other moralists throughout the Middle Ages were as keen on adults setting a good example to the young as on use of the whip. The Catalan scholar Raymond Lully (*c.*1233–*c.*1315) warned parents that surrounding a son with 'vanities and ugly words', romances, songs and instruments risked poisoning his mind with a taste for luxury.[70] Advice manuals in the early modern period advised using corporal punishment as a last resort, and disapproved of immediate, ill-tempered responses to childish faults. What mattered to them was that the child developed a conscience, and internalized the prevailing norms.

It goes without saying that there were always examples of vicious parents (or step-parents) who abused children, the sort 'who beats them about the head, punches and pummels them until he has made them into deaf-and-dumb fools and broken cripples', to quote from a sixteenth-century German source. Samuel Butler provided a vivid account of one such parent, an Anglican clergyman no less, when recalling the 'long and savage cruelty' of his childhood in *The Way of All Flesh* (1903). This partly autobiographical novel made it clear that he could remember no feelings for his father 'but fear and shrinking'.[71] On the other side of the coin, the experience of the odd English and American Puritan that has come down to us suggests that this group may not entirely deserve its fearsome reputation in child-rearing. The diary of Ralph Josselin, written between 1641 and 1683, gave no hint of harsh and authoritarian attitudes to his sons, nor of physical punishments. Similarly, the grandson of the leading American evangelical Jonathan Edwards (1703–58) emphasized the benign approach of the latter's wife, Sarah: 'She had an excellent way of governing her children; she knew how to make them regard and obey her cheerfully, without loud angry words, much less heavy blows.'[72] The historian Simon Schama has noted the way Dutch Protestants in the seventeenth century followed the alternative humanist tradition of cajoling children into learning. Women reformers in nineteenth-century America took a similar line by encouraging mothers to take advantage of their children's affection for them where possible instead of resorting to corporal punishment. In Edwardian England there is evidence from oral testimonies that, outside the industrial north and Midlands, children were not beaten very often, simply because parental authority was rarely challenged.[73]

Moreover, there was always an awareness that excessive discipline would provoke resistance. St Paul himself had warned fathers not to provoke children to anger. The future Mme Roland, of French Revolutionary fame, contrasted her 'sagacious and discreet' mother with her 'despot-like' father. The former realized that the young Marie-Jeanne needed to be governed by reason and affection; the latter failed miserably, his recourse to the rod converting his gentle daughter into 'a lion'. The English writer Edmund Gosse (1849–1928) likewise recalled that a caning from his father when he was 6 provoked only murderous rage.[74]

Conclusion

> To parents who wish to lead a quiet life I would say: Tell your children
> that they are very naughty – much naughtier than most children. Point
> to the young people of some acquaintance as models of perfection and
> impress your own children with a deep sense of their own inferiority.
> You carry so many more guns than they do. This is called moral influ-
> ence, and it will enable you to bounce them as much as you please.[75]

This passage from *The Way of All Flesh* trades on a certain cynicism:
Samuel Butler was after all out for revenge on his parents for an
unhappy childhood. Even so, it is hard to disagree that the early
stages of parent–child relations lend themselves to a gross imbalance
of power. Not all parents in the past chose to exploit this, of course,
but there was a significant group, influenced by religious dogma on
the sinfulness of children, which was determined to exert a formidable 'moral influence'. How children reacted to the grim regime of cold
baths, battles over food, whippings and scoldings is hard to gauge.
Some of the more strong-willed evidently rebelled; others meekly
conformed. Doubtless it is easy to overdo the violence involved, and
to ignore the parental love and concern for spiritual wellbeing that
underpinned such efforts. Most children therefore probably bonded
effectively with their parents – at worst, because they were unaware of any alternative. To quote Butler again, 'young people have
a marvellous faculty of either dying or adapting themselves to
circumstances.'[76]

7

Relations with Parents and the Peer Group during the Third Phase of Childhood

The age of 7 or thereabouts marked a significant turning point in the life of a child in the past, in theory if not always in practice. It might be acknowledged with a little ceremony, above all the 'breeching' of a boy when he was ready to move on from the little gown associated with early childhood. The future Louis XIII discarded his robe for a doublet and breeches; slave boys in America swapped their smocks for trousers or breechcloths. The sons of Russian nobles had to move from the female to the male quarters of their homes somewhere around this age, while poorer boys in America would no longer be allowed to sleep with sisters or female servants.[1] Gender differences, never far below the surface in infancy, became more pronounced. Fathers took over prime responsibility for sons, while mothers continued their instruction of daughters. Life became increasingly complicated for young people at various levels: within their families, among their peers and in the local community. Those from the 'popular classes' were expected to start making a serious contribution to the family economy, minding farm animals, for example, or looking after younger children. At the same time, the peer group came to rival the family as a source of influence. The young tended where possible to group in little 'gangs' separated by no more than three or four years of age. Finally, they gradually joined the community at large, possibly through formal education in the school system, or even through marriage. In canon law, 12 was the minimum age of marriage for a girl, 14 for a boy.[2]

Parent–child relations

Fathers were expected to take a more prominent role in child-rearing at this stage of life. They were thought to have the necessary strength to inculcate the values of respect and obedience in the young. Mothers were considered by moralists during the early modern era to be too indulgent with their offspring – more likely by their perceived emotional nature to spoil children than to discipline them. This was not merely a family matter. The great fear at this period was that an unruly younger generation would threaten the foundations of an ordered society. In the absence of a police force, the family was the basic unit of supervision.

Mothers would continue to influence their sons, providing affection and perhaps occasionally something sterner. Jessica Tovrov notes that in noble circles during the nineteenth century Russian mothers habitually shamed sons into doing better.[3] Sons generally reciprocated these maternal feelings. During the Middle Ages, for example, a long line of medieval saints and clergy, ranging from St Augustine to St Bernard, looked back fondly to pious mothers who had inspired their vocation. Guibert de Nogent was more ambivalent: he was certainly in awe of a mother who was 'beautiful, yet chaste, modest, and steeped in the fear of the Lord', but he bitterly resented her decision to pursue her own religious vocation and leave him as an 'orphan' at the age of 12.[4] One might also cite the valiant little Vivien from the romance *Doon de la Roche*. Although only 9 years of age he threatened to avenge his mother, Olive, when his father repudiated her and proposed to marry again:

> Si je puis vivre tant qu'armes puisse baillir,
> Ce est .i. mariages qui durera petit.

[If I live long enough to take up arms, it is a marriage which will not last long.][5]

Mothers in the past have been accused of 'selective love', favouring sons over daughters, and the eldest over younger sons.[6] This can hardly be denied outright, but probably cannot be sustained very far. It may be that mothers had a particular soft spot for their first-born, whatever its sex. Youngest sons also often convinced themselves that they were the most cherished. Typically, Guibert of Nogent mentioned a mother's 'special affection' for her last-born. There is, moreover, a strong counter-current in the literature to suggest that mothers developed more enduring bonds with daughters than with sons. The latter after all would soon drift off as adolescents into the world of men. By the nineteenth century, as their entry into paid employment was delayed, boys often became restless. 'Who can love boys!' wrote an exasperated middle-class mother in New York state during the 1840s, 'They are awkward, ugly things, always in the way, and always in mischief! they are neither companions nor pets.'[7]

Whatever her relations with her sons, the main role of the mother was to prepare her daughters for life as a wife and mother. She taught them to spin and to sew, how to manage a household, and, it was hoped, those virtues of humility and submissiveness supposedly appropriate to their sex. Girls often developed close bonds of affection with their mothers as they came to depend on them for help and advice. Even among the educated nobility of nineteenth-century Russia, where mothers generally remained aloof from their children during the early years, the onset of adolescence brought a growing intimacy as the young woman tried to make her way in society.[8]

Fathers meanwhile expected to take over the upbringing of their sons. If a noble, during the Middle Ages and beyond, he would prepare a boy for a military career by encouraging him to pursue various physical pursuits such as horseriding, hunting and hawking. To take an extreme example, about 826 the future Charles the Bald joined his father on a hunt at the age of 3, striking with child-sized weapons the 'quivering back' of a young doe specially brought to him.[9] Fathers from the upper and middling ranks in general were also interested in encouraging a little learning. They might take this on themselves. Jerome Cardan (1501–76) recalled that his Milanese father taught him the rudiments of arithmetic and the ways of magic about the age of 9. 'Shortly after', Cardan added, 'he instructed me in the elements of the astrology of Arabia, meanwhile trying to instil in me some system of memorizing', and, to round off, at the age of 12, there were the first six books of Euclid.[10] This was exceptional, however: English aristocrats in the eighteenth century thought that fathers made the best teachers for their sons, but accepted that they would never take up the opportunity.[11] Instead, fathers handed over their sons to tutors or schools for formal education. They did retain an interest in the religious instruction of their children, and in discipline. Martin Luther, echoing St Augustine, proclaimed that the head of the house 'should punish his child like a judge, instruct him like a doctor and preach to him like a parson or a bishop'.[12] Lower down the social scale, learning a trade loomed large early in life, and sons often picked up the basics by helping their fathers around a farm or a workshop. As for daughters, fathers were not directly involved in their upbringing, but they might well regard them with great affection. Sir Thomas More (1478–1535), 'the most loving father of his generation' according to the historian M. J. Tucker, famously reminded his daughters that he had always been an indulgent father and that his whip was 'invariably a *peacock's tail*'.[13] However, conflicts over who might marry could easily sour relations at a later stage.

In the long run, the patriarchal family, with the father ruling the roost over his wife, children and servants, would not survive the transition from an agrarian to an industrial society. In seventeenth-century America, for example, where most families maintained an independent existence on a farm or in a small business, paternal authority was reinforced by control of landed property or a craft skill which could be passed on to children. By the eighteenth and nineteenth centuries, the development of new forms of wealth and increased geographical mobility combined to weaken the authority of fathers. This was particularly the case in the North. Southern fathers, less affected by industrialization, retained a more prominent role. In the Chesapeake, for example, most young men on the plantations were aware that their future prosperity depended on the generosity of their fathers. In Oneida County, New York, by contrast, the writing was on the wall for the traditional patriarchal family by the 1820s and 1830s. Daughters could now find jobs in the factories, sons were going to work in artisan workshops or local stores, and any young person from a farm family could weigh up the benefits of independence through migration. Everywhere the way was open for more informal relations between parents and children. However, it was mothers who stood to gain most from this shift, particularly as the notion of 'separate spheres' encouraged mothers to stay at home and look after children while fathers went out to work.[14] The father became the 'second parent'. As such, children came to exert a hold over him: if he wanted their affection, he would have to work for it by spending more time with them![15]

Dealing with abusive and negligent parents

Before the nineteenth century, the idea that the state should intervene in relationships between parents and their children was almost unthinkable. In *ancien-régime* France, say, as in colonial America, governments expected the head of each family to be responsible for the orderliness of its members, and in return they granted him wide-ranging powers over his wife and children. Even local communities appear to have been reluctant to put pressure on abusive fathers.

They might organize a charivari or 'rough music' to show their disapproval of what they considered an unsuitable marriage, but they appear to have regarded children as almost a form of property for the father.[16] Respect for paternal power would remain potent everywhere well into the nineteenth century. Yet as reformers in various parts of Europe and North America became concerned over such issues as the health, delinquency, morality, poverty and schooling of children, so the logic began to shift inexorably in favour of philanthropic and state intervention in family affairs.

Jacques Donzelot traced the transformation in the relations between the state and the family in France to a long campaign during the late eighteenth and nineteenth centuries for the preservation of children. He depicted doctors, administrators and others lambasting the waste of infant life in foundling hospitals and among wet-nurses, and the heavy burden on the public purse of single mothers. During the 1860s, societies for the protection of children therefore attempted a close surveillance of working-class households, encouraging improved hygiene and regular family life. Soon, however, the reformers found their efforts stymied by the refusal of some families to allow entry into their homes, or the calling back of delinquent children from special correctional institutions. They responded by promoting a series of laws which shifted control from 'morally deficient' families to philanthropists, doctors and magistrates. The 1889 Roussel law on the divestiture of paternal authority deprived parents of their rights if they had been convicted of prostituting their children or committing crimes against them. Moreover, even in the absence of any such conviction, the courts might divest of their rights parents who 'by their habitual drunkenness, their notorious and scandalous misconduct, or by their physical abuse, compromise the health, the safety, or the morality of children'.[17] This took care of parents who were clearly unfit to rear children, but did nothing to cover another group who were merely incompetent. A further law of 1898 gave judges the power to declare the Public Assistance or a person from a charitable society the guardian of a child in all cases where offences had been committed by or against children.[18]

Meanwhile in Britain various reformers began to ponder the advantages of legal intervention in family life. Those investigating juvenile delinquency, notably London philanthropists in 1816, became aware of the role of parental neglect in encouraging criminal behaviour among the young. The 'condition of England' debate of the 1830s and 1840s prompted others to assert the need to 'civilize' the poor in the new urban slums. Reformers blamed parents for the hordes of children in the cities drifting into vagrancy and crime, and took initiatives such as founding industrial schools and reformatories as a response. Renewed interest in the social question during the 1880s led to the foundation of the National Society for the Prevention of Cruelty to Children, and a campaign for statutory reform of family issues.[19] In Germany zealous Protestants set about 'rescuing' wayward children whose families had failed them and placing them in the pious atmosphere of a *Rettunghaus* ('House of Salvation'): in 1847 there were forty-seven such institutions in operation. By the 1870s, however, various critics suggested that these private initiatives were inadequate to combat growing social disorder. As Bismarck himself put it, 'only the state can resolve the social question'. Later the Berlin schoolteacher Franz Pagel found a ready audience for his lurid account of society at the mercy of its restive masses. More specifically, he argued in 1896 that the 'principle of self-preservation' demanded that society take charge of fatherless children, otherwise they risked descending into the ranks of 'those wild hordes . . . who wait in the shadows of houses and trees in the finest quarters of town for the harmless pedestrian and, in the dark of night, threaten the life and property of the peaceful citizen'.[20] 'Child-savers' in America also made their mark during the Progressive era of the late nineteenth and early twentieth centuries, with the familiar combination of private charitable initiatives and government regulation – at the local if not the federal level. To begin with, nineteenth-century charities such as the New York Children's Aid Society (founded in 1853) launched a placing-out movement for abused, neglected and homeless children. Their famous orphan trains, an American speciality, may have taken as many as 200,000 youngsters from the cities of the East to farm families in the Midwest and the Plains. Later on the example of Boston shows class tensions between a native-born Protestant elite and largely Catholic immigrants coming to the fore in the activities of the local Society for the Prevention of Cruelty to Children. Upper-class agents of the society saw themselves helping culturally inferior immigrants achieve 'American' standards of childcare.[21]

What stands out, then, is the way the peculiar atmosphere of the late nineteenth century in particular, with its widespread fear of social unrest and foreign rivals, concentrated minds on the advantages for the nation of encouraging child welfare. Hence all the effort to educate poor parents, provide them with material assistance, and, if necessary, to take over their responsibilities. So, besides French legislation, outstanding examples include the Prussian Law on Compulsory Correctional Education of 1878, which allowed guardianship courts to place child convicts in the *Rettungshaus* or a foster family if it would prevent further 'moral waywardness', and the British Prevention of Cruelty to Children Act of 1889, also known as the Children's Charter. The latter permitted the courts to take a child into care in cases of parental ill-treatment or neglect, and to punish those who ill-treated boys under 14 and girls under 16.[22]

Whether these campaigns did much to improve the lot of children is impossible to determine. It can certainly be stated without undue cynicism that one of the motives behind them was to refashion poor, working-class families in the image of middle-class reformers, which leaves the benefits for children open to question. The 'moral panic' over child abuse during the late nineteenth century may also have caused reformers to exaggerate the evil to further their cause. At the same time, the campaigns did reflect a heightened interest in child welfare, and led to improvements in the mechanisms to help, cajole or punish abusive parents. To take one example, Paul Thompson cited the recollections of a nurse who worked in both rural and urban parts of southern England during the Edwardian era. The conclusion was that the extent of abuse in working-class households can easily be overdone: 'In all my experience I doubt if I have come across as many as twelve cruelly used children; not one of those was persistently ill-treated.'[23]

Mixing with the peer group

There is an argument from the 1990s that peer groups of children and adolescents have more influence on the long-term development of an individual's personality than parents. According to psychologist Judith Rich Harris, parents pass on their genes to their offspring, but 'heritability' will only account for 40 to 50 per cent of the variance in personality characteristics between adults. The rest must be explained by environmental influences – of which the personalities and child-rearing philosophies of parents are not likely to be important. Hence she asserts that assumptions about 'nature and nurture' need rethinking. The earlier stress on nurturing by parents should be abandoned in favour of one on socialization by the peer group. In her own words, 'children learn how to behave outside the home by becoming members of, and identifying with, a social group'. Whether her work will revolutionize the way we think about parent–child relationships, as some have suggested, remains to be seen. She has perhaps over-played a good hand, dismissing rather too easily the influence of parents on their children. At the same time, there is a long tradition of parents blaming 'peers' for leading their children astray.[24] There is also plenty of evidence from the past that young people left home relatively early and spent a good deal of time with others of their own age. Interestingly, the historian François Lebrun concluded several years ago that the influence of families on the socialization of children was 'quite thin', at least among the popular classes. He emphasized instead the role of relatives, friends, neighbours – and other children.[25]

The gang

Boys and girls might play together in the fields or on the streets of a town, but where there were sufficient numbers available, they generally went their separate ways in groups segregated by both age and sex. 'It was degrading to play with girls and in our talk we relegated them to a remote island of life,' wrote Richard Wright (1908–60) of his experience as a black youth in West Helena, Arkansas.[26] Young males from the 'popular classes' tended to form gangs, profiting from their greater freedom to roam away from the house. In British towns during the late nineteenth and early twentieth centuries the lads drifted into street gangs from about the age of 10, and gave up when courtship took over during their late teens. Some of the more delinquent gangs achieved widespread notoriety, such as the fearsome Peaky Blinders in Birmingham and the Redskins in Glasgow, not to mention the 'Hooligan' gangs that supposedly terrorized Londoners during the 1890s, but these were dominated by older teenagers. Their French equivalents included the *Gars de Charonne* and the *Loups de la Butte* among the notorious *Apaches* in Paris, taking their names in these cases from their neighbourhoods. Berlin in its turn had its *Apachenblut* (Apache blood) and the *Galgenvogel* (gallows bird), and towns in the southern United States, during the time of the Civil war, their 'Baconsoles' and 'Pinchguts'.[27] Most of the younger gangs were simply informal groupings of children who happened to play on the same street. Membership fluctuated as families moved around and as older children were drawn into the world of work. Even so they tended to have their own leaders and codes of conduct. Members solemnly supported their oaths with such familiar rhymes as the English:

> Cross my heart and hope to die
> Drop down dead if I tell a lie

or, in a French version:

> Boul' de feu, boul' de fer
> Si j' dis pas vrai, j'vas en enfer
>
> [Ball of fire, ball of iron
> If I lie, I go to hell].[28]

They demanded absolute loyalty, sneaks and traitors being punished mercilessly. Witness the fate of Bacaille in Louis Pergaud's novel *La Guerre des boutons*: having betrayed his comrades' camp to a rival gang, he was stripped, beaten and spat upon, and his clothes were returned heavily soiled with urine and faeces, and with all their buttons missing. The gangs also discouraged any form of effeminate behaviour, boys who played girls' games in the Nivernais, for example, being mocked as Jean-Fillette.[29]

The climate of the urban street gangs was dominated by a strong sense of machismo. The gangs carved out their identity by defending their territory against incursions from rivals in neighbouring parishes or sections of a town. According to a report from Cologne in 1810, repeated brawls during the summer months meant that boys could not go unaccompanied from one district to another. In Lancashire this custom of 'scuttling' involved much ritualized abuse and brandishing of weapons, although in the end the lads preferred to rely on fists and boots in a fight. A gang member insisted from his experiences during the early twentieth century that: 'It wasn't too serious; every party was more or less satisfied with a black eye or a nose bleed.'[30] Public authorities tended to regard male juveniles with a jaundiced eye, not least because of their rowdy street games, their petty theft and their pranks to annoy adults. Such antics had a long pedigree. In 1448 the dean and chapter at Exeter accused young people who had entered their cloisters to play games of scrawling on walls and breaking windows. In the 1590s, there were similar complaints of boys breaking windows and disturbing services at St Paul's Cathedral in London. Boys in Oneida County, New York, kept the local press occupied during the mid-nineteenth century with stories of their practical jokes, such as digging holes in the streets to trip pedestrians and stuffing a butcher's sausage machine with huge amounts of garlic. The socialist militant Georges Dumoulin remembered his gang marauding the gardens of their village in the Pas-de-Calais Departement during the 1880s. Their particular speciality was killing the cats of aged *rentières* and turning them into stew.[31] Street children also indulged in stealing from markets and shops. Court records for Oxford around the town of the twentieth century show petty theft among juveniles concentrating on fruit and vegetables, toys, sweets and cigarettes. The gangs organized lookouts and developed various ruses so that one member distracted the shopkeeper while another pocketed the goods. The pay-off was perhaps something to eat or smoke – and a chance of a little excitement to relieve a humdrum existence. Prowess in pilfering guaranteed enormous prestige among the peer group.[32]

As for the girls, they were more inclined to mix in shifting alliances of twos and threes, defiantly observing and mocking the males.[33] Parents tied them more closely to the home, above all in the Mediterranean culture. Even in northern Europe, custom dictated that they behave modestly and make themselves useful. A study of the village of Minot, in Burgundy, revealed that among the young shepherds and shepherdesses in the fields, boys could play around, while girls had to spend their time knitting, lace-making or mending clothes. Martial Chaulanges recreated this type of scene in his novel *Les Rouges Moissons*, set in the Limousin region during the 1890s. When two shepherd girls meet in the fields, they chat, sing, and eat together, all the while knitting and keeping an eye on their flocks.[34]

Games and entertainment

Last but not least, young people spent as much time as they could playing games among themselves. There is a remarkable continuity in these activities. Iona and Peter Opie remarked that 'if a present-day schoolchild was wafted back to any previous century he would probably find himself more at home with the games being played than with any other social custom.' They noted that the Elizabethans played Bowls, 'King by your Leaue' (a version of Hide and Seek) and 'Sunne and Moone' (Tug of War). Other familiar games can be traced back further, to the Middle Ages, and even into antiquity.[35] There is indeed a familiar air to many of the activities depicted in the famous painting *Children's Games* (1560), by Pieter Bruegel the Elder.[36] This encourages the pleasing notion of a particular 'culture of childhood'. Thomas Jordan talked in terms of a lost Tribe of Children. The task of the historian then becomes one of investigating this tribe like an anthropologist, to see how it transfers the lore of the group to its newest and youngest members – for it is children, not adults, who teach the rules. It must be said that there is a danger here of pushing the young into a ghetto, ignoring the fact that from the very beginning they acquire their language and patterns of thought from adults.[37]

Yet there is no doubting that they liked nothing better than to roam unsupervised in the fields, on waste ground, or around the streets of a town. At first sight, children who lived in rural areas appear best placed to do this. Lucy Larcom (b. 1825) recalled almost 'unlimited liberty' in rural Massachusetts, as she and her friends created a fantasy world of castles and exotic entertainment along the rocky shoreline. Boys preferred hunting, fishing, climbing, and generally exploring every last nook and cranny of their territory. The English poet John Clare confessed to 'robbing the poor birds nests or searching among the prickly firze on the heath poking a stick into the rabbit holes'. The former slave Winger Vanhook in America remembered robbing birds' nests, fishing, riding plough horses, running calves 'an fightin' de old ganders'.[38] Yet many children raised in the towns had the countryside just around the corner. Suburban Los Angeles during the late nineteenth and early twentieth centuries

Pieter Bruegel the Elder, *Children's Games*, 1560.
Kunsthistorisches Museum, Vienna photo AKG London.

was still a haven for middle-class youngsters, as girls and especially boys escaped on horseback to the beach or up into the hills. Marshall Stimson, for example, wrote that by the age of 10 he and three or four other boys were able to ride 'all over the county'. They carried with them 'a skillet, a coffee pot, bacon and bread', and scavenged whatever else they needed on their camping expeditions. Even in the big cities children managed to find sanctuaries from the outside world in such places as graveyards, deserted houses and building sites. The streets themselves were very much children's territory in the towns: areas where, by mutual consent, young and old stayed out of each other's way as far as possible. A survey of children by social workers in Cleveland, Ohio, in 1913 found half of them on the streets, playing games or 'just fooling'.[39]

Children played their games with scrupulous attention to tradition. Karl Friedrich Klöden recalled from his childhood in late eighteenth-century Germany that 'one knew that "Kühler" [marbles] was played only in early spring, ball only at Easter time, kite-flying in the autumn'. The games themselves can be classified under various headings, including chasing, hunting, racing, daring, guessing and pretending, as the Opies have done. Some involved 'wanton acts of barbarism' to animals. Boys, for example, liked to shoot at birds with their catapults, or to tie a cockchafer to a piece of string and watch it fly around until it dropped from exhaustion. Other games involved running, jumping and wrestling, or early versions of modern ball games. It was a simple matter to turn a pig's bladder into a ball or to make a serviceable cricket bat. The English folklorist Lady Alice Gomme, for example, described 'Camp', or 'Kicking Camp', a form of football played by boys in Suffolk. Two teams of ten to fifteen players attempt to 'seize and convey the ball between their own goals', the latter being approximately 150 yards apart.[40] There was an underlying seriousness to these apparently frivolous activities, in so far as local employers kept an eye out for the strongest and most courageous youths. Pierre-Jakez Hélias reported from his Breton village that the whole community watched as its young played games such as trying to push wheelbarrows along a plank over a stream or diving through breakers in the sea. Later those hiring farm-hands used various subtle criteria to judge the worth of the young males, including their repertoire of songs, their accomplishment in dancing the gavotte, and 'their strength and dexterity in local games'. Out in the Far West of America, youngsters took with particular enthusiasm to competitive and aggressive games such as 'prisoner's base' or 'anti-I-over'. These 'achievement' games, according to the historian Elliott West, helped prepare them for the individualism and social mobility of frontier society.[41]

The type of games that a child played, or whether it played them much at all, depended on various influences such as social class, gender, ethnicity and urban or rural residence. Thus one child from a poor background in nineteenth-century London lamented that there was 'never no time to play'. Meanwhile another, daughter of a vicar in London's Poplar and so kept apart from *hoi polloi* by her parents, watched all the varied activities taking place in the street below her: it was 'my theatre, puppet show and pantomime in one'.[42] These differences re-emerged when it came to savouring the entertainments that became increasingly available in urban society. The historian J. H. Plumb listed an impressive array of entertainments designed to instruct as well as amuse in eighteenth-century England, in the form of 'exhibitions of curiosities; museums; zoos; puppet shows; circuses; lectures on science; panoramas of European cities; automata; horseless carriages; even human and animal monstrosities'. These improving activities, however, were largely beyond the reach of working-class families. They had to make do with cheap and cheerful entertainments such as dancing on the streets to a barrel organ or enjoying the hustle and bustle of a street market. Alice Foley delighted in the Bolton market on a Saturday night, with the 'open shop fronts lit by paraffin flares, competing traders bawling their wares, and narrow streets crowded with buyers, or gaping sight-seers'. By the end of the nineteenth century they might be able to afford a ticket to a professional football match, or an evening at one of the more popular music halls or *café-concerts*.[43]

Children themselves influenced what was on offer from the growing entertainment industry. In mid-nineteenth-century London, to the dismay of 'respectable' middle-class opinion, the children of the poor revelled in the lurid productions of cheap theatre. Observers of the 'penny gaffs' noted that most of the customers were young labourers, apprentices and costermongers, ranging in age from about 8 to 20. With spoken dialogue ruled out by the licensing laws, the shows revolved around ballets, singing and dancing. What appealed most to these audiences were dramatizations of the more sensational murders, pantomimes and melodrama, side-by-side with popular songs and dances. A similar market emerged in America during the early twentieth century, as the children of working-class and immigrant families flocked to such spectacles as the 'penny arcades', cheap vaudeville halls and moving-picture theatres. Again reformers balked at the idea of children running loose without adult supervision. Teachers worried that boys would learn about crime and 'how to get money without work'. The Chicago Vice Commission in 1911 fussed over boys and girls mixing in a darkened room: boys, they felt, were encouraged to embrace the girls near them and 'offer certain indignities'. Yet all appeals to the owners of nickelodeons to provide more wholesome fare fell on deaf ears. They were more impressed by the money to be made by catering to juvenile tastes with westerns, comedies, melodramas and the occasional adaptation of a 'classic' like *Ben Hur*.[44]

Leaving home

Philippe Ariès asserted that in medieval times the child 'soon escaped from his own family'. After the age of 7, he specified, children lived with families other than their own. He cited an Italian text from the late fifteenth century which accused the English of a 'want of affection' towards their children, on the grounds that they were accustomed to put them out to 'hard service' in the houses of others at the tender age of 7 to 9. It was of course all grist for his mill in arguing for the lack of sentiment in parent–child relations.[45] No one disputes that during medieval and early modern times, in north-west Europe at least, a very substantial proportion of families routinely sent off their offspring to boarding-school or to another family. A spell as a servant with a farmer or craftsman was a common experience for young people between leaving home and getting married. For example, a census of population in rural Denmark at the end of the eighteenth century revealed well over 50 per cent of adolescents and young adults in service. Some of these children also suffered from the isolation involved: the historian Terence Murphy suggests that feelings of loneliness and anxiety lay behind the remarkably high level of child and adolescent suicides in early modern England. Daniel Rose was a case in point: a 12-year-old from Gloucestershire who hanged himself in his master's garden in 1695, having complained to friends that he was unhappy with his position as an apprentice weaver.[46]

What is more controversial is the age at which children left home. It now seems that historians were rather too impressed with the very quotable Italian visitor. Some children undoubtedly left home to serve in another household about the age of 7. However, these must be seen as an unfortunate minority, drawn largely from the ranks of small peasants and agricultural labourers. Most young people waited until their teens or even their twenties before becoming apprentices or servants. An early census from 1422 for the French town of Reims showed female servants concentrated in the age-group 12 to 22, males that of 12 to 30. Ann Kussmaul calculated from evidence concerning early modern England that 13 to 14 was the most common age for moving into service in husbandry. Richard Wall in his turn drew attention to the village of Colyton, in Devon, during the 1840s. Here, 23 per cent of boys in the age group 10–14 were absent from home, but a further quarter in the age-group 25–9 were still living with their parents. We are bound to follow him in concluding that leaving home was a protracted process, with no mass exodus at one particular age. A few very young children, under 10 years of age, were likely to be away from home, but otherwise the contrasts with the contemporary world were not striking.[47]

Conclusion

So in the final analysis should one emphasize the improvements in parent–child relations over the centuries, or the continuities? Put this baldly, the obvious answer would be to call for a more nuanced approach. There were of course considerable variations created by the familiar influences of class, gender and ethnicity. None the less, the inclination here is to plump for continuities rather than the escape from a nightmarish past. Certainly one can point to the growing interest in child-rearing methods since the eighteenth century, and the decline in the belief that children were fundamentally sinful creatures who needed to be broken in like an animal. We are bound to agree with Lloyd deMause that by the early twentieth century children in the West were less likely to be killed, abandoned or beaten than in the past (reserving judgement for lack of evidence on sexual abuse). With the extremes of poverty gradually receding, the rough edge to parent–child relations may well have been smoothed over: parents were arguably less preoccupied with the basic struggle for existence, and more relaxed in their company. They were also beginning to have fewer children, allowing them to devote more attention and resources to each one. On the other side of the coin, several historians have come to the conclusion that the harshness of parental treatment of children during the medieval and early modern periods has been exaggerated. Children may well have grasped that practices that appear abusive today, such as repeated whippings, were motivated by love and a concern for their interests. There was too an underlying cruel necessity, which pushed parents into heartrending decisions on abandonment or an early age for leaving home. Once again one might note the adaptability of children to different circumstances, and the importance to them of peers and others outside the parental home.

PART III

Children in a Wider World

Although children spent much of their time among family and friends, they were never confined exclusively to such intimate circles. Their activities in the public arena ranged from the respectable to the deviant, from singing in a church choir or earning wages, say, to thieving or prostituting themselves on the streets. Sooner or later, depending on their particular circumstances, they were likely to come into contact with priests, folk healers (or physicians), schoolteachers, employers, customers, and so on. Moreover, by the early twentieth century they might find it difficult to avoid the attentions of a whole army of professionals dedicated to their welfare, including health visitors, charity workers, truancy officers and factory inspectors, not to mention the police. Historians have written countless volumes documenting efforts by voluntary agencies and the state to 'help', 'rescue' and 'improve' young people. Witness the extensive literature in such fields as education, penal reform, factory legislation, and maternity rights. The reasons for this generous coverage are readily discernible. Historians can tap into a long series of impassioned debates, on such issues as child labour and juvenile delinquency. They can gain easy access to the records of the institutions involved. And they can remain safely in the world of conventional politics. The links between children and mainstream adult life are indeed important. Unfortunately, the focus is nearly all on what adults thought was good for children, and on how the old manipulated the young, rather than the juvenile perspective.

8

Children at Work

Child labour is a subject that stirs the passions. People today react indignantly to reports of children still working in 'sweatshops' in Western societies, not to mention the millions employed in the poorer countries of the world. They regard the widespread employment of children in their own past as rather shameful. The climbing boy suffocating up a chimney, or the little mill hand working to the relentless pace of a machine, have become stock images of the Industrial Revolution. Yet such hostility to child labour is a comparatively recent phenomenon. During the early modern period, the majority of families sought work for their children as a matter of routine. Indeed, the authorities worried more about the sins of 'sloth and idleness' among the young than about excessive work.[1] It was the nineteenth and early twentieth centuries that brought profound changes to the role of children as workers. In Europe, as in America, child labour legislation and compulsory education ensured that children would be dependent on their parents and to some extent sheltered from the world of adults. In the much-quoted words of Viviana A. Zelizer, children became economically 'worthless' but emotionally 'priceless'.[2]

The first historians to investigate child labour generally focused on the passing of the nineteenth-century Factory Acts in England and America. They adopted a simple challenge and response model, in which the unprecedented 'exploitation' of child labour in the factories and workshops provoked the state to intervene. As Hugh Cunningham has pointed out, in the British case their story could be dressed up in the form of a romance, with gallant figures such as Lord Shaftesbury rescuing poor factory children from the clutches of cruel

employers. In similar vein the American historian Walter Trattner
lined up child labour reformers, motivated by 'pity, compassion, and
a sense of patriotism', against greedy or ignorant parents and employers.[3] Such a heavy focus on the benevolent influence of the state
on child labour was not to everyone's taste, however. Historians on
the extreme left of the political spectrum countered that social policy,
although superficially responding to the perceived needs of children
and the working class, was, in the words of Michael Lavalette, 'shaped
by a bourgeois ideal of "childhood" and family life'.[4] There was also
a critique from the political right. It emphasized the material and
moral progress brought by the factory system, and the disadvantages
of state intervention for child workers, notably a loss of training and
skill.[5] Some historians since the 1960s have argued that rising real
wages rather than factory legislation were the main influence on the
long-term decline of child labour in various European countries and
the United States.[6] Others have noted the way certain groups of
employers and workers were more receptive to curbs on child labour
than others, which reinforced considerable regional disparities in
the age structure of the labour force.[7] Myron Weiner has recently
asserted that it was compulsory school attendance rather than factory
legislation that finally eliminated children from the workshops in
the past, the former being more readily enforced than the latter.[8]
On a different tack altogether, historians focusing on the process of
growing up or on autobiographical material have attempted to record
the way children themselves felt about work. This leads them to consider differences in the experiences of, say, agricultural and industrial
workers, slave and free children, or males and females.[9] Not surprisingly, perhaps, the historical literature remains skewed towards industrial and urban child labour, and towards Britain and other nations
that industrialized early.

When discussing the history of child labour, it is difficult to
avoid the influence of our own experiences in a modern, bureau-
cratized society. The temptation is to ask at what age children started
work, as if it were the same as starting school today, and whether
they were employed or unemployed, as most adults would now consider themselves. The answers are likely to be misleading, unless one
makes considerable allowance for the peculiar nature of children's
work in the past. Children's entry into the labour force was staggered
over several years, according to personal circumstances and the availability of work in each locality. Some had full-time employment
outside the home, but the majority probably worked without
wages in a family unit, or took on little tasks, such as caring for siblings, which released adults for productive labour. Definitions of 'children' in the labour force varied considerably in different national
contexts: most historians have taken 14, 15 or 16 to be the upper age
limit.

Children and family work routines

Despite the grisly images that loom large in textbooks, much of the work done by children in the past was casual and undemanding. Children gradually drifted into the labour force, mopping up a host of little tasks that were appropriate to their size and experience. They might make themselves useful on a farm or in a workshop about the age of 6 or 7, but were unlikely to start a training in the more skilled and exacting tasks until about the age of 10, at the very earliest. Censuses of population do not lend themselves particularly well to recording this type of routine working and helping. For what it is worth, the British census of 1851 found that only 3.5 per cent of children aged 5 to 9 were occupied. P. E. H. Hair concludes that even allowing for a high margin of error 'the vast majority of children under 10 did not undertake any regular gainful employment'. In the next age group, 10–14, the census found no more than 30 per cent occupied: 37 per cent of boys and 22 per cent of girls. Not until the late nineteenth and early twentieth centuries is there evidence of a crisp transition from childhood into the adult world of work, marked by the ritual of leaving school at the minimum age required by the state.[10]

Work on the land

In both Europe and America, the majority of children lived in the countryside, at least until urbanization steadily impinged from the mid-nineteenth century onwards. Most jobs in agriculture required strength and stamina that were beyond the capacity of children. Even American slaveholders considered children under 10 a net liability. A former slave, John Smith, recalled that 'children were not made to work till dey got twelve or fourteen years old, unless it was some light work around de house – mindin' de table, fannin' flies, an' pickin' up chips to start a fire, scratchin' Master's head so he could sleep in de evenings, an' washin' Missus' feet at night, 'fore she went to bed'.[11] On the small family farms that were characteristic of many regions on both sides of the Atlantic, young children of both sexes were confined to 'helping out' with such simple but time-consuming chores as looking after younger brothers and sisters, fetching water and firewood, gathering fruit and herbs, picking stones, scaring birds, spreading manure and 'minding' pigs and sheep.[12] During the fourteenth century, Jean de Brie began his life as a shepherd at the age of 7 with a few geese and goslings, moved on at 8 to the more demanding task of minding pigs, helped a cowherd at 9, and by 11 was in charge of eighty lambs which 'neither ran away nor hurt him'.[13] The contribution of children was also partly seasonal, reaching a peak with the intensive work routines of the harvest period. Younger juveniles took food out to the labourers in the fields, while older ones bound corn into sheaves behind the harvesters or led the wagon horses.[14]

Some of this work required long, lonely hours in the fields, not to mention spells out in cold or wet weather. A young Yorkshire lad recalled the miseries of preparing cattle fodder in winter during the early twentieth century, as his breeches became soaked in the slops and his hands became swollen and cracked. At the same period Marie-Claire, eponymous heroine of a novel by Marguerite Audoux, struggled with the desolate atmosphere surrounding her as she watched over her sheep in the Sologne region of France. She found the mist hanging in the woods and the absolute silence oppressive: 'There were days when I felt so abandoned that I believed the world had collapsed around me, and when a crow cried out as it flew by in the grey skies, its loud, raucous voice seemed to announce the misfortunes of the world.'[15] Yet children themselves often managed to ease their burdens by combining work and play, either on their own or with others out in the fields. Young shepherds went swimming, climbed trees or carved wood. Early in the sixteenth century, a native of Segovia described mingling his sheep with other flocks so that he and his fellow shepherds could play games along the lines of hockey and racing.[16]

If populations of hard-pressed smallholders were most inclined to find little tasks for young children, the larger farmers might also do so. In isolated cases during the nineteenth century, and indeed creating considerable scandal, children of both sexes joined agricultural gangs. Critics pointed out that the youngsters often had to walk long distances to the fields, work intensively under the gangmasters and miss school for weeks at a time. In Italy, the spread of rice-growing on the irrigated plains of Piedmont and Lombardy led to the widespread mobilization of women and child workers. In Belgium 'weeding groups' of thirty to forty children, aged between 8 and 14, cleaned up beet, oat and flax fields. They regularly awoke at five o'clock in the morning, marched out to the fields for up to an hour, and worked until seven in the evening. In England, particularly in East Anglia and the east Midlands, public gangs of women and children performed similar tasks, weeding, hoeing, pulling roots and stone-picking on the large arable holdings. Others collected shellfish on the Lancashire coast, or picked fruit and vegetables in numerous parts of the country. A Report by the Children's Employment Commission in 1866 discovered that approximately half of the gang members in the eastern counties were between 6 and 18 years of age, and that they might work from 5 a.m. to 7 p.m. Contemporaries were as concerned by the moral dangers posed by male and female, young and old, working together (and sometimes sleeping together in barns) as by the physical hardship of long working hours. The 1867 Gangs Act therefore prohibited public gangs that mixed the sexes, as well as banning children under 8 from such employment, and requiring licences for gangmasters.[17] Slave children on the plantations of the American South faced the bleakest outlook of all. Once out in the fields, they faced the full force of a harsh disciplinary regime, ruthlessly enforced by the whip. As a prelude to this they might work at clearing rocks or care for animals in adolescent 'slave gangs'.[18]

During their early teens, as they moved from childhood to youth, gender differences among young farm workers became more pronounced. Daughters continued to help their mothers around the house, the garden and the dairy, while sons began to work more intensively beside their fathers in the fields and stables. In arable areas, teenage lads often began by working with a pair of oxen or horses, and eventually learned the numerous skills of a farmer, including ploughing, sowing, harvesting and carting. Meanwhile in pastoral regions they took responsibility for larger flocks or herds, and spent nights out alone in the fields. Robert Savage confessed that at the end of the nineteenth century in east Suffolk:

> I was so young, that I dursn't stay out in the dark by myself. I was not man enough to stay with the flock throughout the night; so for a little while my father used to come out wi me at night and sleep in the little ol' cabin along o' me. But I soon got used to it by myself and I took no notice of the queer little noises you hear in the night.[19]

Girls too were affected by crop specialization. In the Midwest of America, for example, during the early twentieth century wheat-producing areas minimized the demand for women and girls to work in the fields, while tobacco farming maximized it.[20]

These conventions for distributing work according to age and gender were often ignored in poor or isolated households. St Alpaix was the first-born of a poor peasant in twelfth-century France. From the age of 12 she helped her father with his plough team of oxen, and carried baskets of manure to the fields and garden, while her younger brothers minded cows and sheep. Arthur Young in eighteenth-century England was most impressed by the way smallholders in the north sometimes turned out their wives and daughters to drive a plough in the depths of winter. Similarly, in the northern United States during the antebellum period, when weather or market conditions put families under pressure, each individual did whatever was required. In the words of an Ohio farmer, 'The rule was that whoever had the strength to work, took hold and helped.' Most spectacularly of all, on the far western frontier in late nineteenth-century America, an acute shortage of labour and dispersed settlement patterns obliged children to take on a range of responsibilities that would have been unthinkable in the more settled east. Sons undertook women's work, and, more commonly, daughters became involved in such activities as herding, harvesting and hunting. Fifteen-year-old Luna Walker, newly arrived in Kansas in 1871, boasted in her diary of bringing home rabbits, ducks and turkeys, and even of attempting to ambush buffalo, while out hunting with her brother. Teams of children, boys and girls alike, might occasionally take on such 'adult' work as ploughing and planting. They also became adept at herding sheep and cattle, and at making a quick profit selling food to the men in the new mining towns. A visitor to Nebraska observed: 'It has been a novel sight to watch a little girl about ten years old herding sheep near town, handling her pony with a masterly hand, galloping around the herd if they begin to scatter out, and driving them into a corral.'[21]

At some stage during childhood or youth, many young people in early modern Europe left home for employment in other households. The proportion of the youthful population involved in farm service varied considerably between regions, being more evident in northwestern Europe than in the south: above all in Scandinavia, the German states, Holland, Britain and France. In Austria, between the seventeenth and early twentieth centuries, a sample of census material from various rural communities reveals that somewhere between a fifth and a half of those in the age-group 15 to 19 were servants.[22] A female farm servant in Bavaria at the end of the nineteenth century started at the age of 13 or 14, helping the peasant's wife with household chores and looking after the children. She would hope to move up the hierarchy of servants as she grew older. The ultimate aim of such girls was to accumulate enough skills and money for a dowry to secure a husband. In Tuscany, during the late eighteenth century, girls preferred to work on larger farms, where they could learn a broader range of skills, and so enhance their marriage prospects.[23] The typical male experience was slightly different, being geared more towards acquiring the skills needed later in life on the land. The young Robert Savage started in the kitchen of a big farm in Suffolk as a 'back'us boy' (back house boy) at the age of 12. By his mid-teens he had moved on to the more obviously 'masculine' work of helping with the horses and assisting a shepherd at lambing season.[24] Ideally, the farm servant was treated as a member of the employer's family, though this was not always the case. Some found themselves relegated to the stables at night, others felt that they were not being fed adequately. As Martial Chaulanges noted, on the basis of his ancestors' experience in the Limousin, there was no question of choosing the work to be done or the tools to be used:

> If someone has to go out and look after the sheep when the weather is bad, or was at *la serbe* when it is freezing hard enough to crack a

stone, it is the servant girl who goes. Is there a border to clear, a tough tree stump to cut up? It is for the *domestique*.[25]

Employment in the towns

In the towns, particularly the major commercial and administrative centres, formal training or paid work for children was also not always easy to come by. Apprenticeships did not usually start until boys, or in some cases girls, had reached their teens: an age when they were considered sufficiently strong or mature to be able to cope with the requirements of the craft. A study of apprenticeship contracts drawn up in the Orléanais region of France between 1380 and 1480 found starting ages of between 7 and 20. However, the large majority of boys began in their mid- to late teens, half being over 16. Most of the girls, it should be added, were under 12, but they were generally orphans: the only category of female likely to have a written contract. English evidence reveals that in a few trades which did not need much in the way of strength or skill, such as nail-making and ribbon-weaving, children might start as apprentices somewhere between 7 and 13 years. England also had its pauper apprentices, who were usually placed with a farmer or a craftsman by the Poor Law authorities about the age of 7 or 8. Otherwise apprentices, like servants, were more often youths than children.[26]

Where children did go into full-time work, the example of nineteenth-century London reveals a minority starting about the age of 6 or 7, but most delaying until they were closer to 12. They began with light work such as making clothes or 'trimmings' for furniture, street selling, or making deliveries. (The streets of any big city offered opportunities for turning an honest, or not-so-honest, penny, ranging from sweeping crossings for pedestrians to begging and prostitution[27]). Even without a full-time job they could help with household chores and perhaps also a domestic trade: many children learned a craft informally by watching a mother or a father at work. Girls in particular looked after younger children for their mothers, or, in the words of the social investigator Henry Mayhew, were 'lent out to carry about a baby to add to the family income by gaining her six-pence weekly'. Their next step, at 12 or 13, was often to become a 'slavey': a telling indicator of the fate that awaited child servants everywhere in Europe.[28] One can find traces of children and adolescents working outside their own families in domestic service as far back as the fifteenth century in Florence. In this case both girls and boys were involved, and the 'little servants' might be 8 years old or little more. From the seventeenth century onwards, outside the Mediterranean area at least, the job gradually became 'feminized'.

The country girl who had come to find work as a servant emerged as a common figure in the towns. In late eighteenth-century Paris, for example, the *bourgeoises* sought to hire girls from the provinces where they themselves had been raised, principally the Ile-de-France, Champagne, Normandy, Picardy, Lorraine and Burgundy. Domestic service was indeed by far the largest employer of female labour in Europe before the First World War. The British census of 1881 recorded 45.3 per cent of all girls under 15 listed with an occupation being in domestic service (compared to 2.8 per cent of boys). As in the villages, the young girl started at the bottom, as maid of all work in a modest household, or as scullery maid in a large one. At this stage her life became one of constant drudgery: cooking, cleaning, running errands and lugging the laundry to and from the wash place.[29]

An overview

In sum, children were perhaps the most flexible workers within the family economy, ranging from full-time employment outside the home to helping their parents with a wide range of light jobs. As such, although it is difficult to measure their precise contribution, they were valued members of a team. Young people were also likely to accumulate a varied experience of work by their late teens. Edward Barlow, to take an example from mid-seventeenth-century England, began his working life in Lancashire as a casual labourer at harvest time and in a colliery. He went on to become an apprentice in the Manchester textile trade, and then tried his hand in London at being successively an errand boy, a post boy, and a vintner's apprentice. He finally settled on a seven-year apprenticeship as a seaman. In late nineteenth-century Germany, the anonymous female author of *Im Kampf ums Dasein!* moved from gluing bags at home to domestic service, later found jobs in a series of factories, and ended up as a waitress.[30] For the most part, the work performed by children in agriculture, the handicraft trades and the service sector remained uncontroversial. Indignation aroused in the late eighteenth century by the fate of the climbing boys employed by chimney sweeps, or *petits savoyards* as they were known in France, gave a hint of battles to come on the industrial front.[31] Otherwise, agricultural gangs apart, it was not until about 1900 that reformers made an issue of young males going into dead-end jobs without any form of training, the 'boy labour' problem. Around the farms, the practice of finding jobs for the young before and after school proceeded unobtrusively well into the twentieth century. Typically, Vesta Finley from North Carolina recalled during the 1970s that, during her childhood, 'Before we went to school in the morning we had to carry in stove wood, and feed the chickens, and carry in enough water from the springs to do Mother during the day.'[32]

Child labour and industrialization

During the eighteenth and early nineteenth centuries, the authorities in many regions were keen to promote industry precisely because they hoped it would provide a reliable source of employment for women and children living in poverty. In 1795 Alexander Hamilton famously argued that 'women and children are rendered more useful, and the latter more early useful, by manufacturing establishments, than they otherwise would be'.[33] Whether industrialization did in the end bring an increase in the proportion of young people who were gainfully occupied is a matter of dispute, particularly among British historians. Some of them assert that since most children in the pre-industrial era had been expected to make a contribution to the family economy, there was little scope for a general increase in child labour during the Industrial Revolution.[34] A more common assumption would be that industrialization did draw in more young children to the labour force – although it is not clear whether the peak in Britain was during the 'proto-industrial' phase of the eighteenth and early nineteenth century, or the later factory-based phase of the 1830s and 1840s. Claudia Goldin and Kenneth Sokoloff assert that in the case of the American North-east the initial period of industrialization during the first half of the nineteenth century created a dispropor-tionate demand for female and child labour. They calculate that females and young males accounted for about 10 per cent of the manufacturing labour force at the beginning of the century, but roughly 40 per cent by 1832. Assuming that few women and children in this particular region had worked in agriculture or household industry during the pre-industrial period, they conclude that partici-pation in the market economy by these types of labour 'must have risen substantially'.[35] Most historians would also accept that indus-trialization generally brought a more intensive work regime for child workers in certain occupations. Children working in, say, cotton mills and urban 'sweatshops' were everywhere a minority, but they faced more regular employment through the year, longer hours and a more sustained level of effort than their peers.[36]

Child labour in the 'proto-industrial' sector

The first signs of change appeared in the countryside of north-west Europe during the seventeenth and eighteenth centuries, when merchants decided to profit from the supply of relatively cheap and docile labour for their manufacturing operations. Families in these 'proto-industrial' workshops were goaded by the pressures of poverty and the seemingly endless round of agricultural and industrial work into erasing the customary division of labour by age and gender. The historian Hans Medick has drawn attention to child labour among rural weavers, spinners and knitters 'which both in its intensity and duration went far beyond that of the corresponding labour of farm peasant householders'. Instead of leaving home to become servants during their adolescence, children in these areas remained to work beside their parents.[37] During the early nineteenth century, among the handloom weaving families of the Saxon Oberlausitz, young children wound bobbins and prepared spools, while both adolescent boys and girls learned to weave. Similarly in England a Royal Commission on the Employment of Children of 1843 reported that the children of knitters in the Leicestershire hosiery industry began work about the age of 6, 7 or 8. The boys worked up to twelve hours a day as winders, the girls as seamers. Boys as young as 10 years of age worked on the stocking frames, and allegedly were soon able to earn nearly as much as their fathers.[38] Other trades that employed countless numbers of children in the countryside included handspinning, lace-making and embroidery, straw-plaiting, nail-making and other forms of metal-working.

Pressure on child workers in the smaller workshops also increased in the towns during the eighteenth and nineteenth centuries, as guilds and apprenticeship regulations crumbled in the face of free markets. Take the example of children employed in the silk industry of Lyons. The development of *grande tire* looms for the production of fancy brocades involved numerous *tireuses* (drawgirls) pulling their heavy cords for up to fourteen hours a day, until the invention of the Jacquard loom in 1807 eventually made them redundant. Silk reelers fared little better. In 1866 the legal authorities of the city investigated the case of 10-year-old Marie Péchard, a so-called apprentice reeler, after she ended up in hospital with a serious eye disease. They found that a certain Dame Bernard was employing Marie and two other girls in their early teens for sixteen hours a day: from five or six in the morning until ten or eleven o'clock at night.[39] In similar fashion, the rise of 'slop-work' or *confection* in the tailoring and shoemaking trades of big cities such as London, Paris, Hamburg, Berlin and New York during the nineteenth century heightened competition between skilled and unskilled labour, and between factory or workshop labour and outworkers. The upshot was that wives had to compete with husbands, and daughters with mothers. In the garment trades, homeworkers maximized output by relying on help from relatives or children. Again there was a grim regime of long hours, frequent unemployment and low wages. In New York City, Rose Cohen described toiling beside her father, a tailor, basting coat edges. With the stiffness of the material, 'my fingers often stiffened with pain as I rolled and basted the edges'. An Italian woman immigrant, employed on the finishing of felt slippers in the 'tenement city' of Little Falls (New York) proudly showed an investigating commission the enlarged joints, the cuts and the callouses on the hands of a 6-year-old child to provide evidence of the work.[40]

Factory children

The climax to the story came, of course, with the massive 'exploitation' of child labour in the cotton mills, coal mines and factories of the Industrial Revolution. Steam power and machinery, it is commonly assumed, allowed women and children to take over work that had previously required the strength and skill of an adult male. Certainly the earliest spinning machinery of the late eighteenth century was designed to be operated by children (strictly, in this case, ousting adult females), in a bid to reduce labour costs. Thus the first spinning mill in the United States used Arkwright's machinery to employ 100 children between 4 and 10 in 1801. By a fortunate coincidence, from the point of view of employers, large numbers of pauper children were available for industrial work on long-term contracts. Robert Owen estimated that he employed 500 parish apprentices in his cotton mill at New Lanark, in Scotland, in 1799. Overall, children under 13 accounted for 40 per cent of the workforce in this mill. Meanwhile in France the upheavals of Revolution and war after 1789 left the authorities saddled with huge numbers of *enfants assistés*. A series of cotton manufacturers seized the opportunity to secure a cheap and docile labour force. In 1796, for example, Delaître, Noël et Compagnie took on twenty children from the Salpêtrière at their mill in L'Epine, while Henry Sykes provided for sixty at Saint-Rémy-sur-Avre.[41]

As a rule, odd exceptions such as very early cotton spinners apart, children continued their customary role of acting as assistants to adults. They took on simple ancillary tasks and at the same time learned the skills and general culture of their trade. Examples are legion: the little piecer who tied broken threads for a mule spinner; the doffer replacing bobbins for a ring-spinner; the winder who prepared yarn for a weaver; the trapper who operated ventilation doors for miners at the coal face, and the carriers of bottles for glass-blowers. Where there was a surge in the employment of women and children during the early phases of industrialization, various organizational changes may have been as important as mechanization in influencing the demand for various categories of labour. Goldin and

Sokoloff note that in the North-east of America innovations such as a more elaborate division of labour within the firm, a more disciplined working environment and a larger scale of operation came into play. These influences were particularly in evidence if one looks beyond the textile trades to others such as boot, shoe, glass and paper manufacturing.[42]

The temptation is always to emphasize that children might start work in the mills 'as young as 7 or 8'. Most, however, probably waited until they were 10 or 12 in the textile trades, and into their teens in a heavy industry such as iron- and steel-making. A parliamentary report on child labour in the cotton manufactures of the United Kingdom found that in mills around Stockport and Manchester in 1818–19 the average age for starting work was about 11½. At the Heilmann spinning mill, in the Alsatian town of Ribeauvillé, an industrial census of 1822–3 listed twenty-seven children aged 8 to 11, but eighty-one aged 12 to 15. Similarly at the Voortman cotton mill in Ghent, which integrated spinning, weaving and printing, there were no boys under 14 in 1842, and girls of that age-group accounted for only 3.1 per cent of the labour force. By contrast, boys aged 15 to 19 accounted for 4.4 per cent of the total, girls 9.5 per cent.[43] Employers liked to argue that the new machinery had taken over the physical effort of work, so that children only had to bestir themselves intermittently. A less partial view would surely stress the long hours and sustained concentration required in the early mills. A piecer in a cotton mill during the 1830s was likely to have to work for thirteen and a half hours a day, and be prepared to rush forward and mend any of up to 500 threads.[44]

Work done by young boys and girls in some cases followed a traditional division of labour by sex, while in others they performed similar tasks. What stands out are the variations between trades and regions.[45] Thus one might contrast 'masculine' trades such as coalmining and basic metallurgy with 'feminine' ones such as lace-making and silk-reeling. Yet girls routinely worked underground in the mines until the 1840s in Yorkshire, Cumberland and Lancashire, and for much of the nineteenth century in Belgium. Conversely Samuel Courtauld employed large numbers of boys as well as girls to wind silk at his Halstead mill in Essex, though he did require them to leave at the age of 15.[46] Trades where juveniles of either sex might be employed to assist adults included spinning, power loom weaving and knitting. Here again there were no hard-and-fast rules. In the east Midlands of England and the lower Champagne region of France, men trained young lads to operate the big Cotton's-patent type of machine, while in the Canadian province of Ontario women trained young girls. The power of organized labour also made itself felt in the Lancashire cotton industry during the 1880s, when male operatives in the fine-spinning branch refused to train female piecers, as a way of preventing women taking over the new self-acting machines.[47]

Table 8.1 Main occupations of boys and girls under fifteen years in Britain in 1851 (thousands)

Boys

		%
Agriculture	120	28.4
Textiles	82	19.4
Navigation and Docks	46	10.9
Mines	37	8.7
Metal Workers and Manufacture of Machinery and Tools	26	6.1
Dress	23	5.4
General Labour	15	3.5
Dealing (various) incl. lodging and coffee houses	12	2.8
Building	11	2.6
Domestic Service	9	2.1
Earthenware	6	1.4
TOTAL EMPLOYED	423	

Girls

		%
Textiles	98	41.3
Domestic Service	71	30.0
Dress	32	13.5
Agriculture	17	7.2
Metal Workers and Manufacture of Machinery and Tools	4	1.7
Navigation and Docks	4	1.7
Earthenware	3	1.3
Dealing (various) incl. lodging and coffee houses	2	0.8
TOTAL EMPLOYED	237	

Source: From C. Booth, 'On Occupations of the People of the United Kingdom, 1801–81; *Journal of the Royal Statistical Society*, 49 (1886), cited by E. H. Hunt, *British Labour History, 1815–1914*, London: Weidenfeld and Nicolson, 1981, p. 14.

There is evidence, then, that the early phase of industrialization, during the eighteenth and nineteenth centuries, brought an increased reliance on child labour. How far this varied between the countries of Europe is difficult to estimate, given the lack of reliable statistics. The safest conclusion must be that child labour in the manufacturing sector was particularly important for the early starters on the path to industrialization, notably Britain, Belgium, France, the western parts of Prussia, and the United States. An industrial enquiry of 1839 to 1843 in France found 143,665 child workers under the age of 16, equivalent to 12.1 per cent of the labour force. Another, but not necessarily comparable one, for Belgium in 1843, counted 10,514 child workers, or 19.5 per cent of the total.[48] A high proportion of child labour was concentrated in a small number of industries, particularly textiles, as can be seen in Table 8.1.[49] The often distressing experiences of factory children were therefore far from typical, yet it was their plight that loomed large in the debates over child labour launched by social reformers.

Child labour and child welfare

The health of child workers

Lurid accounts of harsh working conditions for children in the factories and workshops were grist to the mill for all those who feared that industrialization and urbanization would cause massive social dislocation. The public health movement that emerged in France during the 1820s and 1830s reflected such concerns, notably with the investigations by Dr Louis Villermé into the 'physical and moral condition' of textile workers. There was talk of a 'bastardization of the race' in the wake of industrial expansion. The new manufacturing centres were allegedly producing children described by Villermé as 'pale, enervated, slow in their movements, tranquil in their games' who would later be incapable of defending their country.[50] The heightened economic and imperial rivalry between nations of the late nineteenth century, combined with threats to the established order from the labour movement, only served to reinforce the obsession with 'degeneration' in certain circles throughout Europe. A British doctor, Margaret Alden, warned in 1908 that 'the nation that first recognizes the importance of scientifically rearing and training the children of the commonwealth will be the nation that will survive.'[51]

The first observers to ring the alarm bells were doctors in the industrial towns of Britain who were disturbed by the physical condition of child workers. As early as 1784 a report on conditions in the Lancashire cotton mills by one Dr Percival, following an outbreak of typhus, noted 'the injury done to young persons through confinement and too long-continued labour'.[52] The case against child labour on health grounds was not as straightforward as might be thought. In the first place, the costs of working at a tender age had to be set against the benefits of earning a wage and combating the debilitating effects of poverty. Villermé estimated that during the 1830s a handloom weaving family of four in Rouen needed to earn 912 francs a year to cover basic necessities. But the average wage of men and women in the trade produced only 861 francs. The husband and wife needed above-average earnings, or one of their children to be working, to reach the minimum threshold. Otherwise they were condemned to desperate measures such as leaving rent unpaid, wearing unwashed clothes and basing their diet on bread and potatoes. A recent study of working-class household budgets in England gives even more weight to the contribution from children. During the period 1817–39, it found that children whose fathers were employed in a factory accounted for 28.2 per cent of the total household income, those whose fathers were miners, 23.9 per cent. Even at the end of the nineteenth century, social enquiries in Britain revealed that many poor families still depended on income from their children. Charles Booth, for example, indicated that nearly a third of the families he surveyed in London were unable to survive on the wages of the male head of household. In Philadelphia at the same period, the historian Claudia Goldin describes children as a major economic resource, 'contributing income in normal times, and supporting their families in especially difficult situations'. A more general study of family budgets in the United States and five European countries, covering the period 1889–90, amplifies this conclusion. It found that necessity was the greatest spur to child labour: when, for example, the father's earnings were relatively low, or the mother was not working.[53] Employers, it might be added, liked to emphasize the cleanliness of their factories in comparison to the slums, and the 'moderate degree of healthy exercise' which work involved. The Conseil d'Hygiène of Montluçon, in southern France, argued during the 1870s that work in the local iron industry was a matter of gymnastics for children. Hence nineteenth-century reformers generally argued against the dangers of excessive work for children rather than against work *per se*.[54]

In the second place, providing statistical proof that child labour in industry undermined health was not always easy. Apologists for the factory system asserted that the health of children was undermined more by the poverty of their families than by their working conditions. Villermé was surely right to note the cluster of influences that lay behind the poor physical condition of so many workers in the towns:

> I do not seek to establish whether the poor succumb most readily to their lack of nourishment; to the poor quality of their food; to their excessive work; to the bad air; to illness brought on by their trades, humidity, unhealthy lodgings, squalor or overcrowding; to the anxiety of being unable to raise a family; or even to the intemperate habits common amongst them.[55]

As for the specific influences of child labour on health, reformers first highlighted the strain of a long working day on a small and partially formed body. During the 1840s, for example, children in the cotton mills of Ghent worked from dawn till 10 p.m. in winter, and from 5 or 5.30 a.m. until 8 p.m. in summer. Such long hours produced twisted limbs and curved spines among the poor 'factory cripples', as they were known in Lancashire, and weakened the eyes of the thousand of girls engaged in close work such as lace-making and embroidery.[56] A second set of problems noted by doctors and other observers was the unhealthy environment created in the workshops by dust, noxious fumes, humidity and high temperatures. Adelheid Popp recalled being poisoned by her job with a bronze manufacturer in Vienna during the 1880s. Alice Foley in her turn described a spell working in the basement of a Bolton weaving shed where 'the frames stood on damp, cracked floors and I recall that the captive clouds of dust and lint could never escape'.[57] The young operatives were vulnerable to a sad catalogue of afflictions such as typhus epidemics, 'spinners' phthisis' and other forms of tuberculosis, anaemia, eye infections and white phosphorous poisoning (in the matchstick factories). Industrial accidents were another new hazard for child workers working with machinery. The early factories were a menacing concentration of fast-moving shafts, drive belts, flywheels and gearings which could seize the hair or loose clothing of a passing operative. Piecers were all too often crushed by self-acting mules; 'tenters' on the power looms might be hit in the eye by their shuttles; drawers in the mines fell under their wagons; and children cleaning machinery had fingers and hands mutilated by the moving parts.[58]

A moral decline?

Contemporaries were probably even more perturbed by the threats to the moral and educational development of child workers. They disliked the idea of the young being snatched from the bosom of their family and launched into the rough-and-tumble of life on the shop floor, with its coarse language, licentious horse-play and sometimes outright brutality. Of course, employers' representatives countered that the tight discipline of a well-run factory ruled out such pernicious influences, and some of the larger ones arranged separate workshops for males and females. At the extreme, silk mill owners in southern France brought in nuns to supervise their largely youthful and female labour force. Several dozen religious orders became involved with the industry, some specially formed for the purpose. The most highly developed of the 'silk convents' was the one at Jujurieux, founded in 1835 by Joseph Bonnet. Unusually, the nuns in this establishment were responsible for the running of the workshops as well as the schools, refectories, infirmaries and dormitories attached to it. During the 1850s Louis Reybaud enthused over the 'moral guarantees for young girls fresh in from the countryside'.[59] The American equivalent was the 'Waltham' system, which was applied to certain New England cotton mills during the 1820s and 1830s. In this case it was 'matrons of tried character' running company boarding-houses who kept young working girls on the straight and narrow. Employees had to be in by 10 p.m., they were not allowed to smoke or drink on the premises, and they were expected to attend church on Sundays. Lucy Larcom recalled that the atmosphere in these mills was not overly oppressive. She confessed to finding confinement in the mill wearisome, and she took against the machinery, with its 'buzzing and hissing and whizzing of pulleys and rollers and spindles'. At the same time, she recalled that when starting at the age of 11 she only worked for half of the time, changing bobbins on the spinning frames. This left plenty of opportunity to play with other girls of her own age, 'frolicking around among the spinning-frames, teasing and talking to the older girls, or entertaining ourselves with games and stories in a corner, or exploring with the overseer's permission, the mysteries of the carding-room, the dressing-room, and the weaving-room'. Harriet Robinson largely corroborated this testimony, admitting that she only needed to work fifteen minutes of each hour as a 'doffer'. She did, however, find a working day running from five o'clock in the morning till seven at night a great hardship.[60]

Many children may indeed have enjoyed the sociability of factory life. The young Norbert Truquin, having been battered by his master in a small woolcombing shop in Reims, recalled passing his time cheerfully in a spinning mill. When the foremen were not around, he and his friends amused themselves telling stories, discussing plays and mimicking priests in an improvised pulpit. American boys in the Piedmont region of the South did much the same towards the end of the century, improvising ball games and teasing girls.[61] Other children found entry into the world of work a trying experience. The pauper apprentices of the early Industrial Revolution were doubtless more vulnerable than most to abuse. How representative the experiences of Robert Blincoe were is open to question, but his alleged sufferings at Litton Mill in Derbyshire certainly make grim reading. Older 'stretchers' in the mill regularly kicked and beat him, threw rollers at his head and played sadistic games such as tying him by the wrists to a cross beam so that he had to draw up his legs every time the machinery moved under him.[62] Children suffered at the hands of adults impatient with the quality or the pace of their work. Operatives in the textile mills were notoriously quick to resort to the whip or a fist as a means of spurring on their child workers. Lea Baravalle, who worked as a *sbattitrice* in an Italian silk mill immediately after the First World War, recorded how the throwsters hit her and splashed boiling water in her face if she was slow in supplying them with thread.[63] The historian Clark Nardinelli takes the controversial line that, leaving aside present-day moral considerations, corporal punishment had the effect of raising the productivity of child labour. What can scarcely be doubted is the occasional outburst of out-and-out cruelty in the workshops, which outraged critics of the new industrial regime. Nardinelli cites the spectacular case of a boy in an English factory who was making bad nails: 'somebody in the warehouse took him and put his head down on an iron counter and hammered a nail through one ear'. Apparently the lad made good nails from then on.[64]

Child workers had some scope for escaping from difficult circumstances, by changing jobs, or, if the worst came to the worst, by staying at home or running away. Samuel Greg may have enjoyed a reputation as a humanitarian employer at Quarry Bank Mill, in the Cheshire village of Styal, but he could not entirely avoid problems of truancy with his pauper apprentices. A few risked severe punishment by absconding to visit their families or to enjoy Wilmslow Wakes Week; the odd persistent offender pushed Greg into a dismissal.[65] The turnover of 'free' child labour within firms might also be high in the towns, in cases where employers had to compete for operatives. In short, although the relations between employers and children were far from equal, children were by no means passive victims of exploitation. They were generally eager to start work, as a way of contributing to their family budgets and joining the world of adults. They had some success in turning the shop floor into a playground for themselves, and in subverting the intentions of the adults around them.

Finally, the tension between work and school aroused a series of impassioned debates between family members throughout the nineteenth and early twentieth centuries. During the medieval period, according to Philippe Ariès, 'all education was carried out by means of apprenticeship', meaning that boys learned their trade and their 'human worth' living and working with adults.[66] This type of apprenticeship was gradually replaced by an academic training, but this was a slow process, particularly in the 'mechanical arts'. Young people, particularly the males, continued to follow apprenticeships during the eighteenth and nineteenth centuries, yet it was generally agreed that the whole institution had become seriously debased. An extensive division of labour in the 'sweated' trades and the mechanization of production in the factories permitted so-called 'apprentices' to be exploited as a cheap source of labour. There remained a residual feeling that starting work as early as possible had its benefits, notably acquiring arcane skills and learning the disciplines of the workshop. Glass manufacturers were notoriously reluctant to yield up their child workers well into the nineteenth century. The director of the *cristallerie* at Baccarat, in Lorraine, asserted during the 1840s that 'the apprenticeship must be started early, to avoid the risk of never acquiring the degree of dexterity which makes the skilled workers.' In similar vein, manufacturers in the cotton textile industry of the American South were convinced that the best age for training workers was between 10 and 14.[67] Employers also argued with some justification during the early nineteenth century that children excluded from the workshops would merely idle away their time on the streets, given the absence of school places for them.

Peasant and working-class families had to weigh up the costs and benefits of investing in the schooling of their offspring. The novelist Jules Reboul highlighted their dilemma in staging an argument during the 1870s in the Vivarais region of France between father and mother over the future of their son, Jacques Baudet. The father was willing to make sacrifices for him to continue to attend school, even after he had acquired a basic literacy, in the hope that he might secure a better job. The mother would have none of it, asserting that a school certificate would never be enough to land someone from their background a white-collar occupation: better by far for him to start earning in the hope of building up a landholding. The young Jacques duly started work as a shepherd. Across the Atlantic, Italian immigrants in Buffalo (New York) felt they were best serving the interests of their children by investing in property rather than education, and so pushed them into a relentless work regime. On a slightly different tack, Claudia Goldin has used the case of Philadelphia to show ethnicity as one of several influences on decision-making in this area. About 1880, daughters from immigrant families, in this case from Irish and German backgrounds, were more likely to participate in the labour force than the daughters of native-born heads of households. Part of the process of assimilation into American society, she notes, was 'learning' not to send daughters out to work. Children from black families (up to the age of 16) were in a similar position to the native-born whites, though one cannot be sure from the evidence available whether this was because their mothers generally worked so that they could attend school, or because local employers would not hire them.[68]

If the need to earn a living sometimes ruled out any schooling at all, in other cases it confined time in class to the winter months, allowing children to work on the land during the harvest season, or undermined its effectiveness by requiring them to work before and after class. Heinrich Holeck, born in Bohemia in 1885, had to help his stepmother with her brick-making job by getting up at four in the morning to prepare the clay, and resuming work after school making bricks. Emilie Carlès faced an equally daunting routine in her Alpine village on the eve of the First World War, working around her classes at such tasks as hoeing, weeding, fetching water and minding sheep. As a broad generalization, the schooling of girls was sacrificed to work more readily than that of boys, and country children attended class less regularly than those in the towns. By the late nineteenth century, however, such disparities were fast disappearing as the school triumphed over work.[69]

Child labour in decline

The obvious starting point for analysing the causes of the withdrawal of children from the labour force would be to pinpoint when the process started. If, as Clark Nardinelli claims for the British case, the long-term decline set in before the passing of effective Factory Acts, then one would have to look further afield than state intervention for explanations. Unfortunately, such evidence is hard to come by, not least since many of the statistics on child labour first appeared when states attempted to justify and implement factory legislation. Nardinelli uses data from the textile industry to show that child labour in Britain was decreasing relative to adult labour before inspectors began to enforce the 1833 Factory Act: the first such act to have any teeth. In 1816, he estimates, children under 13 accounted for 20 per cent of the labour force in the cotton industry, but by 1835 the proportion had fallen to 13.1 per cent. He also notes the relative decline of child labour in the silk industry during the 1840s and 1850s, even though its mills were not covered by factory legislation at this period.[70] One can make a similar case for a number of other industrializing nations or regions. In the north-eastern region of America, for example, Goldin and Sokoloff suggest that the share of women and children in the industrial labour force began to decline about 1840: a time when the various states involved were only beginning to experiment with factory legislation.[71]

The broader picture of a gradual elimination of children from the economically active population cannot be documented before 1851, when the British census began to record the occupations of young people. At that point, as noted above, 97 per cent of children in the age-group 5 to 9 were without a 'specified occupation' and from 1881 the census no longer considered it worthwhile counting them.[72] The next group, aged 10 to 14, experienced an uneven decline in the proportion occupied from decade to decade, but the long-term trend was clear: if 30 per cent were occupied in 1851, only 17 per cent were in 1901. By this latter date young people were largely confined to a small niche in the labour market within the service sector. Much of their work was in fact of a part-time nature, such as half-time employment in the mills, selling newspapers, or delivering messages, so that it could be combined with attendance at school. Other countries were less preoccupied with this issue. The American census did not count child workers until the end of the nineteenth century: in 1890 it found that around 18 per cent of those aged 10 to 14 were gainfully employed. The French one did not publish information on the active population by age-group until 1896. In that year only one-fifth of those were occupied, and as in Britain and the United States, most of these would have been aged 13 or 14.[73]

Social reformers in all countries certainly attempted to use state intervention to curb the abuse of child labour. Their motives were largely humanitarian, though other parties might support them for more mercenary reasons. In other words, besides disinterested campaigners such as doctors, civil servants and members of the aristocracy, various business and labour interests might also be involved.[74] Howard Marvel argued that the 1833 Factory Act in Britain was designed to favour the interests of the large urban manufacturers in the textile industry. He reasoned that they employed relatively fewer young children than their rural counterparts, and that with steam rather than water power they rarely needed exceptionally long working hours to compensate for interruptions to production. Such a *cui bono* line of argument is not entirely convincing, for want of direct evidence on motives, but it does at least draw attention to the active role of certain manufacturers in promoting factory legislation. The French case reveals textile magnates of the Société Industrielle de Mulhouse prominent from the 1820s in demanding the passage and the enforcement of legislation to curb abuses of child labour. The last thing they had in mind was to give up their juvenile labour force. Rather, they sought to compel other employers to follow them in what might be called a policy of enlightened self-interest, focused on the health and morality of their workers. One of their number, Jean-Jacques Bourcart, explained in 1828 that a law would improve the quality of labour: 'The master will have a choice of robust workers; he will have workers who are more intelligent and easier to guide.'[75] British factory operatives and weavers in the Ten Hours Movement also agitated during the 1830s and 1840s for shorter working hours for children, making it clear that this was part of a wider campaign to lighten the burden of labour on all workers.

Everywhere the state proceeded by a process of trial and error, gradually extending the scope of factory legislation and tightening the systems of inspection. The British paved the way in 1802 with an act that limited itself to protecting apprentices in the cotton mills, moved on to a broader but still ineffective one in 1819, and had to await Althorp's Act of 1833 for the first workable system of inspection. Among later landmarks, the 1842 Mines Act attempted to ban all females and boys under the age of 10 from underground work, the 1844 Factory Act pioneered the half-time system, permitting children to divide their time between work and school, while the 1867 Factories Extension Act finally branched out beyond the textile industries. Prussia and France in their turn began tentatively about 1840 with child labour laws that were hamstrung by feeble means of enforcement, and went no further until 1853 in the former case, 1874 in the latter. Various American states in the North-east also began to regulate child labour during the 1840s, notably Massachusetts, Connecticut and Pennsylvania, but again they were either poorly enforced or unenforceable. Most states, for example, allowed children to start work below the minimum age or to work longer hours if they had the consent of their parents, were orphans or were supporting disabled parents.

All such legislation aimed to regulate rather than abolish child labour. To begin with it tended to set minimum ages, such as 8 or 9, which made little difference to employers, and concentrated on grading hours according to age, banning night work, insisting on sanitary measures in the workshops, and enforcing a limited amount of schooling. The impact of these laws on child welfare is open to question. On the one hand, they undoubtedly drove some child labour 'underground', into the small workshops which were either exempt from legislation or difficult to inspect. They may even have deprived some needy families of income. On the other hand, they curbed some of the worst abuses of children in the workshops, and encouraged the shift from the workshops to the school benches. Even Nardinelli concedes that the 1833 Althorp's Act in Britain caused what he sees as short-term boost to the secular decline in child labour by placing a 'tax' on it, in the form of the costs incurred by employers in taking responsibility for the education of the children.[76] The fact remains that the clear-cut demands of compulsory education up until the age of 13 or so did more to keep young children out of the workshops than child labour legislation. In the words of Myron Weiner, 'Child-labor laws proved to be unenforceable unless all children were required to attend school.'[77]

Before concluding that state intervention provides the key to removing children from the workplace, however, one should ask why the climate became favourable to legislation during the early nineteenth century, and also why the initial opposition to it from many quarters eventually weakened. Historians have sought answers in both the cultural and the socio-economic spheres. In the first place, they cite the new ideals for childhood of the late eighteenth century, which ultimately made it unthinkable for young people to work. Out went the existing orthodoxy that children were essentially idle creatures who needed to be put to work as soon as possible. In its place, Jean-Jacques Rousseau proposed that people 'love childhood; promote its games, its pleasures, its amiable instinct'. Doubtless the sentimental approach to childhood championed by Rousseau and by the Romantic poets initially reached only a narrow, middle-class audience, and their ideas were always contested by those espousing less sentimental viewpoints. None the less, by the late nineteenth and early twentieth centuries, something of a consensus emerged portraying children, in the words of the historian Harry Hendrick, as 'innocent, ignorant, dependent, vulnerable, generally incompetent and in need of protection and discipline'.[78] Such a construction of childhood went against the grain of earlier peasant and working-class experience, though it did complement demands from the labour movement for a 'family wage': a wage high enough to allow a male breadwinner to support his wife and children without their having to work. It also meshed neatly with the growing interest in formal education among the working classes. By this period opposition to shorter working hours and at least part-time schooling was often associated with 'rougher' elements among the labouring population. Glassworkers provided an egregious example: in 1875 a French Divisional Inspector from Reims described them as 'the most appalling collection of undisciplined good-for-nothings, drunks and idlers that it is possible to imagine'. In the United States it was the regional divide that stood out, with poor whites in the cotton mills of the South conspicuous for their indifference to schooling for their children.[79]

Secondly, changes on the labour market arguably tended to push children away from the world of work. On the one hand, the rising real wages which sooner or later trickled down to workers during the course of economic development made families increasingly reluctant to supply their children to employers. Sections of the working classes remained anxious over the loss of earnings from their children implied by child labour legislation, but they did gradually shift the balance from work to school. On the other hand, technical progress in industry reduced the demand for juvenile workers, cotton spinners, for example, allegedly finding that they needed to employ fewer piecers once the self-actor had replaced the hand mule.[80] Let it be added that there was nothing inevitable about these forms of change on the shop floor. Per Bolin recently highlighted the stubborn persistence of operatives in the Lancashire cotton industry with the employment of their own children in the mills as 'half-timers', even though they were a relatively affluent group of workers. He also documented the diversity of strategies open to employers in deploying different types of labour on the same technology. To return to the example of the self-acting mule, in some cases both girls and boys were taken as piecers, in others only the latter, and it was even possible to dispense with their services entirely by employing an adult 'minder-piecer'.[81]

Conclusion

The virtual elimination of the full-time employment of children in the developed economies of the West was a protracted process.[82]

Campaigns to improve conditions for child workers had to contend with tight family budgets, labour-intensive methods of production, poor communications and established notions of childhood. Change therefore had to take place on a number of fronts before conditions would be ripe for a sea change on the juvenile labour market during the nineteenth and twentieth centuries.[83] At the same time, there is no denying that from an early stage of industrialization efforts at reform made a difference to the welfare of the young. A very mixed bunch of philanthropists, politicians, working-class radicals, journalists, civil servants, industrialists, factory inspectors and schoolteachers contributed in their various ways to imposing a 'modern' conception of childhood. Finally, one should not lose sight of the persistence of part-time child labour in the West right up to the present. From the beginning of the twentieth century, various enquiries noted the relatively large numbers of children in familiar part-time occupations for young people such as serving in shops, selling newspapers and running errands. Many recent commentators have assumed these to be harmless activities, providing children with the opportunity to earn a little cash. However, where there remains an element of economic compulsion, jeopardizing an individual's health and education, this can hardly be the case.[84]

9

Investing in the Future: Health and Education

Campaigners against child labour in the factories liked to appeal to the self-interest of manufacturers, by suggesting that abuses risked compromising the future quality of the industrial workforce. During the 1870s a French factory inspector went a step further by attempting to capitalize on heightened patriotic feelings in the wake of the Franco-Prussian War. While visiting workshops in the Ardennes he told those present 'that the Prussians could all read and write, and that those, like the brutes I had in front of me who were rotting in their ignorance, could only be bad Frenchmen and bad soldiers, who would run away on our day of revenge'.[1] However distasteful many adults in the past might have found the subject of childhood, and however reluctant the rich might have been to subsidize the children of the poor, they could hardly ignore the fact that the young embodied the future of their society. They would therefore have to devote some resources to what would now be called investment in human capital, to produce the next generation of workers and soldiers. The key concerns were always the physical, moral and intellectual development of the young. These loomed large in the atmosphere of intense rivalry between nations on the military and economic fronts that began in the late eighteenth century, and intensified in the run-up to the First World War.

The problem for historians in this area is to avoid an air of triumphalism. One can point to a series of impressive advances for young people in the long term, such as improvements in infant and child mortality, average heights, literacy and school attendance rates. At the same time, the 'meaningless mean' risks masking huge inequalities within societies, the general progressive drift to improvement was interrupted by numerous whirls and eddies, and even in the twenty-first century there is little room in the West for complacency on child welfare among the poor. Fortunately, beside the worthy accounts of the rise of child welfare agencies or the struggle for mass schooling, there is an awareness in the literature of darker forces at work, such as bitter rivalries over professional status, and determined efforts to maintain established class, race and gender inequalities.

Child health, morbidity and mortality

What was it like to be ill as a child in the past? The evidence on this point is fragmentary. References to serious illness in autobiographies are often perfunctory. St Augustine (354–430), for example, only mentioned in passing that 'once as a child I was taken suddenly ill with a disorder of the stomach and was on the point of death'.[2] This appears a little odd, given that everyone must have gone through a series of childhood illnesses, and in many cases, been seriously scarred by them both physically and psychologically. Gerald Strauss may be right in arguing that 'the pains and dangers facing all children in late medieval and early modern Europe made childhood such a traumatic experience that there was a strong incentive to blot out memories of it.'[3] Where autobiographers did go into more detail, one is brought face to face with the grim realities of daily existence before modern medicine. Hermann von Weinsberg came from a relatively wealthy family in Cologne, yet his childhood in the early sixteenth century was blighted by illness. Before he was 9, according to Strauss:

> he had several kinds of fevers, including the sweating disease of which several of his acquaintances died within twenty-four hours, also mysterious temporary paralyses, boils, sores and scabs on his scalp, 'foul flesh in the mouth' that a barber cut out with a pair of shears, worms giving him vertigo, diarrhea and violent vomiting, constant toothache followed by extraction of most of his teeth by hand, hernia, and the plague.[4]

Antoine Sylvère (1888–1963) considered it entirely normal for his whole class at school in the Auvergne to cough their way like a choir through the long winter nights. He felt increasingly ugly as the constant running of his nose flattened his nostrils. The 10-year-old Fritz Pauk (1888–?) suffered even more after a farmer employing him as a servant near Lippe allowed his swollen leg to fester for too long:

> Every day the farmer came and cursed me for being so lazy and not getting up; the cattle had to be fed. But I just couldn't do anything; I

was crying with pain, but the farmer didn't send for the doctor or help me himself.

In the end Pauk had to have a foot amputated. Socialist writers lingered to good effect on the debilitating effects of poverty on a worker's health. Adelheid Popp recalled that during the 1880s she struggled with undernourishment while working in a metal factory, fearing that she might lose consciousness at any time.[5]

Children evidently had various mechanisms for coping with illness and injury. Robert Roberts (1905–74) admitted that when suffering from the occasional bout of neuralgia 'I used to lie on the sofa, moaning loud and making the most of it'. His objective was to have his mother cradle his head on her breast, so that he could drift into oblivion 'on bulbous bliss and Pear's soap'. Antoine Sylvère also enjoyed the respite from everyday life that went with illness, as he retired to his bed and drank herb teas, but his mother gave him short shrift when he cried out for attention. Even a spell in hospital might feel like a pleasant interlude in a harsh existence for a poor child. Adelheid Popp admitted that her time in a mental asylum was the best she had ever had. Everyone was kind to her, the food was good and she had a bed to herself. Much of the time children doubtless looked after themselves as best they could. Pierre-Jakez Hélias, to take a Breton example, knew that if a nail pierced his foot he should allow the wound to bleed, and then piss on it, using the imprint of a cow's hoof on the road as a makeshift receptacle, before sealing it with the secretion of a slug or a snail.[6]

Long-term improvements: height and mortality

Changes over time in the average heights of young people give a first indication of improved health in modern Europe and North America. Much of the data used by historians comes from military records dating from the eighteenth century and onwards. In continental Europe, a system of compulsory military service meant that all young males of conscription age were measured in order to check whether they met the minimum height requirement. This gave a solid base for estimating the mean height of the population, though it inevitably ignored females entirely, and pre-adolescent children.[7] Researchers in this area make the assumption that 'a child's growth rate reflects, better than any other single index, his state of health and nutrition, and often indeed his psychological situation also'.[8] Their surveys leave no doubt about the substantial long-term increases registered in average heights since the eighteenth century, and the rising tempo of growth: the so-called 'secular trend'. On the one hand, in Britain working-class adolescents born at the end of the 1950s were over 11 inches taller than those born in the mid-eighteenth century: the mean heights for 14-year-olds in London rose from approximately 135 cm (53.15 in) to a little under 164 cm (64.57 in) over this period. On the other, data from Norway during the late eighteenth century suggest that young males were still maturing very late by present-day standards: the peak velocity of growth in a sample of men from the north-west of the country took place between the ages of 17.0 and 18.0, far later than in any population group in the world today. Native-born whites in the United States, it might be added, were significantly taller than their European counterparts: the generation of soldiers born a little before the American Revolution were on average 2 to 4 inches taller than the British. Indeed, their mean terminal height of 68.1 inches was close to the Second World War level. The most likely explanation for this American lead is an early and rapid improvement in nutrition. Today well-fed West Europeans and North Americans, whether black or white, attain almost identical average heights.[9]

The research also makes it clear that the increases were far from linear: in other words, the secular growth 'trend' could go into reverse for a while. A number of studies have reported a decline in stature among boys during the late eighteenth century, presumably linked to a deterioration in living standards and a consequent crisis in nutrition. Thus in Vienna, the historical demographer John Komlos noted an 'extraordinary' decline among those orphans in the Josephinische Waisenhaus born between 1760 and 1800, and also among pupils in special schools for the sons of soldiers. He discovered that the difference between the heights reached during the 1760s or 1770s and those of the 1780s ranged from 0.3 to 4.5 cm, depending on age. Roderick Floud and his colleagues found a similar dip among the charity boys of the Marine Society in London during the 'Great Immiseration' of the turn of the nineteenth century. A study of the final heights of American slaves transported by coastal shipping (and measured for identification purposes) in its turn showed that the cohort born in the early 1790s was approximately half an inch shorter than the cohort born in the late 1770s. Some of these studies reveal a further downturn in the cycle about the 1840s, the 'hungry forties'.[10]

Demographers have gleaned further insights into the improved health of children by measuring changes in infant and child mortality. Their starting point is the extreme fragility of life during childhood in early modern Europe. Michael Flinn asserted that until the late eighteenth and early nineteenth century period, under what he called the 'Ancien Régime demographic system', only about half of all children survived to their tenth birthday. More recent authorities prefer to stress the diversity of demographic experience across countries and regions. None the less, the heavy toll taken on young lives in the low-income societies of the past is not in doubt.[11] The first year was particularly precarious. In the absence of any national data before the eighteenth century, historical demographers have to rely on studies of individual parishes to measure infant mortality rates (deaths under the age of 1 per 1,000 live births). A sample of eight parishes in England over the period 1550–1649 produced estimates ranging from a suspiciously low 94 for males and 82 for females at Hartland (Devon), to 219 for males and 188 for females at the market town of Gainsborough (Lincolnshire). Comparable estimates for parishes in early modern France were generally higher, with many of them hovering around the 250 or even 350 mark.[12] Children aged 1 to 5 also remained highly vulnerable to infectious diseases, not least because after weaning they lost the partial immunity provided by their mother's breast milk.

Signs of improvement were slow to materialize, though in the long run they were spectacular. Infant mortality rates declined during the late eighteenth and early nineteenth century in Sweden, England and above all France, but thereafter they generally remained steady for several decades, or even increased a little.[13] It was only during the two or three decades before the First World War that this rate began to fall steadily nearly everywhere in the West. By the end of the twentieth century it had reached single figures in the most favoured areas.[14] Child mortality, in the age-group 1 to 5 years, also began to fall in sustained fashion around 1860 in England, Belgium and France: rare examples, it must be admitted, of countries where the censuses are sufficiently informative to permit this type of calculation. Recent estimates suggest that child mortality levels were also improving in the United States during the late nineteenth century.

The persistence of inequalities

Lurking behind this pleasing image of improvement in average heights and levels of mortality was a series of persistent inequalities, notably between social classes, ethnic groups and regions. 'Anthropometric' studies consistently expose shocking disparities in the heights of rich and poor. Among students attending the elite Carlschule in Stuttgart between 1771 and 1793, the index of stature correlated highly with socio-economic status. The average height of boys aged 15 whose fathers came from a lower-class background was 146.0 cm, compared to 150.1 for those from the middle class, and 158.5 for sons of the upper aristocracy.[15] In London the boys of the Marine Society, drawn from the most destitute sections of the urban population, were very short indeed, shorter than all but a few of the most impoverished populations of the Third World today. The gap during the nineteenth century between their stature and that of the upper-class boys attending the Royal Military Academy at Sandhurst was striking. It was indeed so large, 'that almost all the Sandhurst boys would have been taller than almost all the London boys'.[16] Factory children in England fulfilled contemporary expectations during the 1830s by emerging as slightly shorter than a control group of children from a similar socio-economic background not working in the mills. The young factory operatives were even shorter than American slave children: those aged 9 were about 1 cm below the average for the slaves, and by the end of their growth period, girls were about 5 cm smaller, the boys 8 cm. A peculiar feature of the growth pattern among slaves, it should be added, was a massive 'catch-up' spurt during adolescence. This is attributed by historians to the willingness of plantation owners to supply more food when the slaves began working in the fields.[17] Children from the rural poor fared little better. A study of recruitment operations among 20-year-olds in central, southern and western France during the 1860s found agricultural labourers and farm servants to be the most disadvantaged group in society. No less than 29 per cent of their number were under 1.60 m, compared to only 12.7 per cent of a middle-class group. 'To be born very poor, under the Second Empire, was to have a one-in-three chance of becoming a dwarf', observed Emmanuel Le Roy Ladurie and his colleagues.[18]

Studies of differential mortality rates in their turn exposed glaring differences between socio-professional groups. For what it is worth, the disparities being barely credible, Villermé calculated that in the industrial town of Mulhouse between 1823 and 1835 the 'probable life' of a child born to a merchant or industrialist was 28 years, compared to 12 years for the child of a tailor, and $1\frac{1}{2}$ years for the child of a weaver.[19] Infant mortality rates also varied considerably between the nations during the nineteenth and twentieth centuries. In Scandinavia and some northern countries they were relatively low, Norway scoring 98 per 1,000 during the 1880s, Ireland 95, whilst in southern and eastern Europe they remained high, at 195 in Italy, 247 in Austria, and 268 in Russia. Western European countries fell somewhere in between, as in the case of England (142) and France (168).[20] The numerous studies of the decline in infant mortality in England make it clear that the general pattern of improvement after 1900 conceals as much as it reveals. A closer look at the statistics shows that the beginning of the downturn can be traced back to the 1860s in a number of southern counties, though the rate actually increased during the 1890s in London and in the major industrial centres of the north and South Wales. As a rule, the retreat of infant mortality was more rapid among legitimate than illegitimate children, in rural than in urban-industrial areas, and in the affluent outer suburbs of London than in the impoverished inner ones.[21]

Some explanations: nutrition vs. public health measures

Thomas McKeown set the cat among the pigeons in the 1950s and 1960s by demolishing the orthodox view that medical measures were largely responsible for the modern decline in mortality, and at the same time proposing a contentious alternative of his own.[22] He reasoned that doctors could do little to cure or prevent diseases before the introduction of effective chemotherapy during the 1930s. He also doubted whether fortuitous changes in the character of infections could do much to explain the enormous reduction in mortality. On the dubious principle, borrowed from Sherlock Holmes, that 'when we have eliminated the impossible, whatever remains, however improbable, must be the truth', he concluded that the rise of population in modern Europe must be attributed mainly to improvements in the environment. In particular, he focused on the improvement in nutrition following greater food supplies.[23] His picture becomes more nuanced if one considers his analysis of the fall in mortality among the young in England and Wales during the second half of the nineteenth century. McKeown conceded an important role for medical measures in the decline of smallpox, as vaccination virtually eliminated the disease from the age groups 0–4 and 5–9. He accepted that the substantial reduction of mortality from scarlet fever during childhood stemmed from a change in the nature of the disease. He also linked the decline in mortality from diarrhoeal diseases to the sanitary revolution, whilst noting that young children aged 0–4 continued to die from these in large numbers. Finally, with all age groups experiencing substantial reductions in mortality from tuberculosis, typhus and related fevers, he came round to improved diet increasing resistance to these diseases.[24]

Most historians have followed McKeown in playing down the role of 'medical advances' in reducing mortality before the twentieth century. As far as child health was concerned, medical men tended to leave the matter to midwives and other women. Their repertoire of measures to neutralize 'noxious humours', following in the Hippocratic tradition, revolved around bleeding, emetics and purgation. It was almost certainly unsuited to curing childhood diseases. The only concession they were prepared to make to infancy was a limit on the amount of blood they took.[25] Not surprisingly, their stock among the population at large was very low. Most people dreaded their recommendations, or were too poor to be able to afford them. Oliver Twist, one might recall, began his life during the 1830s gasping for breath in the workhouse. 'Now, if, during this brief period,' Dickens observed tartly, 'Oliver had been surrounded by careful grandmothers, anxious aunts, experienced nurses, and doctors of profound wisdom, he would most inevitably and indubitably have been killed in no time.'[26] Popular medicine, by contrast, had plenty to offer the young. It was an eclectic mixture of herbal remedies, bone-setting techniques, sorcery and healing saints, practised by a motley assortment of men and women. Many of its remedies were hair-raising, even by the standards of modern medicine, as in the case of its slug syrups, powdered viper and magic incantations. Yet it harmonized well enough with the social and cultural context of the pre-industrial village.[27] Eventually, during the eighteenth and nineteenth centuries, physicians were able to establish the authority of medical science, and their own professional status, notably with developments such as smallpox vaccinations and a serum for diphtheria. They were also prominent in campaigning for a range of measures beneficial to child health, ranging from the encouragement of breastfeeding to improved sanitation.[28] Even so, Breton peasants at the beginning of the twentieth century took their sprains and fractures to millers rather than to doctors. They preferred the experience of the former coping with injuries around the mill to the paper qualifications of the latter. Adelheid Popp described the various household remedies applied to her sick brother in Austria:

> My mother brought an ointment from the town, which had been prepared by an old woman and was to have wonderful results. Others came and laid dry, pounded plums, mixed with sugar, on his wounds. Herb baths were made for him, so-called sympathetic treatments were tried – all in vain; his wounds did not heal.

The unfortunate youth died shortly afterwards in hospital.[29]

Where most authorities diverge from McKeown is in playing down his emphasis on improved nutrition. In general his critics wondered whether he had not overemphasized the 'invisible hand' of a rising standard of living at the expense of various types of social intervention.[30] More recent accounts prefer to highlight the multiple influences on mortality. Besides nutrition, living standards and public health, Schofield and Reher mention related factors such as living and working conditions, urbanization, education, medical science, mothering practices, reformers and even climate.[31] Improvements in nutritional status therefore take their place among other influences rather than being the prime mover implied by McKeown. Robert Fogel, for example, concluded that nutritional improvements made a 'substantial contribution' to the decline in American mortality rates after 1700. Quantifying this, he suggested that they accounted for around four-tenths of the decline, though, interestingly, he added that 'this contribution was confined largely to the reduction in infant deaths, particularly to late fetal and neonatal deaths and to deaths during weaning.' On the other side of the coin, the example of slave children on the cotton plantations illustrates the lethal effects of working pregnant women intensively on an inadequate diet, and expecting infants to flourish on gruels and porridges after weaning.[32]

Finally, historians have restored an assortment of politicians, civil servants, philanthropists and social reformers to a prominent role in improving life expectancy and health among the young. The critical period was the late nineteenth and early twentieth centuries. This was when such people agonized over depopulation, racial inferiority, international economic competition, the rise of organized labour, and related issues. Local politicians pushed through sanitary reforms in the towns, helping to combat the water- and food-borne diseases that had been so destructive of child health in earlier periods. The most clear-cut illustration of the point to date comes from France, with the demographers Preston and van de Walle managing to correlate improvements in water and sewerage systems with increases in life expectancy, using Paris, Lyons and Marseilles as case studies.[33] Philanthropic men and women founded voluntary associations, ranging from the Russian Society for the Protection of Infant Lives and Childrearing to the American Association for the Study and Prevention of Infant Mortality. School medical inspectors in a number of countries took advantage of compulsory education to monitor the health of children, and combat the spread of infectious diseases. Reformers promoted a raft of measures concerned with maternal, infant and child welfare. The outcomes included experiments with maternity leave, infant milk depots, well baby clinics, health visitors, crêches and free school meals. There were of course considerable differences as well as similarities between the nations. The priorities for the reformers were the encouragement of maternal breastfeeding, the provision of safe methods of artificial feeding and the diffusion of knowledge on personal hygiene. At the same time, French leaders fretted over the issue of depopulation, after their defeat at the hands of the Prussians in 1870, while at the same period their American counterparts focused on the ethnic composition of the population during a period of heavy immigration. English admirers of the French *Gouttes de lait* found that these milk depots failed to flourish on their side of the Channel. The German state took a confident lead in welfare measures from the 1880s while Britain and particularly the United States lagged behind.[34]

The welfare campaigns struggled against huge odds, and were by no means an unmixed blessing for poor families. Efforts to provide clean milk for infants almost foundered on a series of problems running from the farms to working-class homes; health visitors met with resistance from poor mothers to their stern views on hygiene; and schoolteachers complained of poor facilities in schools when attempting to clean up their pupils.[35] There was the paradox, established with understandable relish by feminist historians, that powerful males often showed scant sympathy for the women and children they were supposed to be helping.[36] Politicians considered the reforms as merely a means to more important ends, such as securing enough recruits for the army, heading off socialism, and exhorting married women to concentrate on being mothers rather than working. In 1906 the medical expert Arthur Schlossmann explained in a speech to Rhineland notables that high infant mortality rates needed to be given a high priority since an increase in population affected Germany's military strength, its labour force and its consumption: 'the unrelenting drive of our times demands a resistant, healthy population'.[37] In this light, welfare legislation emerged as a buttress for existing social and gender divisions. Reformers allegedly attempted to impose 'middle-class' values on working-class mothers, denigrating traditional folk wisdom on child-rearing and demonizing those who went out to work. In the United States there was the added dimension of welfare and charity workers attempting to Americanize poor, immigrant mothers, particularly during the 1900s.[38] Much 'scientific' thinking in this area about 1900 now looks excessively rigid in its rules for feeding times and its distrust of the mother's inclinations.[39] The common notion in medical and official circles that mothers working outside the home were responsible in some way for high infant mortality also looks distinctly shaky in retrospect. It ignored the realities of impossibly tight family budgets, and the fact that it was restricted opportunities for maternal breastfeeding rather than work in itself that mattered.[40] The result of all this moral blackmail was presumably to make mothers feel guilty about their supposed inadequacies. Even so, Deborah Dwork found evidence that working-class mothers in England generally appreciated the advice and aid on offer.[41]

Conclusion

From the health perspective, there are good reasons for being born in the West sometime after the Second World War. Children today suffer less than their ancestors from hunger, repeated illness and the strains and stresses associated with extreme poverty. The point need hardly be laboured that children have benefited over the past 250 years or so from a series of advances, notably in nutritional status (the balance between the intake of nutrients and energy expended), and both public and private health. One no longer expects to read about young people fainting from exhaustion around farms or workshops, as Adelheid Popp described in her autobiography. In the final analysis, it is worth looking beyond these immediate causes to the underlying change in attitudes that made child health a prominent issue in the political sphere. Historians have come to focus above all on the nineteenth century, a period when the old fears of overpopulation receded, yielding ground to a concern with avoiding the waste of human life during infancy and producing more robust citizens.

The child and the school

A suitable ending to a history of childhood must surely be an account of the shift from work to school as the principal occupation for young people. Nowadays we take it for granted that childhood ought to be an age for play, education and a progressive preparation for life as an adult.[42] Many families in the West were either unable or unwilling to think in these terms until the early twentieth century. Efforts by governments to dragoon all children into the schools have a long history, but they faced considerable material and cultural obstacles. Protestant countries in northern Europe led the way. The city of Weimar, in Saxony, was apparently the first to make attendance at school compulsory, requiring in 1619 that all children aged 6 to 12 be in class for the whole year, the harvest month apart. The Hohenzollerns in Brandenburg-Prussia issued equally ambitious regulations during the eighteenth century, but it is doubtful whether any of the states which adopted this policy of 'enthusiastic regulation' was in a position to enforce it. There were simply too few trained teachers and school buildings to make any headway. None the less, they did stand out from areas where school places were still relatively few and far between at this period, notably in much of eastern Europe, Scandinavia, Ireland and southern Italy.[43]

A more significant turning point came during the eighteenth century, when various reformers in continental Europe began to think in terms of a national system of education. In Prussia, philanthropic noblemen floated a number of schemes for educating the lower orders, and military defeat at Jena in 1806 quickened interest in education as a means to national regeneration. Wilhelm von Humboldt and his successors promoted the vision of a structure for elementary, secondary and higher education: the *Volksschule*, *Gymnasium* and university. According to one estimate, by the late 1830s 80 per cent of Prussian children aged 6 to 14 were being systematically educated in the elementary schools. Other countries followed the Prussian lead, slowly prising the schools from the hands of the churches, and making primary education free and compulsory. Britain finally opted for the latter in 1880, as did France in 1882, and the American states in a protracted process that began in 1852 with Massachusetts and ended (for white children) with Texas and ten southern states early in the twentieth century. It remained only to enforce more regular attendance during the following decades to complete this huge push for mass schooling: the age of the 'economically useless but emotionally priceless' child had arrived.[44]

Educational reformers, fired up by the ideals of the Enlightenment, made huge claims for their policy of investing in schools. It would, they believed, reduce crime and disorder, make workers more productive, and, above all, instil moral values in the 'great unwashed'.[45] If this sounds wildly optimistic, even today most people would probably have to admit to some residual faith in the more modern notion of education as an emancipatory force. Historians, as exemplary products of the system, have often depicted a heroic battle against the odds to establish free, state-run schools. Such a 'whiggish' approach tends to be cast in the form of a struggle between enlightenment and obscurantism.[46] It exalts innovations in the form of purpose-built schools, trained teachers, a broad curriculum, and so on, while denigrating older methods of teaching or opponents of change. But were informal methods of socialization within the family and the local community necessarily inferior to formal education within the schools? Were the down-at-heel characters who tried their hand at teaching not better attuned to what peasant families wanted than the products of teacher training colleges? And if the schools were such a boon to the population, why did ruling elites have to compel parents to send their children to them? Indeed, why did publicly funded schooling for the masses itself come under attack during the late twentieth century? During the 1970s, for example, Ivan Illich pursued his 'deschooling' campaign by arguing that to equate the laudable aim of equal educational opportunity with obligatory schooling was to confuse salvation with the Church.[47] What this section focuses on, then, is the shift in ways children were prepared for adulthood and responses to it from the young people themselves and their families.

Service and apprenticeship

Philippe Ariès argued that the medieval period had no idea of education. Instead of being taught basic literacy and 'what is essential to know to get along in life' within the primary school system, children acquired such elementary and empirical knowledge during a period of service with another family. In other words, sent away from home as a servant or an apprentice, they learned by practice alongside adults. 'It was by means of domestic service that the master transmitted to a child, and not his child but another man's, the knowledge, practical experience, and human worth which he was supposed to possess'. This type of general education by means of apprenticeship, to be understood in a broader sense than purely vocational training, lasted until the schools began to quarantine children from the world of adults during the sixteenth and seventeenth centuries. Among the 'lower orders' it remained largely intact until the nineteenth century. Ariès was in no doubt that the older approach had its advantages. He contrasted the freedom it allowed children, as they roamed wherever people were working or relaxing, 'even in taverns of ill repute', with the confinement imposed by the schools.

Critics of Ariès have duly drawn attention to the idealized nature of his account of master–servant relationships. They have queried his willingness to lump together under the heading of 'service' the experiences of such diverse groups as young noblemen attending a royal court, apprentices learning a skilled trade, and domestic servants working in a peasant household. Some of these were paying for the privilege serving a highborn or skilled master, others expected a wage for their manual labour. It is hard to imagine anyone from a humble background complaining that it was beneath his dignity to serve at table, as one aristocratic child did when placed in service with the Abbot Benedict (*c.*480–*c.*547).[48] Finally, there is the suspicion that Ariès underestimated the number of children who learned their trade from their parents. David Nicholas argues that in medieval Europe most apprentices came from broken homes, usually by death, where no proper training was possible within the family. He notes that in Ghent only one master in ten among the numerous weavers had an apprentice. The institution of craft apprenticeship in any case evolved only gradually during the medieval period, perhaps from the twelfth or thirteenth centuries onwards.[49] None the less, Ariès usefully draws our attention to the widespread practice of expecting young people to learn the 'art of living' informally among adults.[50]

Parents of a young, aristocratic male eager to learn the profession of arms, to take a well-documented example, would try to place him at a royal court for a few years, or send him to another noble family. The age at which he made this move varied considerably, but somewhere about puberty appears to have been the most common. Georges Duby cites the example of William Marshal, who in 1155 left his parental home at the age of 11 or 12 to serve with his uncle, William of Tancarville. In the new household, the boy would have to work his way up a hierarchy, starting with menial tasks at table or with the horses, and ending with more virile activities such as riding, hunting and jousting. The ideals of knighthood gradually evolved from their early medieval origins, so that in twelfth- and thirteenth-century French romances, for example, they combined military valour and courtly manners. To help him achieve these qualities the boy had an older knight to supervise his progress. On the one hand, the master sought to toughen up his charge for the field of battle. This meant encouraging him to take up running, jumping, wrestling, throwing the javelin and similar athletic pursuits; to follow lessons in archery and swordsmanship; and to help look after horses, dogs and hawks. On the other hand, the master provided a training in morality so that the future knight could bear arms wisely. He would also give advice on more mundane matters, such as what to wear or how to behave at table, and see to the teaching of dancing, singing and music. Eventually the young squire was dubbed a knight, thereby formally leaving the world of childhood for the violent one of the aristocratic youth. Meanwhile young girls in the aristocracy underwent a similar, if less elaborate 'apprenticeship'. They too would have a mistress to help them acquire skills including riding, dancing and a little reading. To take an early modern English example, Sir Edmund Molyneaux sent his two daughters to a cousin to be raised 'in virtue, good manners and learning to play the gentlewomen and good housewives, to dress meat and oversee their households'.[51] Both males and females in the elite probably had the best part of that 'combination of play and adult imitation' which characterized informal methods of education in the past.[52]

Lower down the social scale, many young people in northern and western Europe hoped to learn from their experience as apprentices or, more commonly, servants with another household.[53] Ideally the master would treat them as members of his family. Benedicti's *Somme des Péchez*, published in 1584, insisted that the master show concern for the salvation of his servants. Authors of domestic manuals during the early modern period expected master craftsmen to give their apprentices guidance on religious and moral affairs, as well as to pass on the secrets of their trade. At the same time, these authorities recognized that servants and apprentices had a contractual relationship with their masters, which distinguished it from the blood tie between a father and his children. Historians have also noted that servants, unlike apprentices, did not usually stay for long with any individual employer. Most were on one-year engagements, and the English case reveals that somewhere between a half and two-thirds did not renew the contract.

It is therefore hardly surprising that many experiences fell far short of the ideal. The more pious employers doubtless took an interest in the spiritual welfare of their servants, but others allowed their own material interests to prevail, working servants on the Sabbath, for example. The Frenchman Jean-Roch Coignet, born during the 1770s, found himself living in squalor in a cattle shed for three years while employed as a young farm servant, only entering the farmhouse once a year on St Martin's Day.[54] Small farmers in England usually ate with their servants and lodged them in their homes, but larger ones made irksome distinctions, seating them apart and constructing special houses for them. The young responded by walking out on abusive masters, and moving around in a bid to broaden their range of skills. Take the case of Joseph Mayett, born in 1783 at Quainton (Buckinghamshire). He moved no fewer than eleven times during his seven years of service. His masters and mistresses veered between various extremes, including a scholarly minded couple who encouraged him to read, a hypocritical Baptist mistress and a violent, hard-drinking character who laid about his servants with a walking-stick. Mayett was by no means helpless, however, leaving a master whose non-stop swearing offended him after three days.[55] Apprentices probably stood a better chance of establishing a good rapport with a master or mistress, given their long-term contracts and the supervision of guild authorities. Again, though, some masters proved of better character than others, and parents from rural areas in particular were poorly placed to discriminate. Apprentices sometimes escaped from violent and abusive masters, or registered complaints about not being taught their trade properly. In early modern Spain the young Alonso de Contreras ran away from an apprenticeship with a silversmith after refusing to carry water for the mistress: 'I said to her that I had not come to be a servant but to learn a craft.'[56]

Children in the medieval and early modern periods had many other opportunities to absorb the skills, knowledge and values that would carry them through adult life. As noted above, their education began in the family, with basic religious and moral instruction, and the passing on of know-how concerning, say, herbal remedies, riding, hunting or weather forecasting.[57] This could develop in various directions. Some children were taught to read and write by their parents. Early modern Sweden provides the outstanding example: inspired by the Protestant Reformation, a Church Law of 1686 stipulated that children and servants should 'learn to read and see with their own eyes what God bids and commands in His Holy Word'. The onus was on parents to do the teaching, and on Lutheran priests to hold regular examinations in reading and the catechism. The example of the parish of Skanör reveals 58 per cent of the population able to read in 1702, and 92 per cent by 1740.[58] Everywhere in the West the churches took it upon themselves to instruct young people in the Christian faith, by means of sermons and catechism classes. The very wealthiest parents in medieval and Renaissance Europe often hired a private tutor to teach their children at home. Charles, son of Louis the Pious, had the scholarly Walahfrid Strabo between 829 and 838; Guibert of Nogent an obscure local schoolmaster during the late eleventh century. The trials and tribulations endured by Guibert at the hands his tutor have been well aired. Guibert doubted that the six years he spent under instruction had been worth the effort, and especially the numerous unjust floggings, given that the tutor was himself barely competent in grammar and composition. Several centuries later the philosopher John Locke made a very late plea for private tutoring as opposed to schooling in his *Some Thoughts Concerning Education* (1693). The tutor, he felt, would be better able to preserve the innocence and modesty of the child, and besides, he was likely to have only three or four children to supervise, compared to the three or four score of the schoolmaster. 'I am sure, he who is able to be at the charge of a Tutor at home, may there give his son a more genteel Carriage, more manly Thoughts, and a sense of what is worthy and becoming, with a greater Proficiency in Learning into the Bargain.' Needless to say, as the Spanish case makes clear, incompetent or immoral tutors were as thick on the ground as good ones.[59] Other young people picked up the techniques of a trade from their parents, or, in the case of landowning families, the practicalities of estate management. In the latter case Linda Pollock noted that daughters as well as sons of the English gentry learned the ropes while accompanying their fathers on their daily routines around his estate.[60] The young also became familiar with the popular culture of the villages, within their families, during festivals, and at a *veillée* or a *Spinnstube* (spinning circle) during winter evenings. That is to say, they learned the songs, dances, poems and legends of their region. Martin Nadaud (1815–98) recalled from his childhood in the Creuse Department of France that he used to come home in terror from the *veillées* after listening to the old women of his village tell stories of ghosts, werewolves and Bluebeard.[61]

In sum, peasants and labourers who had little or no schooling were far from being ignorant, depraved, culturally deprived, or even illiterate. The system of education through 'apprenticeship' in the family and the local community did have much to recommend it, besides the freedom to mingle with adults noted by Ariès. Historians have observed that it encouraged a less solitary, and hence less stressful, exercise of individual aptitudes. It was self-evidently useful for a job or a particular station in life. And it could readily be tailored to the different career paths that people followed within each family, depending on whether they were male or female, and the oldest son or a younger sibling.[62] Yet it gradually withered on the vine from the sixteenth century onwards. Not least of its drawbacks was an inherent conservatism, as each generation merely handed down what it knew from its own experience in a particular calling and region. It was doubtless appropriate to a relatively stable, agrarian society, but not to a more restless commercial and urbanized one.

The rise of the schools

If the school came to loom increasingly large in the lives of young people, it did so in an extremely long-drawn-out process. It is not the intention here to attempt a potted history of education, but a number of points stand out for our purposes. To begin with, many of the early 'schools' were more closely linked to the adult world than would later be the case. The experience for the young people in them was perhaps not too far removed from that of an informal 'apprenticeship'. A ninth-century commentary on the Rule of St Benedict shows that child oblates in the monasteries divided their time between formal instruction in class and practising in the choir. Thus they had *magistri* to instruct them in various subjects, including grammar and arithmetic. But they also learned by participating in the regular activities of the community, singing antiphons beside the monks, and reading in a group during the daily *lectio* session.[63] The episcopal and parish schools of the early Middle Ages were also rudimentary in organization. The former began as small classes, usually with a single master in charge of all ages, geared to the needs of young men preparing to become parish priests or administrators of a diocese. The latter were even more informal arrangements whereby parish priests and clerks assembled a few boys for basic instruction in religious matters.[64] From the twelfth century onwards schools in Europe diversified and became more full-fledged institutions. Even so, some of the small, private schools that flourished throughout the late medieval and early modern periods concentrated more on manual than literacy skills. As late as the 1850s, a schools inspector in the Vosges region of France was outraged to find that parents were sending their children to school on the express condition that the pupils would devote all their time to lace-making, rather than learning to read and write.[65]

Schooling was for a long time confined to that minority of the population which, it was generally felt, needed literacy to fulfil its functions in society. (Members of this group might be taught to read and write at home, of course.) In England at the end of the fifteenth century perhaps 10 per cent of men could sign their name, while nearly all women remained illiterate. During the later Middle Ages, book learning remained a specialized form of knowledge required mainly by clerics, administrators and merchants. Aristocrats did not always learn to read and write: they simply called upon a literate member of their household to help when the need arose. Children who did not attend school were therefore unlikely to feel hard done by. For centuries peasants comforted themselves with the thought that the sun shone alike on those who could read and those who could not. In the more recent past, when a host of other reasons to become literate had come into play, the link between occupation and literacy remained significant. A sample from twenty-three English villages covering the years 1754–84 revealed considerable disparities between occupational groups in their ability to sign a marriage register. At the extremes, only 5 per cent of retailers were illiterate, compared to approximately 50 per cent of those employed in construction and mining. A 'common-sense interpretation', according to R. S. Schofield, suggests that this was because the former had to trade and deal with the public, while the latter spent more time exercising their muscles.[66]

Given that occupation and wealth are closely related, it follows that the influence of social inequalities runs like a red thread through the history of education. Simply stated, the wealthy 'sought or bought literacy', and literacy in its turn generated more wealth for them.[67] Before the twentieth century, the custom everywhere was to teach children to read first, then to write. The scale of fees charged to pupils rose accordingly: in early modern Castile, the elementary schools charged two *reales* a month to teach a child to read, four for reading and writing, and six for the three Rs. Richard Kagan calculates that the full programme was well beyond the means of most working families in Castile.[68] Where elementary schooling developed early, as in colonial New England, the link between social status and basic literacy soon ended. If in 1660 a good 60 per cent of farmers worth over £400 had been able to sign their names, compared to 45 per cent worth less, by the late eighteenth century such differences were all but swallowed up in near universal male literacy. In much of Europe, by contrast, the divergence in literacy rates persisted for longer A study of military conscripts in the Loir-et-Cher Department in France found that, as late as 1840, all of the professional men, landowners and white-collar workers were able to read and write, while 81 per cent of wage earners were not.[69] The advanced studies of the grammar schools were even more inaccessible to the masses. The admissions register at Colchester Free Grammar School during the 1630s and 1640s reveals the vast majority of boys coming from aristocratic, professional and trading backgrounds, with none at all from the ranks of husbandmen and labourers. The sons of yeomen were the only group among the English 'peasantry' with any realistic chance of attending the school, and by the 1670s even they had disappeared entirely.[70]

Besides wealth and status, other factors influencing access to the schools included gender, race and region. Girls fared particularly poorly in the educational sphere during the early modern period. Where literacy campaigns involved parents teaching in the home, as in seventeenth- and eighteenth-century Sweden, rates for the two sexes tended to level out at an early stage.[71] Otherwise, females were excluded from the grammar schools and universities, and disadvantaged even in the time granted for elementary instruction. In 1587, for example, in Venice 4,595 boys were attending school compared to only 30 girls.[72] Most men assumed with a good conscience that females merely needed to be prepared for a future domestic role. In *Emile* (1762), Jean-Jacques Rousseau famously lavished attention on the education of his eponymous male hero, but offered Emile's wife-to-be Sophie little more than needlework, some drawing, and experience of how to govern a household.[73] The gap between male and female literacy rates remained stubbornly persistent, even in colonial New England. Whereas nearly all males in these colonies could sign their name by the period 1787–95, only about half of all females could do so. In the more peripheral areas of Europe, their plight was far worse, though males were not much better off either. Census material reveals a staggering 86 per cent of all females in Spain unable to read or write in 1860, together with 65 per cent of males. In the Russian Empire the respective figures were 87 and 71 per cent in 1897. As for racial influences, plantation owners in the southern United States took a dim view of schooling for their slaves. After 1820 it was even illegal for a while. Towards the end of the century only about half of black children aged 10 to 14 were attending school in the South, compared to 78 per cent of whites. Moreover, the spread of schools proceeded unevenly across the regions of different countries. They usually took a lead in the more economically developed parts of a country: in the New England colonies, say, or north of the famous Saint-Malo to Geneva line in France.[74]

The drift to the schools ebbed and flowed in the very long term. It is tempting to focus on the impact of seemingly apocalyptic events such as the Reformations or the French Revolution. In the case of the French Revolution, defenders of the Republic during the nineteenth century believed that the emancipation of the people through education began only in 1789. Catholic historians retorted that the Church had established thousands of elementary schools for the people under the *ancien régime* which the revolutionaries wantonly destroyed.[75] Now that the dust has settled on some of the ideological battles that fuelled this type of perspective, most historians have plumped for a more evolutionary picture. Historians have certainly acknowledged that the Protestant and Catholic Reformations spurred the churches into a battle for young minds. Puritans in England and America, it will come as no surprise to hear, were eager to lead children from their depravity with guidance from religious books. *The Office of Christian Parents* (1616) argued that they risked becoming 'idle . . . vile and abject persons, liars, thieves, evil beasts, slow bellies and good for nothing'.[76] Yet there were other forces at work besides religious ones, such as the humanist ideals of Renaissance thinkers, the development of commercial and industrial activity, and a concern to control a rising tide of poor. The early modern period, between say the late fifteenth and late eighteenth centuries,

emerges as a long transitional phase in the schooling of the population. It began with formal education limited to a small minority of
specialists, and ended with the first hints of universal literacy in a few
favoured regions. An impressive 85 per cent of males in New England
could sign their wills in 1760. Similarly, in Amsterdam 85 per cent of
bridegrooms signed their marriage registers in 1780. However, the
seventeenth century stands out as a period of waning enthusiasm for
popular schooling after the surge of interest during the sixteenth
century.[77] At the very end of the period, the early stages of the Industrial Revolution in their turn began to undermine working-class
schooling in various parts of western Europe.[78]

Most thinkers on education during the early modern period were
entirely at ease with the notion that schools should reinforce
rather than undermine existing social hierarchies. A hard-liner like
Bernard Mandeville was prepared to attack eighteenth-century
charity schools on the grounds that they gave the poor ideas beyond
their station: he preferred to see a largely ignorant labour force.
Across the Channel, at Rennes, La Chalotais criticized the Christian
Brothers for teaching children to read and write when they would
have been better employed learning how to handle a plane or a file.
Even many Enlightenment figures in eighteenth-century France displayed a measure of 'obscurantism' on education. Although they
asserted that all men were equal, they envisaged a Classical or scientific training for men like themselves, and little or no education for
the labouring poor. Destutt de Tracy followed suit in 1800, arguing
that all civilized societies could be divided into two classes, a working
class and a learned class. Of the former, he wrote that they needed
to begin work early, and so could hardly afford to 'languish' in the
schools for very long.[79] Plans for national systems of education in the
late eighteenth century made this type of class distinction perfectly
explicit. They invariably proposed a school for the people and
another for the notables. Poland, one of the first countries to institu-
tionalize the ideas of the Enlightenment, developed a system of
grammar and parish (elementary) schools. A statute of 1783 stated
that the goal of the parish schools was 'instructing the people in religion, informing them about the duties of their estate, about labour
and craft appropriate for that estate'.[80]

A radical humanist riposte to this line envisaged the school as a
liberating force. During the French Revolution, the Marquis de Con-
dorcet presented a report on primary education which called for a
national system of education. He included among its aims that all
humans should be able 'to develop to the utmost the talents with
which nature has endowed them and, in so doing, to establish among
all citizens a true equality and thus make real the political equality
realised by the law'.[81] In the event, nineteenth-century governments
shied away from the threat this implied to the existing political and

social order. They veered more to what has been called the 'herds-man's' approach to education: that the masses must be disciplined, civilized and trained for their particular roles in society.[82] To this end, they generally limited elementary schooling to a programme of reading, writing and ciphering (arithmetic), combined with moral and religious instruction. In Prussia, once the initial enthusiasm for thor-oughgoing reform associated with Baron Karl vom Stein had cooled, conservatives like Ludolf von Beckedorff returned during the 1820s to the familiar notion that schools should be promoting orders or estates rather than an 'artificial equality'. The French Guizot law of 1833 had a more liberal background, yet the historian Maurice Gontard drew attention to its 'poverty of vision': the deliberate refusal to build on the great principles of the Revolution. The explicit aim of the law was 'to make the school an instrument of popular moralization, political stabilization, social conservation and economic progression'. In the United States the absence of 'aristocratic' hostil-ity to popular education did not stop school advocates emphasizing collective rather than individualistic goals, notably the potential for social stability.[83] Even when education became free, compulsory and supposedly 'egalitarian', primary and secondary schools had a ten-dency to remain stratified by class as well as age. No less importantly, educators took it for granted that boys and girls (and in the United States, whites and blacks as well) needed a different curriculum. To prepare girls for their domestic role, and of course to combat high infant mortality, they recommended subjects described by an English educational expert in 1910 as the domestic arts of cooking, cleaning and clothing. Similarly, to channel American blacks into manual labour, they proposed basic industrial and domestic training.[84]

Popular attitudes to schooling

Most schools legislation was passed without much 'pressure from below'. Politicians, civil servants and reformers forced the pace of change assuming that they knew what was best for the masses. They constituted, in effect, 'a kind of educational dictatorship'.[85] This does not mean that peasant and working-class families were uninterested in education. Rather, they had their own agenda, which differed in significant respects from the official one.[86] Patrician commentators in Europe often referred to parental 'hostility' or 'indifference' to education, suggesting in the nineteenth century that the new working class was incapable of raising its offspring in a responsible manner. The implication was that the schools and their teachers would have to take over some of these functions. In 1846 a clergyman who was also a schools inspector in Lancashire wrote of 'the shamelessness and filthy habits, the want of chastity, the ignorance and carelessness with regard to religion, the neglect of public worship, the brutality, recklessness, and almost animal state' of some of the labouring classes, and the beneficial effects of separating children from such parents.[87] However, besides being a ludicrous travesty of the popular culture, such criticism underestimated the heavy sacrifices involved in forgoing earnings from children, and the careful approach to the costs and benefits of schooling taken by poor families.

On the one hand, as already observed, literacy or book learning was a luxury that was of little use in many occupations. On the other, parents were willing to spend money on the schooling of their sons and, to a lesser extent, their daughters, when they could do so on their own terms. Their motives, depending on circumstances, included a need for literacy skills in a craft or trade, a desire for religious instruction, and hopes of political emancipation or social mobility. There was too the search for a convenient child-minding service. Lucy Larcom recorded that the large families in her part of rural New England expected little more than 'temporary guardianship' to keep children out of mischief from 'Aunt Hannah' and her little dame school.[88] The historian T. W. Laqueur is surely right to argue that parents and children were not simply the passive victims of new, repressive institutions. They helped lift school enrolments to the extent that most children in the more developed parts of the West were probably receiving some schooling by the time primary education was made compulsory. But what they generally wanted was a relatively short and possibly intermittent spell for children on the school benches, to acquire a basic literacy, with teachers whose values were close to their own. By paying fees, they could exercise some control over what went on in class, rejecting teachers who were drunk or violent, for example. The small, private schools and the untrained teachers that they favoured left few traces in the archives, except when campaigns by officials to eliminate them gathered momentum during the nineteenth century. The schools financed by charities, churches, municipalities and the state had much to recommend them. Yet it is worth emphasizing that eventually the notion that parents were the best judges of their children's interests was overridden in this sphere.[89]

Working-class autobiographies often reflect the tenuous hold of the schools on children as late as the nineteenth century. For many, time in class barely rates a mention, or comes over as a pleasant interlude in a laborious existence. Compulsory schooling meant only that lessons were squeezed in between jobs around the farms, workshops and streets. Agricol Perdiguier, born near Avignon in 1805 to a carpenter and a seamstress, recalled that he spent no more than two or three years at school, learning the three Rs, 'though not very well'. From an early age, he had to work. About 1880 Aurelia Roth struggled in her Bohemian village with long hours grinding glass, often having to miss her lessons. 'I didn't get much time to learn, and still less to play', she wrote, 'but it hurt me the most if I had to skip school.' During the same period, Fritz Pauk described the classroom as a welcome relief from heavy work on the farm, but admitted that there was not much to learn at his little village school beyond the catechism and 'innumerable Bible passages'.[90] There was of course a formidable contingent of writers from 'humble' backgrounds who did well at school and went on to make careers in literature or education.[91] Others had searing memories of harsh treatment at the hands of teachers. They particularly resented beatings they considered unjust. Take the sad tale recounted by Ludwig Turek, born in 1898 in Hamburg:

> One day in gym class the teacher beat me with his long stick as far as he could reach as I climbed up the rope. That really galled me. He knew how good I usually was at gymnastics, and he called me mean, lazy, and unruly. There being no beds, I'd slept badly and frozen the night before, and I was also hideously hungry. The few bread crusts we'd gotten by begging were not exactly made to strengthen me. For these reasons I was as limp as a wet mouse. The beating really ate at my guts.

Turek was writing as a revolutionary, and it may be that political militants chose to stress or even fabricate the grimness of their early existence as a suitable prelude for their conversion to socialism.[92] None the less, it is hardly surprising to hear that children reacted with hostility to the rough justice and heavy indoctrination of many schools.

The stock image of a schoolmaster down the centuries is of a fearsome character wielding his authority literally with a birch or a rod: the principle of 'No lickin', no larnin'', as a parent in *The Hoosier Schoolmaster* (1871) neatly put it. On the American frontier, in an interesting variant, the odd one carried a gun, including the character who restored order from time to time by shooting a moose head hanging at the back of the room.[93] Historians have tried to convey a more nuanced picture, noting attempts as far back as the Middle Ages to make lessons interesting, and the counter-current of advice against heavy reliance on corporal punishment.[94] The underlying problem for teachers was always boredom in the class. The traditional method of teaching a child to read was to drill him or her first in the letters of the alphabet, secondly in syllables and finally in recognizing words. The children spent a few minutes with the teacher individually going over their work, while the rest were left to their own devices. The result was generally anarchic, prompting hard-pressed teachers to lay into their restless and unruly charges in an attempt to maintain some control.[95] New teaching methods introduced during eighteenth and

Le Grand Calendrier et Compost des Bergers, Troyes, *c.*1657, illustrating an occupation for the month of February. It reveals the fearsome image of the schoolmaster. Reproduced from Emile Socard, *Etude sur les almanachs et les calendriers de Troyes, 1497–1881*, Troyes: Dufour-Bouquot, 1882. Bibliothèque Municipale de Troyes.

nineteenth centuries, such as the monitorial system and more class-based teaching, combined with a broader curriculum, doubtless improved matters. Even so, teachers continued to rely on much rote learning and fear of the rod. A schools inspector from London mentioned during the late 1880s 'the dolorous chant' produced by whole classes spelling out the letters of words together.[96] Children had various strategies to cope with their predicament, ranging from falling asleep and playing up in class to truancy and occasionally a strike. Attitudes to education varied considerably, even within the working classes, but it does not seem unduly pessimistic to conclude that most children could not get away quickly enough from a school system that had little to offer them.

Conclusion

Two cheers, then, for that disparate group of reformers which campaigned to improve the health and education of children. They had certainly achieved a number of tangible benefits for young people by the early twentieth century, but at the cost of riding roughshod over any opposition to their agenda. Children were generally in better physical shape than earlier generations and more aware of a national literate culture. At the same time, some groups continued to fare better than others, according to their class, gender, race and so on, and parents faced increasing interference from agents of the state. In the end the mighty ambitions of reformers for the 'resocialization' of a new generation were far from being realized, not least because resources for public health and public education programmes were never forthcoming on a sufficient scale. What did emerge was a range of institutions dedicated to child welfare. These included hospitals, schools, crèches, orphanages, reformatories and industrial schools. Their founders were in part motivated by genuine philanthropy, let it be emphasized, but there is no disputing efforts to create what Michel Foucault called a 'disciplinary society'.[97] Fortunately children and ordinary people in general had some success in manipulating the system to their own ends.

Conclusion

What emerges when one attempts the Olympian stance of a twenty-first century perspective on childhood and children down the ages? First, there is the persistence of various themes in the cultural history of childhood in the West. Far from 'discovering' the innocence and weakness of childhood at some particular period, people debated these and related issues from the early medieval period to the twentieth century. Certainly educated opinion tended to favour the contrary view of infant depravity during the medieval and early modern periods, and parents had an interest in toughening up young people for work as early as possible. But at various stages educators, moralists and others challenged these orthodoxies, with varying degrees of success. The assumption here is that there is no essential child for historians to discover, rather that commentators have shuffled around a limited repertoire of themes stemming from the biological immaturity of children. Some of the issues faded from view during the late twentieth century, while others continue to provoke discussion. Sociologists might consign the debate over whether children are born innocent or depraved to a 'presociological' phase, and most people now accept the 'middle-class' conception of a 'long' childhood. That is to say, we take for granted the separateness of childhood from the world of adults, with the young cooped up in schools, playgrounds, their own rooms, and so on. Conversely, the nature/nurture debate continues to interest researchers, though in muted form, and the nature of gender relations during the early years remains controversial. Most parents and educators like to play down differences between boys and girls but old gender stereotypes are difficult to overthrow.

A second, and related, point that stands out from a long-run perspective is the survival until the late nineteenth century of a gradual transition from early childhood to adulthood for most people. This does not mean following Philippe Ariès in his assertion that there was no awareness of childhood until a relatively late stage. Pushed to its limits the thesis leads to absurdities such as the line from Linda Hannas that 'Until the middle of the eighteenth century there was no child in England over the age of seven.'[1] It merely suggests the absence of an established sequence for starting work, leaving home and setting up an independent household. Today the age-graded classes of the school system and child labour laws impose precisely this type of order. But this was far from being the case even in 'modern' American cities such as Philadelphia or the mill town of Manchester (New Hampshire) during the nineteenth century. The key stage occurred between the ages of 7 and 12, when children 'slowly and erratically' joined the world of adults.[2] The upshot was that childhood was less distinct from adulthood than in the early twenty-first century.

Finally, one can discern a growing momentum to social and cultural changes affecting children from the eighteenth century onwards. Philosophers, poets, novelists, educators, doctors and others produced an increasing volume of works devoted to childhood. Reformers in private charities and state bureaucracies founded a range of institutions dedicated to child welfare. Families became smaller and more child-orientated. And school took over from the farms and workshops as the principal site for the work of children. How far young people benefited from these developments is a moot point. Various indicators suggest significant improvements in their health, education, and perhaps moral welfare. The end of the belief in infant depravity may also have removed a hard edge to parent-child relations, as the desire to break the will of the young receded. Increasing affluence trickled down to children in the form of wider opportunities for leisure activities. At the same time, some children gained more from these changes than others, depending on the usual divisions of class, gender and race, and there was perhaps some trade-off between less time spent on wage labour and more on a 'curricularized' life organized by the school and ambitious families. Of course, children were by no means passive victims here: they had some capacity to select, manipulate, resist and above all escape with their friends. Whether the very recent emphasis among researchers on challenging the established asymmetrical pattern of age relations will bear fruit remains to be seen. Perhaps one should never underestimate the power of a child.

Notes

Full details for works cited in the Select Bibliography may be found there; for these short titles only are given in the notes.

Introduction

1 Emile Guillaumin, *The Life of a Simple Man*, transl. Margaret Crosland (Hanover, NH: University Press of New England, 1983), p. 3.
2 See ibid., pp. 1–36 and the editor's introduction by Eugen Weber, pp. vii–xxi.
3 For example, George Sturt, *A Small Boy in the Sixties* (Cambridge: Cambridge University Press, 1932); A. S. Jasper, *Hoxton Childhood*; 'An Old Potter' [C. Shaw], *When I Was a Child* (Wakefield: SR Publishers, 1969 [1903]); Alice Foley, *Bolton Childhood*; J. D. Burn, *The Autobiography of a Beggar Boy* (London: Europa, 1978); Robert Roberts, *A Ragged Schooling*; Angélina Bardin, *Angélina, une fille des champs* (Paris: Editions André Bonne: 1956); Antoine Sylvère, *Toinou*; Richard Wright, *Black Boy*; and Lucy Larcom, *New-England Girlhood*.
4 Larcom, *Girlhood*, p. 17.
5 'Fritz Pauk, Cigar Maker', in Alfred Kelly (ed.), *The German Worker*, pp. 399–427.
6 John Burnett (ed.), *Destiny Obscure*, p. 23. Other recent studies and collections of working-class autobiographies include John Burnett (ed.), *Useful Toil: Autobiographies of Working People from the 1820s to the 1920s* (London: Allen Lane, 1974); David Vincent, *Bread, Knowledge and Freedom*; Thea Thompson, *Edwardian Childhoods*; Mary Jo Maynes, *Taking the Hard Road*. See also Roy Pascal, *Design and Truth in Autobiography* (London: Routledge and Kegan Paul, 1960), p. 64.

7   St Augustine, *Confessions*, book 1; John F. Benton, *Self and Society in Medieval France: The Memoirs of Abbot Guibert of Nogent* (Toronto: University of Toronto Press, 1970), *passim*.

8   James A. Schultz, *Knowledge of Childhood*, p. 13; Peter Coveney, *The Image of Childhood*, p. 29; Keith Thomas, 'Children in Early Modern England', p. 48.

9   Schultz, *German Middle Ages*, pp. 244–51.

10 J. A. Burrow, *The Ages of Man*, pp. 5–8; Robert Pattison, *Child Figure*, p. 2.

11 Egle Becchi, 'Le XIXe siècle', in Egle Becchi and Dominique Julia (eds), *Histoire de l'enfance*, pp. 147–217 (pp. 151–3).

12 This paragraph is indebted to Alan Prout and Allison James, 'A New Paradigm for the Sociology of Childhood? Provenance, Promise and Problems', in James and Prout (eds), *Constructing and Reconstructing Childhood*, pp. 7–34.

13 Hans Peter Dreitzel (ed.), *Childhood and Socialization*, p. 5; Martin P. M. Richards (ed.), *The Integration of a Child into a Social World* (Cambridge: Cambridge University Press, 1974), editor's introduction, pp. 1–10.

14 Robert MacKay, 'Conceptions of Children and Models of Socialization', in Dreitzel, *Socialization*, pp. 27–43 (pp. 27–8).

15 Prout and James, 'New Paradigm', and Allison James, Chris Jenks and Alan Prout, *Theorizing Childhood*, ch. 2.

16 Prout and James, 'New Paradigm', p. 7. See also Nicholas Tucker, *What is a Child?* pp. 13–15, 99; Richards, *Integration;* Frank S. Kessel and Alexander W. Siegel (eds), *The Child and Other Cultural Inventions* (New York: Praeger, 1983); and Martin Richards and Paul Light (eds), *Children of Social Worlds: Development in a Social Context* (Cambridge: Polity, 1986).

17 See William Kessen, 'The American Child', 815–20; and Harry Hendrick, *Children, Childhood and English Society*, p. 12.

18 Frank McCourt, *Angela's Ashes: A Memoir of Childhood* (London: Flamingo, 1997), p. 1.

19 Dreitzel, *Socialization*, pp. 14–15; MacKay, 'Models', p. 31; Jens Qvortrup, 'Childhood Matters: An Introduction', in Jens Qvortrup, Marjatta Bardy, Giovanni Sgritta and Helmut Wintersberger (eds), *Childhood Matters: Social Theory, Practice and Politics* (Avebury: Aldershot, 1994), pp. 1–23 (pp. 3–5).

20 Prout and James, 'New Paradigm', pp. 22–9; Qvortrup et al., 'Childhood Matters', pp. 5–7; Diana Gittins, *Child in Question*, p. 44.

21 Richard T. Vann, 'The Youth of *Centuries of Childhood*', 277.

22 Conspicuous examples include Ivy Pinchbeck and Margaret Hewitt, *Children in English Society*; and Robert H. Bremner (ed.), *Children and Youth in America*.

23 Philippe Ariès, *Centuries of Childhood*, p. 124; Vann, 'The Youth', 283–4; Kessen, 'The American Child and Other Cultural Inventions', 815. Other influential contributions to the cultural history of childhood include Jerome Kroll, 'The Concept of Childhood'; Luke Demaitre, 'The Idea of Childhood and Child Care'; Shulamith Shahar, *Childhood*; C. John Sommerville, *Discovery of Childhood*; Hugh Cunningham,

The Children of the Poor; Carolyn Steedman, *Childhood, Culture and Class*.

24   Recent surveys of the history of childhood, anthologies and research guides concerning these debates include C. John Sommerville, *Rise and Fall of Childhood*; Joseph M. Hawes and N. Ray Hiner, *American Childhood*; Harvey J. Graff (ed.), *Growing up in America*; Joseph M. Hawes and N. Ray Hiner (eds), *Children in Historical and Comparative Perspective*; Hugh Cunningham, *Children and Childhood*; Becchi and Julia, *Histoire de l'enfance*, vol. 2, 'Du XVIIIe siècle à nos jours' (Paris: Editions du Seuil, 1996); Hugh Cunningham, 'Histories of Childhood', *American Historical Review*, 103 (1998), 1195–1208; Paula S. Fass and Mary Ann Mason (eds), *Childhood in America*.

25   Here one might cite as distinguished examples Carol Dyhouse, *Girls Growing up*; Elliott West, *Growing up*; Karin Calvert, *Children in the House*; Barbara A. Hanawalt, *Medieval London*; Harvey J. Graff, *Conflicting Paths*; Anna Davin, *Growing up Poor*.

26   David Nasaw, 'Children and Commercial Culture: Moving Pictures in the Early Twentieth Century', in Elliott West and Paula Petrick (eds), *Small Worlds*, pp. 14–25; and Miriam Formanek-Brunell, *Made to Play House*, ch. 1. From a similar perspective see also Stephen Humphries, *Hooligans or Rebels*; Thomas, 'Children in Early Modern England'; and Catherine Panter-Brick and Malcolm T. Smith, *Abandoned Children*.

27   Recent examples include George K. Behlmer, *Child Abuse*; Colin Heywood, *Childhood*; Lee Shai Weissbach, *Child Labor Reform*; Harry Hendrick, *Child Welfare*; Bernard Harris, *The Health of the Schoolchild: A History of the School Medical Service in England and Wales* (Buckingham: Open University Press, 1995); Edward Ross Dickinson, *The Politics of German Child Welfare*; LeRoy Ashby, *Endangered Children*.

28   Roger Cox, *Shaping Childhood*, p. 6. See also J. Calvet, *L'Enfant dans la littérature française* (2 vols, Paris: Lanore, 1930); Coveney, *The Image of Childhood*; Pattison, *Child Figure*; David Grylls, *Guardians and Angels*; James Holt McGavran Jr. (ed.), *Romanticism and Children's Literature in Nineteenth-Century England* (Athens: University of Georgia Press, 1991); Carolyn Steedman, *Strange Dislocations*.

29   Michael Anderson, *Approaches to the History of the Western Family, 1500–1914* (Cambridge: Cambridge University Press, 1980), ch. 3.

30   Ludmilla Jordanova, 'New Worlds for Children', 78–9.

31   Pascal, *Design and Truth*, pp. 3 and 11.

32   Regenia Gagnier, *Subjectivities: A History of Self-Representation in Britain, 1832–1920* (New York: Oxford University Press, 1991), pp. 138–70 (p. 159).

33   Steedman, *Strange Dislocations*, p. 6, referring to Cunningham, *Children of the Poor*.

Part I (introductory)

1   Pierre de Bérulle, *Opuscules de piété*, 69 (Lyons, 1666), cited by Georges Snyders, *Pédagogie en France*, p. 194.

2   Jerome Kagan, *Nature of the Child*, pp. 4–6.
3   Tucker, *What is a Child?*, pp. 13, 98.
4   See Sommerville, *Discovery of Childhood*, p. 3.
5   See e.g. Ludmilla Jordanova, 'Children in History', p. 5.
6   David Archard, *Children: Rights and Childhood* (London: Routledge, 1993), ch. 2 (pp. 17, 22–4).

Chapter 1   Conceptions of Childhood in the Middle Ages

1   Philippe Ariès, *Centuries of Childhood*, pp. 10, 125–30, 186 and 395–6.
2   Notably Jacques Le Goff, *Medieval Civilization, 400–1500*, transl. Julia Barrow (Oxford: Basil Blackwell, 1988 [1964]); F. R. H. Du Boulay, *An Age of Ambition: English Society in the Late Middle Ages* (London: Thomas Nelson, 1970); John Demos, *A Little Commonwealth*; Edward Shorter, *Modern Family*; S. Ryan Johansson, 'Centuries of Childhood'.
3   Jean-Louis Flandrin, 'Enfance et société'; Adrian Wilson, 'The Infancy', 150, 152.
4   See Vann, 'The Youth of *Centuries of Childhood*', 286–7; and Judith Ennew, 'Time for Children or Time for Adults?', in Jens Qvortrupet et al., *Childhood Matters: Social Theory, Practice and Politics* (Aldershot: Avebury, 1994), pp. 125–43 (p. 126).
5   Martin Hoyles, 'History and Politics', in *Changing Childhood*, pp. 1–14.
6   Ariès, *Centuries of Childhood*, p. 31; Le Goff, *Medieval Civilization*, p. 288.
7   Adrian Wilson, 'The Infancy', 146; though compare this to a more sympathetic approach to Ariès in Andrew Martindale, 'The Child in the Picture'. This section also relies on F. Garnier, 'L'Iconographie de l'enfant au moyen âge'; Ilene H. Forsyth, 'Children in Early Medieval Art' 36–7; Peter Fuller, 'Uncovering Childhood', in Hoyles, *Changing Childhood*, 71–108; Anthony Burton, 'Looking forward from Ariès?', 210; Colin Morris, *The Discovery of the Individual, 1050–1200* (London: SPCK, 1972), pp. 86–91.
8   Adrian Wilson, 'The Infancy', *passim*; Timothy Ashplant and Adrian Wilson, 'Present-Centred History and the Problem of Historical Knowledge', *Historical Journal*, 31 (1988), 253–74; Doris Desclais Berkvam, 'Nature and *Norreture*', 165–80 (165).
9   Notably Urban T. Holmes, 'Medieval Childhood'; Kroll, 'Concept of Childhood'; Barbara A. Hanawalt, *Ties that Bound*, ch. 11; Shahar, *Childhood, passim*; Linda M. Paterson, *World of the Troubadours*, ch. 10.
10 Jean-Pierre Cuvillier, 'L'Enfant dans la tradition féodale germanique', *Senefiance*, 9 (1980), 45–59; F. L. Attenborough (ed.), *The Laws of the Earliest English Kings* (Cambridge: Cambridge University Press, 1922), pp. 127, 157, 169; Mathew S. Kuefler, '"A Wryed Existence"', 826.
11 Mayke de Jong, 'Growing up in a Carolingian Monastery'.
12 Jean-Noël Biraben, 'Médecine et l'enfant', 73–5; Demaitre, 'The Idea of Childhood and Child Care'.

13   See Holmes, 'Medieval Childhood', *passim*; Pierre-André Sigal, 'Le Vocabulaire de l'enfance et de l'adolescence dans les receuils de miracles latins des XIe et XIIe siècles', *Senefiance*, 9 (1980), 141–59; Shahar, *Childhood*, ch. 2. They are discussed by Ariès in *Centuries of Childhood*, ch. 1, in ambivalent fashion: 'Nowadays we may consider this jargon empty and verbose, but it had a meaning for those who read it' (p. 19).

14   Elizabeth Sears, *The Ages of Man*, pp. 29–30.

15   Ibid., p. 5; Burrow, *The Ages of Man*, p. 92.

16   Schultz, *Knowledge of Childhood*, pp. 39–40.

17   Burrow, *Ages of Man*, pp. 20, 92–3.

18   See above, p. 10.

19   Pierre Riché and Danièle Alexandre-Bidon, *L'Enfance*, pp. 22–7; Pierre Riché, *Education and Culture*, pp. 10–12, ch. 10; Shahar, *Childhood*, ch. 1.

20   Donald Weinstein and Rudolph M. Bell, *Saints and Society*, p. 19.

21   Schultz, *Knowledge of Childhood*, p. 6.

22   Shahar, *Childhood*, ch. 2; Weinstein and Bell, *Saints and Society*, ch. 1.

23   Richard B. Lyman, 'Barbarism and Religion: Late Roman and Early Medieval Childhood', in DeMause, *History of Childhood*, pp. 75–100 (p. 77); Robert Pattison, *Child Figure*, pp. 20–1, 45.

24   It should be said that there is an extensive debate over whether the image of a lost pearl in *Pearl* symbolizes the death of a child, or provides an allegory for a purely spiritual event. See Ian Bishop, *Pearl in its Setting: A Critical Study of the Structure and Meaning of the Middle English Poem* (Oxford: Basil Blackwell, 1968), pp. 5–9; and Malcolm Andrew and Ronald Waldron (eds), *The Poems of the Pearl Manuscript* (London: Edward Arnold, 1978), p. 32, n.7.

25   Shahar, *Childhood*, p. 15; Riché, *Barbarian West*, pp. 11, 449; D. H. Farmer (ed.), *The Age of Bede* (Harmondsworth: Penguin, 1988), pp. 43–4; Schultz, *Knowledge of Childhood*, p. 240.

26   John Boswell, *The Kindness of Strangers*, pp. 26–36; Berkvam, 'Nature and *Norreture*', 165–6; Schultz, *Knowledge of Childhood*, ch. 2; Christiane Klapisch-Zuber, 'Childhood in Tuscany at the Beginning of the Fifteenth Century', in *Women, Family, and Ritual*, pp. 94–116 (p. 96); Paterson, *World of the Troubadours*, p. 286; de Jong, 'Magister Hildemar and his Oblates', 102–3.

27   Doris Desclais Berkvam, *Enfance et maternité*, ch. 5; eadem, 'Nature and *Norreture*', 169; Klapisch, 'Attitudes', 64–5; Schultz, *Knowledge of Childhood*, ch. 9.

28   See e.g. Norbert Elias, *The Civilizing Process*, vol. 1, p. xiii; and Ruth Benedict, 'Continuities and Discontinuities in Cultural Conditioning', *Psychiatry*, 1 (1938), 161–7.

29   Hanawalt, *Ties that Bound*, pp. 188–90.

30   Riché, *Barbarian West*, pp. xiv–xv.

31   Cuvillier, 'Tradition féodale germanique', 49.

Chapter 2   The Quest for a Turning Point

1   Adrian Wilson, 'Philippe Ariès', 144.

2   Ariès, *Centuries of Childhood*, esp. pp. 125–30, 316 and 395–9.

3 Ibid., p. 129.

4 Jordanova, 'Children in History', p. 10.

5 Pierre Riché, *De l'éducation antique à l'éducation chevaleresque*, pp. 30–5; idem, *Education and Culture*, pp. 453–4.

6 Jacques Le Goff, *Medieval Civilization, 400–1500*, transl. Julia Barrow (Oxford: Basil Blackwell, 1988 [1964]), p. 288; Colin Morris, *The Discovery of the Individual, 1050–1200* (London: SPCK, 1972), ch. 2; R. W. Southern, *Western Society and the Church in the Middle Ages* (Harmondsworth: Penguin, 1970), ch. 2.

7 See Joseph H. Lynch, *Simoniacal Entry into Religious Life from 1000 to 1260* (Columbus: Ohio State University Press, 1976), pp. 36–50; Boswell, *Kindness of Strangers*, ch. 5; Mayke de Jong, *In Samuel's Image*, ch. 1.

8 Riché, *Education and Culture*, pp. 453–4; Kuefler, '"A Wryed Existence"', 825; and Janet L. Nelson, 'Parents, Children, and the Church', pp. 86–8. See also Paterson, *World of the Troubadours*, pp. 281–6.

9 Mary Martin McLaughlin, 'Survivors and Surrogates: Children and Parents from the Ninth to the Thirteenth Centuries', in Lloyd deMause (ed.), *The History of Childhood*, pp. 101–81 (p. 139); Lorraine C. Attreed, 'From *Pearl* Maiden to Tower Princes', p. 47; Roland Carron, *Enfant et parenté dans la France médiévale*, p. 173.

10 David Herlihy, 'Medieval Children', pp. 120–1. See also Southern, *Western Society*, pp. 34–43; Morris, *The Discovery*, ch. 3; Le Goff, *Medieval Civilization, passim*; and Jacques Rossiaud, 'The City-Dweller and Life in Cities and Towns', in Jacques Le Goff (ed.), *The Medieval World*, transl. Lydia G. Cochrane (London: Collins and Brown, 1990), pp. 139–79.

11 See Kagan, *Nature of the Child*, p. 26 (discussing the seventeenth century).

12 Morris, *The Discovery*, p. 47; Betty Radice (ed.), *The Letters of Abelard and Heloise* (Harmondsworth: Penguin, 1974), p. 57; M. T. Clanchy, *Abelard: A Medieval Life* (Oxford: Blackwell Publishers, 1997), pp. 47–50.

13 Herlihy, 'Medieval Children', pp. 120–6.

14 Morris, *The Discovery*, chs 3, 4 and 6.

15 Sommerville, *Discovery of Childhood*, pp. 3–10; David Leverenz, *Language of Puritan Feeling*, ch. 5.

16 On the background to the doctrine of original sin, see below, pp. 32–4.

17 Snyders, *Pédagogie en France*, ch. 4.

18 Max J. Okenfuss, *Discovery of Childhood in Russia*, pp. 22 and 74.

19 See e.g. Pat Thane, 'Childhood in History', p. 10.

20 Margaret M. J. Ezell, 'John Locke's Images of Childhood'. *Concerning Education* is conveniently summarized in Maurice Cranston, *John Locke: A Biography* (Oxford: Oxford University Press, 1985), ch. 18; and W. M. Spellman, *John Locke* (Basingstoke: Macmillan, 1997), ch. 4.

21 John Locke, *Concerning Education*, p. 265.

22 Ibid., pp. 23–4 (editors' Introduction); J. A. Passmore, 'The Malleability of Man in Eighteenth-Century Thought', in Earl R. Wasserman, *Aspects of the Eighteenth Century* (Baltimore: Johns Hopkins University Press, 1965), pp. 21–46 (p. 21); W. M. Spellman, 'The Christian Estimate of Man in Locke's *Essay*', *Journal of Religion*, 67 (1987), 474–92.

23   Locke, *Concerning Education*, pp. 107, 134–5 and 141; Ezell, 'Images of Childhood', *passim*.
24   Coveney, *The Image of Childhood*, p. 33. Other useful works on Rousseau's view of childhood include J. H. Broome, *Rousseau* (London: Arnold, 1963), ch. 5; John Charvet, *The Social Problem in the Philosophy of Rousseau* (Cambridge: Cambridge University Press, 1974), ch. 3; Maurice Cranston, *The Noble Savage: Jean-Jacques Rousseau, 1754–1762* (Chicago: University of Chicago Press, 1991), ch. 7; Grylls, *Guardians and Angels*, ch. 1; and Cox, *Shaping Childhood*, ch. 3.
25   Jean-Jacques Rousseau, *Emile*, p. 37.
26   Ibid., pp. 89–90.
27   Ibid., pp. 92–3, 100 and 107.
28   Grylls, *Guardians and Angels*, p. 35.
29   See Egle Becchi, 'Le XIXe siècle', in Becchi and Julia, *Histoire de l'enfance*, vol. 2, pp. 147–223 (151–2).
30   Cited in Charles Strickland, 'Transcendentalist Father', 8.
31   Anne Higonnet, *Pictures of Innocence*, pp. 15–30; Calvert, *Children in the House, passim*.
32   Claude Salleron, 'La Littérature au XIXe siècle et la famille', in R. Prigent (ed.), *Renouveau des idées sur la famille* (Paris: Presses Universitaries de France, 1954), pp. 60–80 (p. 67).
33   Barbara Garlitz, 'The Immortality Ode: Its Cultural Legacy', in *Studies in English Literature, 1500–1900*, 6 (1966), 639–49. See also Coveney, *Image of Childhood*, p. 80.
34   See Coveney, *Image of Childhood*, ch. 3; Robert Pattison, *Child Figure*, ch. 3; Cox, *Shaping Childhood*, ch. 4; Becchi, 'XIXe siècle', n. 26; and Sylvia D. Hoffert, *Private Matters*, ch. 5.
35   F. J. Harvey Darton, *Children's Books*, p. 169, cited by Cox, *Shaping Childhood*, pp. 104–5.
36   Coveney, *Image of Childhood*, pp. 31–2.
37   Viviana A. Zelizer, *Pricing the Priceless Child*, pp. 3–6.
38   Steedman, *Childhood, Culture and Class*, ch. 3; and 'Bodies, Figures and Physiology: Margaret McMillan and the Late Nineteenth-Century Remaking of Working-Class Childhood', in Roger Cooter (ed.), *In the Name of the Child*, pp. 19–44. Steedman explores the Mignon theme and idea of the 'child' in more detail in *Strange Dislocations*.
39   John R. Gillis, *Youth and History: Tradition and Change in European Age Relations, 1770–Present* (New York: Academic Press, 1974), chs. 3–4; Joseph F. Kett, *Rites of Passage: Adolescence in America, 1790 to the Present* (New York: Basic Books, 1977), ch. 8; John Springhall, *Coming of Age: Adolescence in Britain, 1860–1960* (Dublin: Gill and Macmillan, 1986), ch. 1; Harry Hendrick, *Images of Youth: Age, Class, and the Male Youth Problem, 1880–1920* (Oxford: Clarendon Press, 1990), ch. 4; John Davis, *Youth and the Condition of Britain: Images of Adolescent Conflict* (London: Athlone Press, 1990), ch. 3; Christine Griffin, *Representations of Youth: The Study of Youth and Adolescence in Britain and America* (Cambridge: Polity, 1993), ch. 1; Agnès Thiercé, *Histoire de l'adolescence, 1850–1914* (Paris: Belin, 1999).

40 On recapitulation theory, see George Boas, *The Cult of Childhood* (London: Warburg Institute, 1966), ch. 4; Hendrick, *Images of Youth*, pp. 104–6; and Cunningham, *Children of the Poor*, pp. 123–32.

41 G. Stanley Hall, *Adolescence: Its Psychology and its Relations to Physiology, Anthropology, Sociology, Sex, Crime, Religion and Education* (2 vols, New York: Appleton, 1904), vol. 1, pp. viii–xiii. See also Dorothy Ross, *G. Stanley Hall: The Psychologist as Prophet* (Chicago: University of Chicago Press, 1972), ch. 15; and Rolf E. Muuss, *Theories of Adolescence* (3rd edn, New York: Random House, 1975), ch. 2.

42 Barbara A. Hanawalt argued that 'the European medieval world certainly recognized and defined adolescence', though in a different way to the nineteenth and twentieth centuries, in 'Historical Descriptions and Prescriptions for Adolescence', *Journal of Family History*, 17 (1992), 341–51 (342). James A. Schultz countered that, in the Middle High German texts he studied, there was nothing that corresponds to our modern notion of adolescence; 'Medieval Adolescence: The Claims of History and the Silence of the German Narrative', *Speculum*, 66 (1991), 519–39 (533).

43 Natalie Zemon Davis, 'The Reasons of Misrule: Youth Groups and Charivaris in Sixteenth-Century France', *Past and Present*, 50 (1971), 41–75 (55); Michel Mitterauer, *A History of Youth*, transl. Graeme Dunphy (Oxford: Basil Blackwell, 1992), p. 156; Georges Duby, 'In Northwestern France: The "Youth" in Twelfth-Century Aristocratic Society', in Fredric L. Cheyette (ed.), *Lordship and Community in Medieval Europe* (New York: Holt, Rinehart and Winston, 1968), pp. 198–209; Hanawalt, *Ties that Bound*, ch. 12; Kathryn L. Reyerson, 'The Adolescent Apprentice/Worker in Medieval Montpellier', *Journal of Family History*, 17 (1992), 353–70; Anne Yarborough, 'Apprentices as Adolescents in Sixteenth-Century Bristol', *Journal of Social History*, 13 (1979), 68–71; S. R. Smith, 'The London Apprentices as Seventeenth-Century Adolescents', *Past and Present*, 61 (1973), 149–61.

44 Muuss, *Theories of Adolescence*, p. 34.

45 Hall, *Adolescence*, p. x; Muuss, *Theories of Adolescence*, pp. 35–6.

46 Karen Offen, 'Depopulation, Nationalism, and Feminism in Fin-de-Siècle France', *American Historical Review*, 89 (1984), 648–76; Paul Weindling, *Health, Race and German Politics between National Unification and Nazism, 1870–1945* (Cambridge: Cambridge University Press, 1989), pp. 241–62.

47 G. R. Searle, *The Quest for National Efficiency* (Oxford: Basil Blackwell, 1971), *passim*; Sir Robert Baden Powell, *Scouting for Boys: A Handbook for Instruction in Good Citizenship* (12th edn, London: C. Arthur Pearson, 1926), p. 281.

48 Daniel Pick, *Faces of Degeneration: A European Disorder, c.1848–c.1918* (Cambridge: Cambridge University Press, 1989); Geoffrey Pearson, *Hooligan: A History of Respectable Fears* (London: Macmillan, 1983); Thomas E. Jordan, *The Degeneracy Crisis and Victorian Youth* (Albany: State University of New York Press, 1993); Adrian Woolridge, *Measuring the Mind: Education and Psychology in England, c.1860–c.1990* (Cambridge: Cambridge University Press, 1994), ch. 2; Robert A. Nye,

'Degeneration, Neurasthenia and the Culture of Sport in Belle Epoque France', *Journal of Contemporary History*, 17 (1982), 51–68; idem, *Crime, Madness and Politics in Modern France* (Princeton: Princeton University Press, 1984), ch. 6; Weindling, *Health, Race*, chs 1–3.

49   Hall, *Adolescence*, vol. 1, p. xv.
50   *The Child Welfare Annual*, p. vii, cited by Woolridge, *Measuring the Mind*, p. 23.
51   Neil Postman, *The Disappearance of Childhood* (New York: Vintage Books, 1994), pp. 4–5.
52   See the interesting discussion in Chris Jenks, *Childhood* (London: Routledge, 1996), ch. 5.

Chapter 3   Some Themes in the Cultural History of Childhood

1   David Archard, *Children: Rights and Childhood* (London: Routledge, 1993), p. 27. For some pertinent discussion of these points from a sociological point of view, see James, Jenks and Prout, *Theorizing Childhood*, ch. 1; and Gittins, *Child in Question*, ch. 5.
2   St Augustine, *Confessions*, p. 27; Pattison, *Child Figure*, p. 17.
3   Richard B. Lyman Jr, 'Barbarism and Religion: Late Roman and Early Medieval Childhood' in deMause, *History of Childhood*, pp. 75–100 (p. 88).
4   Steven Ozment, *When Fathers Ruled*, p. 164; Gerald Strauss, *Luther's House*, pp. 94–100.
5   Leverenz, *Language of Puritan Feeling*, pp. 156–8; Philip Greven, *The Protestant Temperament*, p. 28.
6   Snyders, *Pédagogie en France*, ch. 4.
7   Janet L. Nelson, 'Parents, Children, and the Church', p. 89.
8   Michael Goodich, 'Bartholomaeus Anglicus on Child-Rearing', 78.
9   Greven, *Protestant Temperament*, pp. 156–9.
10   Malcolm Andrews, Introduction to Charles Dickens, *The Old Curiosity Shop* (Harmondsworth: Penguin, 1972), p. 27; Coveney, *The Image of Childhood*, pp. 32–4, ch. 5; Cunningham, *Children of the Poor, passim*.
11   Berkvam, *Enfance et maternité*, ch. 5 (p. 85) and eadem, 'Nature and Norreture, *passim*; Schultz, *Knowledge of Childhood*, pp. 43, 98–105. Medievalists like to point out the recent reaction among psychologists to established ideas on the continuities between infancy and adulthood. They cite Jerome Kagan and his exploration of the 'possibility of serious discontinuity, where some earlier characteristics vanish completely and new ones emerge with relatively short histories'; Kagan, *Nature of the Child*, p. 11.
12   Pierre Riché, *Education et culture dans l'Occident médiéval* (Paris: Variorum, 1993), p. 296; Danièle Alexandre-Bidon and Didier Lett, *Les Enfants*, p. 73.
13   Locke, *Concerning Education*, p. 83.
14   Ibid., p. 265.
15   See Jean-Gaspard Itard, *The Wild Boy of Aveyron*, transl. George and Muriel Humphrey (New York: Century, 1932); Harlan Lane, *The Wild*

Boy of Aveyron (London: George Allen and Unwin, 1977); and Roger Shattuck, *The Forbidden Experiment: The Story of the Wild Boy of Aveyron* (London: Secker and Warburg, 1980).

16 Karl Pearson, *Nature and Nurture* (London: Dulau, 1906), cited by Leon J. Kamin, *The Science and Politics of I.Q.* (New York: John Wiley, 1974), p. 1.

17 Kamin, *Politics of I.Q.*, ch. 1; Stephen Jay Gould, *The Mismeasure of Man* (Harmondsworth: Penguin, 1997), ch. 5; Steven Rose, R. C. Lewontin and Leon J. Kamin, *Not in Our Genes: Biology, Ideology and Human Nature* (Harmondsworth: Penguin, 1990), ch. 5.

18 Gillian Sutherland, *Ability, Merit and Measurement: Mental Testing and English Education, 1880–1940* (Oxford: Clarendon Press, 1984), ch. 4; Gould, *Mismeasurement of Man*, ch. 6; Rose et al., *Not in Our Genes*, pp. 86–8; Adrian Woolridge, *Measuring the Mind: Education and Psychology in England, c.1860–c.1990* (Cambridge: Cambridge University Press, 1994), p. 2 and passim.

19 See below, chs 7–8.

20 Kroll, 'Concept of Childhood', 388.

21 Cited in Herlihy, 'Medieval Children', 121.

22 Maris A. Vinovskis, 'Changing Perceptions and Treatment of Young Children in the United States', in Arlene Skolnick (ed.), *Rethinking Childhood: Perspectives on Development and Society* (Boston: Little, Brown, 1976), pp. 99–112 (102).

23 André Burgière, 'De Malthus à Max Weber: le mariage tardif et l'esprit d'entreprise', *Annales ESC*, 27 (1972), 1128–38; Jean-Louis Flandrin, 'Mariage tardif et vie sexuelle: discussions et hypothèses de recherche', *Annales ESC*, 27 (1972), 1351–78; and 'Repression and Change in the Sexual Life of Young People in Medieval and Early Modern Times', *Journal of Family History*, 2 (1977), 196–210.

24 Snyders, *La Pédagogie*, pp. 208–10.

25 Robert H. MacDonald, 'The Frightful Consequences of Onanism: Notes on the History of a Delusion', *Journal of the History of Ideas*, 28 (1967), 423–31; Angus McLaren, 'Some Secular Attitudes toward Sexual Behavior in France: 1760–1860', *French Historical Studies*, 8 (1974), 604–25; R. P. Neuman, 'Masturbation, Madness, and the Modern Concepts of Childhood and Adolescence', *Journal of Social History*, 8 (1974–5), 1–27; Michael Stolberg, 'An Unmanly Vice: Self-Pollution, Anxiety, and the Body in the Eighteenth-Century', *Social History of Medicine*, 13 (2000), 1–21.

26 Deborah Gorham, 'The "Maiden Tribute of Modern Babylon"'.

27 Stephen Kern, 'Freud and the Discovery of Child Sexuality'.

28 Skolnick, 'Introduction: Rethinking Childhood', in *Rethinking Childhood*, p. 4.

29 Paterson, *World of the Troubadours*, pp. 286, 295; Schultz, *Knowledge of Childhood*, ch. 2 and pp. 256–9; Ariès, *Centuries of Childhood*, p. 56.

30 Deborah Gorham, *The Victorian Girl*, pp. 42–4; and 'Maiden Tribute', 570–1.

31 *The Mother's Companion*, 1 (1987), p. 62, cited by Gorham, *Victorian Girl*, p. 75; see also ch. 4 in general.

32 Claudia Nelson, 'Sex and the Single Boy'.

33 Thomas Hughes, *Tom Brown's Schooldays* (Harmondsworth: Penguin, 1994 [1857]), pp. 222–7; David Newsome, *Godliness and Good Learning: Four Studies on a Victorian Ideal* (London: John Murray, 1961), *passim*.

34 Cited by Carolyn Steedman, in *Strange Dislocations*, p. 23.

35 James R. Kincaid, *Child-Loving*, p. 365. See also the extended discussion of gender and sexuality in childhood in Cox, *Shaping Childhood*, ch. 6.

Part II (introductory)

1 L. deMause, 'The Evolution of Childhood', in deMause, *History of Childhood*, pp. 1–73 (pp. 17, 52); Lawrence Stone, *The Family*, p. 99; and Elisabeth Badinter, *The Myth of Motherhood: An Historical View of the Maternal 'Instinct'*, transl. Roger DeGaris (London: Souvenir Press, 1981), p. xxiii.

2 Influential examples include Barbara A. Hanawalt, 'Childrearing'; eadem, *Ties that Bound*, ch. 11; Emmanuel Le Roy Ladurie, *Montaillou*, ch. 13; Louis Haas, *Renaissance Man*; Gélis, Laget and Morel, *Entrer dans la vie*; Ralph A. Houlbrooke, *English Family*, ch. 6; Ozment, *When Fathers Ruled*; Keith Wrightson, *English Society*, pp. 104–18; Ferdinand Mount, *The Subversive Family: An Alternative History of Love and Marriage* (London: Jonathan Cape, 1982), ch. 7; and Stephen Wilson, 'Myth of Motherhood'.

3 Ozment, *When Fathers Ruled*, p. 162.

4 Linda Pollock, *Forgotten Children*, p. 268.

Chapter 4   Parent–Child Relations: The First Stages

1 Cited by Angus McLaren, *A History of Contraception: From Antiquity to the Present Day* (Oxford: Basil Blackwell, 1990), p. 117.

2 Shahar, *Childhood*, pp. 9–14; Le Roy Ladurie, *Montaillou*, pp. 206–7; Madeleine Jeay, 'Sexuality and Family in Fifteenth-Century France: Are Literary Sources a Mask or a Mirror?', *Journal of Family History*, 4 (1979), 328–45; Berkvam, *Enfance et maternité*, ch. 1; Danièle Alexandre-Bidon and Monique Closson, *L'Enfant à l'ombre des cathédrales*, ch. 1; Christopher Brooke, *The Medieval Idea of Marriage* (Oxford: Clarendon Press, 1989), *passim*; Clarissa W. Atkinson, *The Oldest Vocation: Christian Motherhood in the Middle Ages* (Ithaca, NY: Cornell University Press, 1991), ch. 3. Riché and Alexandre-Bidon, *L'Enfance*, ch. 4; D. L. d'Avray and M. Tausche, 'Marriage Sermons in *Ad Status* Collections of the Central Middle Ages', *Archives d'histoire doctrinale et littéraire du Moyen Age*, 47 (1980), 71–119 (79, 118).

3 Le Roy Ladurie, *Montaillou*, p. 209.

4 David Herlihy, 'Tuscan Names, 1200–1530', *Renaissance Quarterly*, 41 (1988), 561–82 (566); Riché and Alexandre-Bidon, *L'Enfance*, p. 185.

5 Weinstein and Bell, *Saints and Society*, p. 20.

6 This paragraph relies on Alexandre-Bidon and Closson, *L'Enfant à l'ombre des cathédrales*, ch. 1; Riché and Alexandre-Bidon, *Moyen Age*, pp. 39–42; and Haas, *Renaissance Man*, ch. 1; Sally Crawford, *Childhood in Anglo-Saxon England*, pp. 57–8.

7 Berkvam, *Enfance et maternité*, pp. 13–14; Atkinson, *Oldest Vocation*, ch. 6.

8 Pollock, *Forgotten Children*, pp. 204–8. See also Angus McLaren, *Reproductive Rituals: The Perception of Fertility in England from the Sixteenth Century to the Nineteenth Century* (London: Methuen, 1984), chs 1–2; Patricia Crawford, 'The Construction and Experience of Maternity in Seventeenth-Century England', in Valerie Fildes (ed.), *Women as Mothers in Pre-Industrial England* (London: Routledge, 1990), pp. 3–38; and Jane Turner Censer, *North Carolina Planters*, pp. 24–6.

9 Pollock, *Forgtten Children*, pp. 208–11; Gélis, Laget and Morel, *Entrer dans la vie*, p. 44; Wrightson, *English Society*, p. 104; Houlbrooke, *English Family*, p. 127.

10 Cited by Pollock, *Forgotten Children*, p. 206.

11 J. Hajnal, 'European Marriage Patterns in Perspective', in D. V. Glass and D. E. C. Eversley (eds), *Population in History* (London: Edward Arnold, 1965), pp. 101–43.

12 David Herlihy, *Medieval Households* (Cambridge, Mass.: Harvard University Press, 1985), pp. 146–9. St Augustine, during late antiquity, mentioned that it was common for men to have sex with their wives with the *intent* of avoiding conception; see Brent D. Shaw, 'The Family in Late Antiquity: The Experience of Augustine', *Past and Present*, 115 (1987), 3–51 (44–5).

13 Le Roy Ladurie, *Montaillou*, p. 173; John M. Riddle, *Eve's Herbs: A History of Contraception and Abortion in the West* (Cambridge, Mass.: Harvard University Press, 1997), ch. 1.

14 John M. Riddle, *Contraception and Abortion from the Ancient World to the Renaissance* (Cambridge, Mass.: Harvard University Press, 1992), p. 156. For a very sceptical assessment of this work, see the review by Helen King in *Medical History*, 42 (1998), pp. 412–14. See also Linda Gordon, *Woman's Body, Woman's Right: A Social History of Birth Control in America* (Harmondsworth: Penguin, 1977), ch. 2.

15 See P. P. A. Biller, 'Birth Control in the West in the Thirteenth and Early Fourteenth Centuries', *Past and Present*, 94 (1982), 3–26.

16 R. P. Neuman, 'Working Class Birth Control in Wilhelmine Germany', *Comparative Studies in Society and History*, 20 (1978), 408–28 (426).

17 Angus McLaren, *A History of Contraception: from Antiquity to the Present Day* (Oxford: Basil Blackwell, 1990), *passim*. Jean-Louis Flandrin, *Families in Former Times*, pp. 212–16; Randolph Trumbach, *Rise of the Egalitarian Family*, ch. 14; John E. Knodel, *The Decline of Fertility in Germany, 1871–1939* (Princeton: Princeton University Press, 1974), *passim*; and James Woycke, *Birth Control in Germany, 1871–1933* (London: Routledge, 1988), chs 1–2; James Reed, *From Private Vice to Public Virtue: The Birth Control Movement and American Society since 1830* (New York: Basic Books, 1978), ch. 1.

18 Mireille Laget, 'Childbirth in Seventeenth- and Eighteenth-Century France: Obstetrical Practices and Collective Attitudes', in Robert

Forster and Orest Ranum (eds), *Medicine and Society in France* (Baltimore: Johns Hopkins University Press, 1980), pp. 137–76 (p. 147).

19   Patrick P. Dunn, '"That Enemy is the Baby": Childhood in Imperial Russia', in deMause, *History of Childhood*, pp. 383–405 (pp. 385–6); Samuel C. Ramer, 'Childbirth and Culture: Midwifery in the Nineteenth-Century Russian Countryside', in David I. Ransel (ed.), *The Family in Imperial Russia*, pp. 218–35 (pp. 228–9).

20   Berkvam, *Enfance et maternité*, p. 37.

21   Haas, *Renaissance Man*, p. 44; Houlbrooke, *English Family*, p. 129; Catherine M. Scholten, '"On the Importance of the Obstetrick Art": Changing Customs of Childbirth in America, 1760 to 1825', *William and Mary Quarterly*, 34 (1977), 426–45; Judith Walzer Leavitt, *Brought to Bed: Childbearing in America 1750 to 1950* (New York: Oxford University Press, 1986); Richard W. Wertz and Dorothy C. Wertz, *Lying-in: A History of Childbirth in America* (New Haven: Yale University Press, 1989), p. 47; Hoffert, *Private Matters*, ch. 1; Sally G. McMillan, *Motherhood in the Old South*, ch. 3; Jean Donnison, *Midwives and Medical Men: A History of the Struggle for the Control of Childbirth* (2nd edn, London: Historical Publications, 1988), *passim*; Adrian Wilson, *The Making of Man-Midwifery: Childbirth in England 1660–1770* (London: UCL Press, 1995).

22   Jean Towler and Joan Bramall, *Midwives in History and Society* (London: Croom Helm, 1986), chs. 2–3; Jacques Gélis, *History of Childbirth*, ch. 7; Adrian Wilson, 'The Ceremony of Childbirth and its Interpretation', in Fildes, *Women as Mothers* (n. 8 above), pp. 3–38.

23   Ramer, 'Russian Countryside', *passim*.

24   The diversity of experience with midwifery, both between and within countries, is well conveyed by Hilary Marland (ed.), *The Art of Midwifery: Early Modern Midwives in Europe* (London: Routledge, 1993). For early origins, see Michel Salvat, 'L'Accouchement dans la littérature scientifique médiévale', *Senefiance*, 9 (1980), 87–106 (92).

25   Wertz and Wertz, *Lying-in*, pp. 63–5; Irvine Loudon, *Death in Childbirth: An International Study of Maternal Care and Maternal Mortality 1800–1950* (Oxford: Clarendon Press, 1992), chs 23 and 24.

26   See R. V. Schnucker, 'English Puritans', 640–2; and Laget, 'Childbirth', p. 147.

27   This section is indebted to Gélis, *History of Childbirth*, *passim*.

28   Ibid., p. 97.

29   Crawford, *Anglo-Saxon England*, pp. 59–60.

30   Alexandre-Bidon and Closson, *L'Enfant à l'ombre des cathédrales*, pp. 54–66.

31   Anon., *The Common Errors in the Education of Children and their Consequences* (London, 1744), p. 10, cited by Dunn, 'Imperial Russia', p. 388.

32   Gélis, *History of Childbirth*, p. 177.

33   Berkvam, *Enfance et maternité*, p. 45.

34   Haas, *Renaissance Man*, p. 65.

35   Hanawalt, *Medieval London*, p. 44.

36   Riché and Alexandre-Bidon, *L'Enfance*, p. 182.

37   Gélis, *History of Childbirth*, pp. 194–6.

38   Crawford, 'Experience of Maternity' (n. 8 above), p. 11; Merry E. Wiesner, 'The Midwives of South Germany and the Public/Private

Dichotomy', in Marland, *Art of Midwifery* (n. 24 above), pp. 77–94 (pp. 85–6).

39   Dunn, 'Imperial Russia', pp. 388–9.
40   Hanawalt, *Medieval London*, p. 45; Alexandre-Bidon and Closson, *L'Enfant à l'ombre des cathédrales*, pp. 74–8; François Lebrun, *La Vie conjugale sous l'ancien régime* (Paris: Armand Colin, 1975), pp. 118–24; John Bossy, *Christianity in the West, 1400–1700* (Oxford: Oxford University Press, 1985), pp. 14–19.
41   Joseph H. Lynch, *Godparents and Kinship in Early Medieval Europe* (Princeton: Princeton University Press, 1986), *passim*; Haas, *Renaissance Man*, p. 72.
42   Janet L. Nelson, 'Parents, Children and the *Church*', pp. 103–4.
43   John Bossy, 'Blood and Baptism: Kinship, Community and Christianity in Western Europe from the Fourteenth to the Seventeenth Centuries', in Derek Baker (ed.), *Sanctity and Secularity: The Church and the World* (Oxford: Basil Blackwell, 1973), pp. 129–43 (p. 133).
44   Pierre-Jakez Hélias, *Horse of Pride*, p. 34.
45   Leon Battista Alberti, *The Family in Renaissance Florence: I libri della famiglia* (Columbia, University of South Carolina Press, 1969), pp. 122–3, cited by Haas, *Renaissance Man*, p. 82.
46   Christiane Klapisch-Zuber, 'L'Attribution d'un prénom à l'enfant en Toscane à la fin du Moyen-Age', *Senefiance*, 9 (1980), 73–85; Hanawalt, *Ties that Bound*, pp. 173–5; and *Medieval London*, pp. 46–8.
47   Riché and Alexandre-Bidon, *L'Enfance*, pp. 185–9; Herlihy, 'Tuscan Names', *passim*; Haas, *Renaissance Man*, pp. 82–7.
48   Sommerville, *Discovery of Childhood*, pp. 21–2; Ellen Ross, *Love and Toil: Motherhood in Outcast London, 1870–1918* (New York: Oxford University Press, 1993), pp. 131–2 (this list may be compared with the one in Hanawalt, *Medieval London*, p. 47).
49   Lebrun, *Vie conjugale*, pp. 121–2; Gélis, *History of Childbirth*, ch. 15.
50   Stephen Wilson, *The Means of Naming: A Social and Cultural History of Personal Naming in Western Europe* (London: UCL Press, 1998), ch. 9.
51   Ralph Gibson, *A Social History of French Catholicism, 1789–1914* (London: Routledge, 1989), pp. 163–4; Hugh McLeod, *Religion and Society in England, 1850–1914* (London: Macmillan, 1996), pp. 73–4; Ross, *Motherhood*, pp. 132–3.
52   Gélis, *History of Childbirth*, ch. 14.
53   Alan Macfarlane, *Josselin*, p. 81.
54   Yann Brékilien, *La Vie quotidienne des paysans bretons au xixe siècle* (Paris: Hachette, 1966), p. 145; Gélis, *History of Childbirth*, p. 193; Klapisch-Zuber, *Women, Family, and Ritual*, pp. 101–2.
55   Linda Pollock, *Lasting Relationship*, pp. 43–7; David L. Ransel, *Mothers of Misery*, p. 130.
56   Asser, *Life of King Alfred*, transl. Simon Keynes and Michael Lapidge, in *Alfred the Great* (Harmondsworth: Penguin, 1983), pp. 67–110 (p. 90); Janet L. Nelson, 'Reconstructing a Royal Family: Reflections on Alfred', in Ian Wood and Niels Lund (eds), *People and Places in Northern Europe, 500–1600: Essays in Honour of Peter Hayes Sawyer* (Woodbridge: Boydell Press, 1991), pp. 47–66 (p. 59); Carron, *Enfant et*

parenté, ch. 5; and David Nicholas, *Domestic Life of a Medieval City*, ch. 8.

57   Jean Meyer, 'Illegitimates and Foundlings in Pre-industrial France', in Peter Laslett, Karla Oosterveen and Richard M. Smith (eds), *Bastardy and its Comparative Perspective* (London: Edward Arnold, 1980), pp. 249–63 (p. 250). See also Beatrice Gottlieb, *The Family in the Western World from the Black Death to the Industrial Age* (New York: Oxford University Press, 1993), p. 211.

58   Robert V. Wells, 'Illegitimacy and Bridal Pregnancy in Colonial America', in Laslett et al., *Bastardy*, pp. 349–61 (pp. 355–6).

59   Sheilagh C. Ogilvie, 'Coming of Age in a Corporate Society'. For a discussion of attitudes in eighteenth-century England, see Susan Staves, 'British Seduced Maidens', *Eighteenth-Century Studies*, 14 (1980–1), 109–31.

60   Stephen Wilson, 'Infanticide, Child Abandonment, and Female Honour'.

61   John R. Gillis, *For Better, for Worse: British Marriages, 1600 to the Present* (New York: Oxford University Press, 1985), ch. 4.; and Lola Valverde, 'Illegitimacy and the Abandonment of Children in the Basque Country, 1550–1800', in John Henderson and Richard Wall (eds), *Poor Women and Children*, pp. 51–64.

62   See e.g. Jacques Depauw, 'Illicit Sexual Activity and Society in Eighteenth-Century Nantes', in R. Forster and O. Ranum (eds), *Family and Society: Selections from AESC* (Baltimore: Johns Hopkins University Press, 1976), pp. 145–91; Cissie Fairchilds, 'Female Sexual Attitudes and the Rise of Illegitimacy: A Case Study', *Journal of Interdisciplinary History*, 8 (1978), 627–77; John R. Gillis, 'Servants, Sexual Relations and the Risks of Illegitimacy in London 1801–1900', *Feminist Studies*, 5 (1979), 142–73; Wells, 'Colonial America', p. 357.

63   Lebrun, *La Vie conjugale*, p. 111.

64   Roger Schofield, 'Did the Mothers Really Die? Three Centuries of Maternal Mortality in "The World We Have Lost"', in Lloyd Bonfield, Richard M. Smith and Keith Wrightson (eds), *The World We have Gained* (Oxford: Basil Blackwell, 1986), pp. 231–60 (p. 250); J.-P. Bardet, K.-A. Lynch, G.-P. Mineau, M. Hainsworth and M. Skolnick, 'La Mortalité maternelle autrefois: une étude comparée (de la France de l'Ouest à l'Utah)', *Annales de démographie historique* (1981), 31–48 (41); Leavitt, *Brought to Bed* (n. 21 above), p. 28.

65   B. R. Mitchell, *European Historical Statistics, 1750–1970* (London: Macmillan, 1975), p. 39. See below, p. 149.

66   Ariès, *Centuries of Childhood*, pp. 36–7; Stone, *The Family*, p. 81.

67   Pollock, *Lasting Relationship*, p. 126. See also Riché and Alexandre-Bidon, *L'Enfance*, p. 89; Ozment, *When Fathers Ruled*, p. 167; Houlbrooke, *English Family*, p. 136; Censer, *North Carolina Planters*, pp. 29–30.

68   Riché and Alexandre-Bidon, *L'Enfance*, p. 89; Nicholas Orme, *From Childhood to Chivalry: The Education of the English Kings and Aristocracy 1066–1530* (London: Methuen, 1984), pp. 3–4; Hanawalt, *Medieval London*, pp. 61–2; Ozment, *When Fathers Ruled*, p. 166; Michael MacDonald, *Mystical Bedlam: Madness, Anxiety, and Healing*

in Seventeenth-Century England (Cambridge: Cambridge University Press, 1981), ch. 3.

69   Riché and Alexandre-Bidon, *L'Enfance*, p. 88; Ozment, *When Fathers Ruled*, p. 168; Pollock, *Lasting Relationship*, p. 124; David Cressy, *Birth, Marriage and Death: Ritual, Religion, and the Life-Cycle in Tudor and Stuart England* (Oxford: Oxford University Press, 1997), p. 388.

70   Alexandre-Bidon and Closson, *L'Enfant à l'ombre des cathédrales*, p. 227; Flandrin, *Families in Former Times*, pp. 212–42; Henk van Setten, 'Album Angels', 820–1.

71   Riché and Alexandre-Bidon, *L'Enfance*, p. 89.

72   G. L. Prentiss, *The Life and Letters of Elizabeth Prentiss* (1882), cited in Pollock, *Lasting Relationship*, p. 132.

73   Haas, *Renaissance Man*, p. 88.

Chapter 5   Caring for Infants?

1   This phrase, describing a new-born child, is from Guillaume de Saint-Thierry, *Physica corporis et animae*, and it is cited by Pierre Riché in *Education et culture dans l'Occident médiéval* (Paris: Variorum, 1993), p. 284.

2   Notably the works by deMause, Shorter and Badinter, cited above, ch. 1 n. 2 and p. 41 n. 1.

3   Françoise Loux, *Le Jeune Enfant et son corps dans la medicine traditionnelle* (Paris: Flammarion), pp. 17–19.

4   Goodich, 'Bartholomaeus Anglicus on Child-Rearing', 80; Mary Martin McLaughlin, 'Survivors and Surrogates: Children and Parents from the Ninth to the Thirteenth Centuries', in deMause, *History of Childhood*, pp. 101–81 (p. 115); Alexandre-Bidon and Closson, *L'Enfant à l'ombre des cathédrales*, pp. 112–15; Clarissa W. Atkinson, *The Oldest Vocation: Christian Motherhood in the Middle Ages* (Ithaca, NY: Cornell University Press, 1991), pp. 58–9.

5   Steven Ozment, 'The Family in Reformation Germany: The Bearing and Rearing of Children', *Journal of Family History*, 8 (1983), 159–76 (164).

6   Simon Schama, *Embarrassment of Riches*. This paragraph is indebted to: Schnucker, 'English Puritans', 644–5; Patricia Crawford, ' "The Sucking Child" ', 29–33; Mary Lindemann, 'Love for Hire', 383; Nancy Senior, 'Aspects of Infant Feeding in Eighteenth-Century France', *Eighteenth-Century Studies*, 16 (1983), 367–88 (378–9).

7   See Rousseau, *Emile*, pp. 44–6.

8   Klapisch-Zuber, 'Blood Parents and Milk Parents: Wet Nursing in Florence, 1300–1530', in *Women, Family, and Ritual*, pp. 132–64 (p. 133).

9   Valerie A. Fildes, *Breasts*, and eadem, *Wet Nursing*.

10   George D. Sussman, *Selling Mother's Milk*, chs 2, 3 and 7.

11   Maurice Garden, *Lyon et les lyonnais au XVIIIe siècle* (Paris: Belles Lettres, 1970), pp. 135–7. See also details on parental occupations in Paul Galliano, 'La Mortalité infantile (indigènes et nourrissons) dans la banlieue sud de Paris à la fin du XVIIIe siècle (1774–1794)', *Annales de démographie historique* (1966), 139–77 (172–4); and Alain Bideau, 'L'Envoi des jeunes enfants en nourrice: l'exemple d'une petite ville:

Thoissey-en-Dombes, 1740–1840', and Jean Ganiage, 'Nourrissons parisiens en Beauvaisis', both in *Hommage à Marcel Reinhard: sur la population française au XVIIIe et au XIXe siècles* (Paris: Société de démographie historique, 1973), pp. 49–58 (51–20) and 271–90 (283–7). For nineteenth-century developments, see André Armengaud, 'Les Nourrices du Morvan au XIXe siècle', in *Etudes et chronique de démographie historique* (1964), 131–9; Sussman, 'The Wet-Nursing Business', 304–28; Fanny Fay-Sallois, *Les Nourrices à Paris au XIXe siècle* (Paris: Payot, 1980); James R. Lehning 'Family Life and Wetnursing in a French Village', *Journal of Interdisciplinary History*, 12 (1982), 645–56 (647–8).

12 See e.g. Shorter, *Modern Family*, pp. 176–84; Fildes, *Wet Nursing, passim*.
13 Lindemann, 'Hamburg', 380.
14 Garden, *Lyon*, p. 123.
15 James Bruce Ross, 'The Middle-Class Child in Urban Italy, Fourteenth to Early Sixteenth Century', in DeMause, *History of Childhood*, pp. 183–228 (p. 195); Galliano, 'Mortalité infantile', 161–4; Pollock, *Forgotten Children*, p. 218. See also George D. Sussman, 'Parisian Infants and Norman Wet Nurses in the Early Nineteenth Century: A Statistical Study', *Journal of Interdisciplinary History*, 7 (1977), 637–53, for further evidence on the impact of women's work on the land and mortality among nurselings.
16 A critical stance is taken by Ross, 'Middle-Class Child', p. 190. Evidence that parents did visit their infants regularly comes from Haas, *Renaissance Man*, pp. 116–18; he also doubts that changing nurses traumatized infants (p. 120).
17 Sussman, *Mother's Milk*, p. 67; Jean-Pierre Bardet, 'Enfants abandonnés et enfants assistés à Rouen dans la seconde moitié du XVIIIe siècle', in *Hommage à Marcel Reinhard*, pp. 19–47.
18 Fildes, *Breasts*, p. 265; M. W. Beaver, 'Population, Infant Mortality and Milk'.
19 Ross, 'Middle-Class Child', p. 187.
20 Haas, *Renaissance Man*, pp. 96, 103; Crawford, 'Sucking Child', 33; Senior, 'Aspects', 383.
21 Ross, 'Middle-Class Child', p. 186.
22 Rudolf Dekker, *Children, Memory and Autobiography in Holland*, p. 99.
23 See e.g. Lehning, 'Family Life', 651.
24 Ross, 'Middle-Class Child', p. 195; Sussman, *Selling Mother's Milk*, pp. 79–80; Barbara Alpern Engel, 'Mothers and Daughters: Family Patterns and the Female Intelligentsia', in Ransel, *The Family in Imperial Russia*, pp. 44–59 (pp. 45–6). See also Dekker, *Childhood*, p. 97.
25 Schnucker, 'English Puritans', 645.
26 Haas, *Renaissance Man*, p. 104.
27 Fildes, *Wet Nursing*, p. 21.
28 Klapisch-Zuber, 'Blood Parents', pp. 138–9, 141–3; Haas, *Renaissance Man*, p. 90.
29 See e.g. Galliano, 'Mortalité infantile', 173; Bideau, 'Thoissey-en-Dombes', p. 53.
30 Fildes, *Wet Nursing*, ch. 13.
31 Anne Martin-Fugier, 'La Fin des nourrices', *Le Mouvement Social*, 105 (1978), 11–32 (27–30); Fay-Sallois, *Les Nourrices*, pp. 72–117; Carlo A.

Corsini, 'Enfance et famille au XIXe siècle', in Becchi and Julia (eds), *Histoire de l'enfance en Occident*, vol. 2, 'Du XVIIIe siècle à nos jours', p. 285.

32 Sussman, *Selling Mother's Milk*, ch. 7.

33 Sussman, 'Norman Wet Nurses', 652.

34 P. J. Atkins, 'White Poison? The Social Consequences of Milk Consumption, 1850–1930', *Social History of Medicine*, 5 (1992), 207–27 (221); McMillan, *Motherhood in the Old South*, p. 116; and Samuel H. Preston and Michael R. Haines, *Fatal Years*, p. 28.

35 Sussman, *Selling Mother's Milk*, ch. 7; Fildes, *Wet Nursing*, *passim*; eadem, *Breasts*, ch. 11; John Knodel and Etienne van de Walle, 'Breast Feeding, Fertility and Infant Mortality: An Analysis of Some Early German Data', *Population Studies*, 21 (1967), 109–31; John Knodel, 'Breast-Feeding and Population Growth', *Science*, 198 (1977), 1111–15; Jörg Vögele, 'Urbanization, Infant Mortality and Public Health in Imperial Germany', in C. A. Corsini and P. P. Viazzo (eds), *The Decline of Infant and Child Mortality*, pp. 109–27 (p. 116).

36 Fildes, *Breasts*, p. 120; Crawford, 'Sucking Child', 31.

37 Leslie Howard Owens, *This Species of Property: Slave Life and Culture in the Old South* (New York: Oxford University Press, 1976), p. 199; and John W. Blassingame, *The Slave Community: Plantation Life in the Antebellum South* (rev. edn, New York: Oxford University Press, 1979), p. 179.

38 Dunn, 'Imperial Russia', p. 387.

39 Fildes, *Breasts*, ch. 8.

40 Ibid., ch. 15; Elizabeth Wirth Marvick, 'Nature versus Nurture: Patterns and Trends in Seventeenth-Century French Child-Rearing', in deMause, *History of Childhood*, pp. 259–301 (p. 297 n. 112); Richard Wall, 'Inferring Differential Neglect of Females from Mortality Data', *Annales de démographie historique* (1981), 119–39 (135). See also Pollock, *Forgotten Children*, pp. 219–22.

41 Fildes, *Breasts*, chs 15–17; Gélis, Laget and Morel, *Entrer dans la vie*, pp. 124–7; Alexandre-Bidon and Closson, *L'Enfant à l'ombre des cathédrales*, pp. 137–9; Mary Martin McLaughlin, 'Survivors and Surrogates' (n. 4 above), p. 116; David Hunt, *Parents and Children in History*, p. 133; Knodel and Van de Walle, 'Breast Feeding', 118–19; Ralph Frenken, 'Changes in German Parent–Child Relations', 244; Foley, *Bolton Childhood*, p. 4.

42 Rousseau, *Emile*, p. 43.

43 Jane Sharp, *The Midwives Book* (London, 1671), pp. 372–3, cited in David Cressy, *Birth, Marriage and Death: Ritual, Religion, and the Life-Cycle in Tudor and Stuart England* (Oxford: Oxford University Press, 1997), p. 82.

44 This paragraph relies on Alexandre-Bidon and Closson, *L'Enfant à l'ombre des cathédrales*, pp. 91–102; Riché and Alexandre-Bidon, *L'Enfance*, pp. 65–8; Gélis et al., *Entrer dans la vie*, pp. 115–18; Beatrice Gottlieb, *The Family in the Western World: From the Black Death to the Industrial Age* (New York: Oxford University Press, 1993), p. 141; David Hunt, *Parents and Children in History*, pp. 126–31; Dunn, 'Imperial Russia', pp. 386–7; Calvert, *Children in the House*, pp. 19–27, 61–5.

45 Hélias, *Horse of Pride*, p. 32,
46 Alexandre-Bidon and Closson, *L'Enfant à l'ombre des cathédrales*, pp. 79–88.
47 Pierre Charrié, *Le Folklore du Haut-Vivarais* (Paris: Editions FERN, 1968), p. 15.
48 See Gélis et al., *Entrer dans la vie*, p. 120.
49 Hoffert, *Private Matters*, p. 143.
50 This section is indebted to Gélis et al., *Entrer dans la vie*, pp. 209–32; Luc Boltanski, *Prime éducation et morale de classe* (Paris: Mouton, 1969), *passim*; Christina Hardyment, *Dream Babies*, ch. 3.
51 The term 'infanticide' has been understood in various ways by historians. A rigorous definition must surely be the murder of a new-born baby, or at least an infant under 1 year of age, but some commentators have gone as far as to include the killing of any child under 9 years of age. See Mark Jackson, *New-Born Child Murder*, pp. 6–7.
52 Barbara A. Kellum, 'Infanticide in England in the Later Middle Ages', *History of Childhood Quarterly*, 1 (1974), 367–88 (371); Hanawalt, 'Childrearing', 9; R. W. Malcolmson, 'Infanticide in the Eighteenth Century', in J. S. Cockburn (ed.), *Crime in England 1550–1800* (London: Methuen, 1977), pp. 187–209 (p. 191); Richard C. Trexler, 'Infanticide in Florence: New Sources and First Results', *History of Childhood Quarterly*, 1 (1973), 98–116 (99); Keith Wrightson, 'Infanticide in Earlier Seventeenth-Century England', *Local Population Studies*, 15 (1975), 10–22 (10). For a note of caution on the assumption of a 'dark figure' of crime unknown to the authorities, see Jackson, *New-Born Child Murder*, p. 12.
53 Emily Coleman, 'L'Infanticide dans le Haut Moyen Age', *Annales ESC*, 29 (1974), 315–35; Olwen H. Hufton, *The Poor of Eighteenth-Century France 1750–1789* (Oxford: Oxford University Press, 1974), p. 349. Note that some historians have argued that abandonment rather than infanticide lies behind the evidence marshalled by Emily Coleman; see Boswell, *Kindness of Strangers*, pp. 261–4.
54 Behlmer, *Child Abuse*, pp. 17–18; Lionel Rose, *The Massacre of the Innocents: Infanticide in Britain 1800–1939* (London: Routledge, 1986), pp. 7–8.
55 M. W. Stein-Wilkeshuis, 'The Juridical Position of Children in Old Icelandic Society', in *Receuils de la Société Jean Bodin pour l'histoire comparative des institutions*, 36, 'L' Enfant', part 2 (Brussels: Editions de la Librairie Encyclopédique, 1976), 363–79 (365–9); Jenny Jochens, 'Old Norse Motherhood', in John Carni Parsons and Bonnie Wheeler (eds), *Medieval Mothering* (New York: Garland Publishing, 1996), pp. 201–22 (pp. 204–6); Nicole Belmont, 'Levana; or, How to Raise up Children', in Robert Forster and Orest Ranum (eds), *Family and Society* (Baltimore: Johns Hopkins University Press, 1976), pp. 1–15; and McLaughlin, 'Survivors and Surrogates' (n. 4 above), pp. 120–1.
56 Y.-B. Brissaud, 'L'Infanticide à la fin du Moyen Age, ses motivations psychologiques et sa répression', *Revue historique de droit français et étranger*, 50 (1972), 229–56; W. L. Langer, 'Infanticide: A Historical Survey', *History of Childhood Quarterly*, 1 (1973), 353–65; Trexler, 'Infanticide in Florence' (n. 52 above), *passim*; Hanawalt, 'Medieval Childrearing', 10; R. H. Helmholz, 'Infanticide in the Province of Can-

terbury during the Fifteenth Century', *History of Childhood Quarterly*, 2 (1974–5), 379–90; Jean-Louis Flandrin, 'L'Attitude à l'égard du petit enfant et les conduites sexuelles dans la civilisation occidentale', *Annales de démographie historique* (1973), 143–210; Hufton, *The Poor*, pp. 323–4; Peter C. Hoffer and N. E. H. Hull, *Murdering Mothers*, ch. 1; Malcolmson, 'Infanticide', pp. 196–7; Ransel, *Mothers of Misery*, ch. 2.

57   Flandrin, 'L'Attitude', *passim*; Regina Schulte, 'Infanticide in Rural Bavaria in the Nineteenth Century', in Hans Medick and David Warren Sabean, *Interest and Emotion* (Cambridge: Cambridge University Press, 1984), pp. 77–102 (p. 91); R. Sauer, 'Infanticide and Abortion in Nineteenth-Century Britain', *Population Studies*, 32 (1978), 81–93.

58   Kellum, 'Infanticide in England' (n. 52 above), *passim*.

59   Wrightson, 'Infanticide' (n. 52 above), 12; Hoffer and Hull, *Murdering Mothers*, pp. 107–9 (86 per cent of those accused in Massachusetts were women). See also Ann Jones, *Women who Kill* (London: Victor Gollancz, 1991), pp. 45–66, for early American material; J. M. Beattie, *Crime and the Courts in England, 1660–1800* (Oxford: Clarendon Press, 1986), pp. 113–24, for material on the county of Surrey; Deborah A. Symonds, *Weep Not for Me: Women, Ballads, and Infanticide in Early Modern Scotland* (Pennsylvania: Pennsylvania State University Press, 1997), p. 72; Richard Lalou, 'L'Infanticide devant les tribunaux français (1825–1910), *Communications*, 44 (1986), 175–200 (182–6); James M. Donovan, 'Infanticide and the Juries in France, 1825–1913', *Journal of Family History*, 16 (1991), 157–76 (169); and Jackson, *New-Born Child Murder*, ch. 2.

60   Behlmer, *Child Abuse*, ch. 2; Rose, *Massacre*, *passim*; Ann R. Higginbotham, '"Sin of the Age": Infanticide and Illegitimacy in Victorian London', *Victorian Studies*, 32 (1981), 319–37; Margaret L. Arnot, 'Infant Death, Child Care and the State' 271–311.

61   See above, p. 58.

62   Jackson, *New-Born Child Murder*, p. 43; Lalou, 'L'Infanticide', 185.

63   Schulte, 'Infanticide', *passim*.

64   Hoffer and Hull, *Murdering Mothers*, p. 90.

65   Langer, 'Infanticide', 361–2; Susanne Ward, 'Women as Children, Women as Childkillers: Poetic Images of Infanticide in Eighteenth-Century Germany', *Eighteenth-Century Studies*, 26 (1992–3), 449–66; Hoffer and Hull, *Murdering Mothers*, ch. 3; Beattie, *Crime and the Courts*, pp. 117–24; Behlmer, *Child Abuse*, *passim*; Arnot, 'Infant Death', *passim;* Jackson, *New-Born Child Murder*, ch. 7; Lalou, 'L'Infanticide', 186–95; Donovan, 'Infanticide', *passim*.

66   James Boswell, '*Expositio* and *Oblatio*: The Abandonment of Children and the Ancient and Medieval Family', *American Historical Review*, 89 (1984), 10–33; idem, *Kindness of Strangers*, part II. Note that Mayke de Jong rejects the thesis that oblation was a form of abandonment in *In Samuel's Image*.

67   Joseph H. Lynch, *Simoniacal Entry into the Religious Life from 1000 to 1260: A Social, Economic and Legal Study* (Columbus: Ohio State University Press, 1976), p. 45.

68   Philip Gavitt, *Charity and Children in Renaissance Florence*, p. 21.

69   Rachel Ginnis Fuchs, *Abandoned Children*, p. 77; David L. Ransel, 'Abandonment and Fosterage of Unwanted Children: The Women of the

Foundling System', in *The Family in Imperial Russia*, pp. 189–217 (p. 192); Volker Hunecke, 'The Abandonment of Legitimate Children in Nineteenth-Century Milan and the European Context', in Henderson and Wall (eds), *Poor Women and Children*, pp. 117–35 (p. 125). See also Jean-Pierre Bardet, 'La Société et l'abandon', and Volker Hunecke, 'Intensità e fluttuazioni degli abbandoni dal XV al XIX secolo', in *Enfance abandonné*, pp. 3–26 (pp. 7–8) and pp. 27–72 (pp. 27–38) respectively; Jean-Pierre Bardet and Olivier Faron, 'Des Enfants sans enfance: sur les abandonnés de l'époque moderne', in Becchi and Julia, *Histoire de l'enfance en Occident*, vol. 2, pp. 112–46 (pp. 117–21); Pier Paolo Viazzo, Maria Bortolotto and Andrea Zanotto, 'Five Centuries of Foundling History in Florence: Changing Patterns of Abandonment, Care and Mortality', in Panter-Brick and Smith, *Abandoned Children*, pp. 70–91 (pp. 75–7).

70   Alain Molinier, 'Enfants trouvés, enfants abandonnés et enfants illégitimes en Languedoc aux XVIIe et XVIIIe siècles', in *Hommage à Marcel Reinhard*, pp. 445–73 (p. 454).

71   Claude Delasselle, 'Les Enfants abandonnés à Paris au XVIIIe siècle', *Annales ESC*, 30 (1975), 187–218 (213).

72   Otto Ulbricht, 'The Debate about Foundling Hospitals', 214, 235–6; Wladimir Berelowitch, 'Les Hospices des enfants trouvés en Russie (1763–1914), in *Enfance abandonné*, pp. 167–217, mentions nurses in the Foundling Hospital in Moscow routinely having to feed up to four children by the late eighteenth century (p. 190); Valerie Fildes, 'Maternal Feelings Re-Assessed: Child Abandonment in London and Westminster, 1550–1800', in Fildes, *Women as Mothers* (see ch. 4 n. 8 above), pp. 139–78 (p. 167).

73   Mary Lindemann, 'Love for Hire' (n. 6 above), 385; A. Chamoux, 'L'Enfance abandonné à Reims à la fin du XVIIIe siècle', *Annales de démographie historique* (1973), 263–85 (277); Jean-Pierre Bardet, 'Enfants abandonnés et enfants assistés à Rouen dans la seconde moitié du XVIIIe siècle', in *Hommage à Marcel Reinhard*, pp. 19–47 (p. 27); Ransel, *Mothers of Misery*, table 12.1, p. 259.

74   Boswell, *Kindness of Strangers*, pp. 24–6.

75   See e.g. C. Billot, 'Les Enfants abandonnés à Chartres à la fin du Moyen Age', *Annales de démographie historique* (1975), 167–86 (esp. figure 1).

76   Paolo Viazzo usefully points out that southern European countries established their lead in establishing foundling hospitals well before the Reformation, in 'Family Structures and the Early Phase in the Individual Life Cycle: A Southern European Perspective', in Henderson and Wall, *Poor Women*, pp. 31–50 (p. 36). Moreover, Catholic France began to adopt the system of foundling hospitals only in the late seventeenth century, and Protestant London had its Foundling Hospital in the mid-eighteenth century. See Ernest Caulfield, *The Infant Welfare Movement in the Eighteenth Century* (New York: Paul B. Hoeber, 1931) and Ruth K. McClure, *Coram's Children: The London Foundling Hospital in the Eighteenth Century* (New Haven: Yale University Press, 1981).

77   See above, p. 57.

78   The work of Volker Hunecke is particularly helpful here, notably 'European Context' and 'Abbandoni'. See also the excellent survey by Brian

Pullen in *Orphans and Foundlings in Early Modern Europe* (Reading: University of Reading, 1989), and the outline of the debate for and against foundling hospitals in Germany in Ulbricht, 'Foundling Hospitals'.

79 Trexler, 'Foundlings of Florence', 266–8; Herlihy and Klapisch-Zuber, *Tuscans*, p. 145; Gavitt, *Charity and Children*, pp. 195 and 210–16; Ransel, *Mothers of Misery*, ch. 7.

80 Boswell, *Kindness of Strangers*, ch. 6.

81 Fildes, 'Maternal Feelings', pp. 153–4.

82 Jean-Claude Perrot, *Genèse d'une ville moderne: Caen au XVIIIe siècle* (2 vols, Paris: Mouton, 1975), vol. 2, pp. 846–53; Ransel, *Mothers of Misery*, ch. 8.

83 McClure, *Coram's Children*, p. 9.

84 David I. Kertzer, *Sacrificed for Honor*, ch. 2.

85 Bernd Weisbrod, 'How to Become a Good Foundling in Early Victorian London', *Social History*, 10 (1977), 193–209 (205).

86 Trexler, 'Foundlings', 270; Kertzer, 'Gender Ideology', 14; Fuchs, *Abandoned Children*, p. 66; Caroline B. Brettell and Rui Feijó, 'Foundlings in Nineteenth-Century Northwestern Portugal: Public welfare and Family Strategies', in *Enfance abandonnée*, pp. 273–300 (278–9).

87 See e.g. McClure, *Coram's Children*, pp. 83–4; Delasselle, 'Paris', 210; Bardet, 'Rouen', p. 37; Peyronnet, 'Limoges', 418; Isabelle Robin and Agnès Walch, 'Les Billets trouvés sur les enfants abandonnés à Paris aux XVIIe et XVIIIe siècles', in *Enfance abandonnée*, pp. 981–91.

88 Viazzo, 'Family structures', p. 43; Robin and Walch, 'Les Billets trouvés', p. 986.

89 Berelowitch, 'Russie', p. 176.

90 Hunecke, 'European Context', *passim*; Viazzo, 'Family Structure', 44.

91 On abandonment as a 'catch-all term', see Catherine Panter-Brick, 'Nobody's Children? A Reconsideration of Child Abandonment', in Panter-Brick and Smith, *Abandoned Children*, pp. 1–26 (pp. 1–4).

92 Strickland, 'Transcendentalist Father', 16.

Chapter 6   Parent–Child Relations during the Second Phase of Childhood

1 Bogna W. Lorence, 'Parents and Children'; and Greven, *Protestant Temperament*, *passim*. Lawrence Stone proposed a more elaborate scheme for England, with six different modes, in *The Family*, pp. 449–80.

2 Claire Tomalin (ed.), *Parents and Children*, pp. 14–16.

3 Yvonne Knibiehler and Catherine Fouquet, *L'Histoire des mères du moyen âge à nos jours* (Paris: Editions Montalba, 1980), p. 8.

4 Ralph V. Turner, 'Eleanor of Aquitaine and her Children: An Inquiry into Medieval Family Attachment', *Journal of Medieval History*, 14 (1988), 321–35; and Lois L. Huneycutt, 'Public Lives, Private Ties: Royal Mothers in England and Scotland, 1070–1204', in John Carni Parsons and Bonnie Wheeler (eds), *Medieval Mothering* (New York: Garland Publishing, 1996), pp. 295–311. See also Mary Martin McLaughlin,

'Survivors and Surrogates: Children and Parents from the Ninth to the Thirteenth Century', in deMause, *History of Childhood*, pp. 101–81 (p. 127); and Alexandre-Bidon and Closson, *L'Enfant à l'ombre des cathédrales*, p. 200.

5 See e.g. Greven, *Protestant Temperament*, p. 22 (in relation to 'evangelical' parents) and Leverenz, *Language of Puritan Feeling*, ch. 3.

6 David Hunt, *Parents and Children*, p. 94; and Barbara Alpern Engel, 'Mothers and Daughters: Family Patterns and the Female Intelligentsia', in Ransel, *The Family in Imperial Russia*, pp. 44–59 (p. 46). See also Lorence, 'Eighteenth-Century Europe', 1–13; and Stone, *The Family*, 'The Aristocracy: The Negligent Mode', pp. 451–2.

7 Adelheid Popp, *Autobiography of a Working Woman*, p. 15. See also Standish Meacham, *A Life Apart: The English Working Class, 1890–1914* (London: Thames and Hudson, 1977), pp. 159–60; Burnett, *Destiny Obscure*, pp. 53–6; West, *Growing up*, pp. 156–7; and Maynes, *Taking the Hard Road*, pp. 64–8.

8 James Mellon (ed.), *Bullwhip Days: The Slaves Remember* (New York: Weidenfeld and Nicolson, 1988), p. 35.

9 *Narrative of the Life of Frederick Douglass, an American Slave, Written by Himself* (New York: Dolphin Books 1963 [1845]), p. 2. The passage is discussed in more detail in Herbert G. Gutman, *The Black Family in Slavery and Freedom, 1750–1925* (New York: Pantheon Books, 1976), p. 98.

10 Eugene D. Genovese, *Roll, Jordan, Roll: The World the Slaves Made* (New York: Pantheon Books, 1974), pp. 502–19; Leslie Howard Owens, *This Species of Property: Slave Life and Culture in the Old South* (New York: Oxford University Press, 1976), ch. 9; John W. Blassingame, *The Slave Community: Plantation Life in the Antebellum South* (rev. edn, New York: Oxford University Press, 1979), ch. 4; and Lester Alston, 'Children as Chattel', in West and Petrick, *Small Worlds*, pp. 208–31.

11 Thomas Cobbett, *A Fruitfull and Usefull Discourse touching the Honour due from Children to Parents and the Duty of Parents towards their Children* (London, 1656), cited in Edmund S. Morgan, *The Puritan Family: Religion and Domestic Relations in Seventeenth-Century New England* (New York: Harper and Row, 1966), pp. 106–7. See also Levin L. Schücking, *The Puritan Family: A Social Study from the Literary Sources*, transl. Brian Battershaw (London: Routledge and Kegan Paul, 1969 [1929]), p. 74.

12 Mrs Housman, *The Power and Pleasure of the Divine Life* (London, 1744), cited in Pollock, *Forgotten Children*, pp. 101–2.

13 Lorence, 'Eighteenth-Century Europe', 13–18; Stone, *The Family*, pp. 463–8.

14 Leverenz, *Puritan Feeling*, pp. 70–9.

15 David E. Stannard, *The Puritan Way of Death: A Study in Religion, Culture, and Social Change* (Oxford: Oxford University Press, 1972), ch. 3; Cox, *Shaping Childhood*, ch. 2.

16 See 'Happy Families', a review of Stone's book by E. P. Thompson in *New Society*, 8 September 1977, 499–501.

17 Stone, *The Family*, *passim*; Greven, *Protestant Temperament*, part 4; Daniel Blake Smith, *Inside the Great House: Planter Family Life in*

Eighteenth-Century Chesapeake Society (Ithaca, NY: Cornell University Press, 1980), ch. 1 (p. 44). See also Trumbach, *Rise of the Egalitarian Family*, ch. 5; and Censer, *North Carolina Planters*, p. 39.

18 Greven, *Protestant Temperament*, p. 27.

19 Houlbrooke, *English Family*, pp. 192–4; Larcom, *New-England Girlhood*, pp. 26–8; John F. Walzer, 'A Period of Ambivalence: Eighteenth-Century American Childhood', in deMause, *History of Childhood*, pp. 351–82 (p. 356); and Sylvère, *Toinou*, pp. 1–2, 73–88.

20 Gutman, *Black Family*, ch. 5; Owens, *Species of Property*, ch. 9.

21 Trumbach, *Egalitarian Family*, pp. 237–8; Roberts, *A Ragged Schooling*, p. 13; Jasper, *Hoxton Childhood*, p. 9; Robert L. Griswold, *Fatherhood in America: A History* (New York: Basic Books, 1993), pp. 2–3.

22 Schama, *Embarrassment of Riches*, p. 541; Larcom, *New-England Girlhood*, p. 41; Riché and Alexandre-Bidon, *L'Enfance*, p. 100; Foley, *Bolton Childhood*, pp. 10–12.

23 Riché and Alexandre-Bidon, *L'Enfance*, p. 105.

24 Emilie Carlès, *Une soupe aux herbes sauvages* (Paris: Simoën, 1977), p. 47.

25 Davin, *Growing up Poor*, pp. 88–91; and Genovese, *Roll, Jordan, Roll* (n. 10 above), pp. 508–9. Riché and Alexandre-Bidon also give a positive assessment of relations between brothers and sisters; *L'Enfance*, p. 105.

26 Sylvère, *Toinou*, p. 6.

27 Christopher Lasch, *Haven in a Heartless World: The Family Besieged* (New York: Basic Books, 1977).

28 Schama, *Embarrassment of Riches*, p. 557.

29 David Hunt, *Parents and Children*, p. 141.

30 Cited in Trumbach, *Egalitarian Family*, pp. 227–8.

31 Alexandre-Bidon and Closson, *L'Enfant à l'ombre des cathédrales*, pp. 187–92; Riché and Alexandre-Bidon, *L'Enfance*, p. 78; Gélis, Laget and Morel, *Entrer dans la vie*, p. 127; Joseph Illick, 'Child-Rearing in Seventeenth-Century England and America', in deMause, *History of Childhood*, pp. 303–50 (p. 312).

32 Demaitre, 'The Idea of Childhood and Child Care', 466; and Alexandre-Bidon and Closson, *L'Enfant à l'ombre des cathédrales*, pp. 192–4.

33 This section relies on Arnold Van Gennep, *Manuel de folklore français contemporain*, vol. 1 (Paris: Picard, 1972 [1943]), pp. 152–65; Antonina Martynova, 'Life of the Pre-Revolutionary Village as Reflected in Popular Lullabies', in Ransel, *Imperial Russia*, pp. 171–85; Iona and Peter Opie (eds), *The Oxford Dictionary of Nursery Rhymes* (Oxford: Oxford University Press, 1997); and Bettina Hürlimann, *Children's Books*, ch. 1.

34 Cf. Van Gennep, *Manuel*, p. 152; and Reinhard Sieder, ' "Vata, derf i aufstehn?" '.

35 Opie and Opie, *Nursery Rhymes*, Introduction; Hürlimann, *Children's Books*, pp. 7–9.

36 Riché and Alexandre-Bidon, *L'Enfance*, pp. 113–16; Nicholas Orme, 'Children and the Church', 566–7.

37 David Hunt, *Parents and Children*, p. 182; Robert Darton, 'Peasants Tell Tales: The Meaning of Mother Goose', in *The Great Cat Massacre*

(Harmondsworth: Penguin, 1984), pp. 17–78; and Gillian Avery, 'The Beginnings of Children's Reading, to *c.*1700', in Peter Hunt (ed.), *Children's Literature*, pp. 1–25 (p. 3).

38   Ozment, *When Fathers Ruled*, ch. 4; Houlbrooke, *English Family*, pp. 146–7; Elias, *The Civilizing Process*, vol. 1, p. 140.

39   Bernard Mergen, 'Made, Bought, and Stolen: Toys and the Culture of Childhood', in West and Petrik, *Small Worlds*, pp. 86–106 (p. 88).

40   P. N. Denieul, 'Histoire de jouer', in Denieul et al., *Jeux et jouets* (Paris: Aubier, 1979), pp. 89–107; Jean Drouillet, *Folklore du Nivernais et du Morvan* (La Charité-sur-Loire: Editions Thoreau, 1959), p. 87; and Pollock, *Forgotten Children*, p. 237.

41   Nicholas Orme, 'The Culture of Children', 51–8, reveals a fascinating series of early toys. See also Françoise Piponnier, 'Les Objets de l'enfance', *Annales de demographie historique* (1973), 69–71; Alexandre-Bidon and Closson, *L'Enfant à l'ombre des cathédrales*, pp. 174–86; J. Grange, 'Histoire du jouet et d'une industrie', in Denieul et al., *Jeux et jouets*, pp. 224–76 (p. 245); Joseph Strutt, *The Sports and Pastimes of the People of England* (London: Thomas Tegg, 1838), pp. 385–6; and Formanek-Brunell, *Made to Play House*, ch. 1.

42   Cited in Hardyment, *Dream Babies*, p. 145.

43   This section relies on Linda Hannas, *The English Jigsaw Puzzle, 1760–1890* (London: Wayland Publishers, 1972), *passim*; J. H. Plumb, 'The New World of Children in Eighteenth-Century England', *Past and Present*, 67 (1975), 64–95; Kenneth D. Brown, *The British Toy Business: A History since 1700* (London: Hambledon Press, 1996), chs 1–3; and George Sturt, *A Small Boy in the Sixties* (Cambridge: Cambridge University Press, 1932), ch. 16.

44   Darton, *Children's Books in England*, p. 1.

45   Monica Kiefer, *American Children through their Books*, pp. 6–7.

46   See James Janeway, *Token for Children* (London: Religious Tract Society, n.d.), pp. 8, 19, 26, 44, 72 and 111.

47   Kiefer, *American Children*, ch. 4; Geoffrey Summerfield, *Fantasy and Reason: Children's Literature in the Eighteenth Century* (London: Methuen, 1984), pp. 72–81; Elizabeth A. Francis, 'American Children's Literature, 1646–1880', in Hawes and Hiner (eds), *American Childhood*, pp. 185–233; Gillian Avery, 'The Puritans and their Heirs', in Gillian Avery and Julia Briggs (eds), *Children and their Books* (Oxford: Clarendon Press, 1989), pp. 95–118; eadem, 'The Beginnings of Children's Reading to *c.*1700' and Anne Scott MacLeod, 'Children's Literature in America from the Puritan Beginnings to 1870', both in Peter Hunt, *Children's Literature*, pp. 1–25 and 102–29.

48   Yann Brékilien, *La Vie quotidienne des paysans bretons* (*au XIXe siècle*) (Paris: Hachette, 1966), p. 90; Hélias, *Horse of Pride*, p. 97.

49   Hürlimann, *Books in Europe*, p. xiii; Darton, *Children's Books in England*, ch. 5; Victor E. Neuburg, *The Penny Histories: A Study of Chapbooks for Young Readers over Two Centuries* (London: Oxford University Press, 1968): idem, *Popular Literature: A History and Guide* (Harmondsworth: Penguin, 1977), ch. 3; Summerfield, *Fantasy and Reason*, ch. 2; Mary V. Jackson, *Engines of Instruction*, ch. 3; Robert Mandrou, *De la culture populaire aux XVIIe et XVIIIe siècles: la bib-*

liothèque bleue de Troyes (Paris: Stock, 1964); Geneviève Bollème, *La Bibliothèque bleue* (Paris: Julliard, 1971).

50 Hürlimann, *Books in Europe*, Introduction; Darton, *Children's Books*, ch. 7.

51 Adelaide O'Keefe, Ann and Jane Taylor, *Original Poems for Infant Minds*, cited by Kiefer, *American Children*, p. 22.

52 Alison Lurie speculates that the reason British and American authors dominate the world of children's books is that in these two countries more people never quite grow up! In the background, she suggests, is the impact of Romantic notions of childhood as something wonderful and unique. But one might wonder whether it is really the case that in other countries boys and girls are expected to become little adults after the age of 4 or 5. See her 'Not for Muggles', in the *New York Review of Books*, 16 December 1999.

53 From an extremely large and attractive historiography, one might cite here Darton, *Children's Books in England, passim*; Hürlimann, *Children's Books, passim*; Peter Hunt, *An Introduction to Children's Literature*, chs 3–4; idem, *Children's Literature*, chs 3–9; Gillian Avery, *Nineteenth Century Children: Heroes and Heroines in English Children's Stories 1780–1900* (London: Hodder and Stoughton, 1965), *passim*; Jackson, *Engines of Instruction, passim*; Francis, 'American Children's Literature', pp. 205–22; Kirsten Drotner, *English Children and their Magazines, 1751–1945* (New Haven: Yale University Press, 1988); Dennis Butts, 'The Adventure Story', in Butts (ed.), *Stories and Society: Children's Literature in its Social Context* (London: Macmillan, 1992), pp. 65–83; Hans-Heino Ewers, 'La Littérature moderne pour enfants: son évolution historique à travers l'exemple allemand du XVIIIe au XXe siècle', in Becchi and Julia, *Histoire de l'enfance*, vol. 2, pp. 434–60; Mary Cadogan and Patricia Craig, *You're a Brick Angela! A New Look at Girls' Fiction from 1839 to 1975* (London: Victor Gollancz, 1976), chs 1–6.

54 Julia Briggs, 'Transitions' and 'Children's Literature in America 1870–1945', both in Peter Hunt, *Children's Literature*, pp. 167–91 and 225–51; Marie-José Chombart de Lauwe, *Un Monde autre: l'enfance* (Paris, 1971); Patrick A. Dunae, 'Penny Dreadfuls'; Jean-Jacques Darmon, *Le Colportage de librairie en France sous le Second Empire: grands colporteurs et culture populaire* (Paris: Plon, 1972).

55 Van Gennep, *Manuel*, pp. 156–60.

56 Bernard de Gordon, *Liber pronosticorum*, cited in Demaitre, 'Child Care', 466.

57 Larcom, *New-England Girlhood*, p. 30; and Olivier Perrin, *Galerie Bretonne, ou vie des Bretons armoriques* (3 vols, Paris: Isidore Pesron, 1835), vol. 1, p. 85.

58 Hanawalt, 'Childrearing', 15–16, and eadem, *Ties that Bound*, ch. 11. See also Eleanora C. Gordon, 'Accidents among Medieval Children as Seen from the Miracles of six English Saints and Martyrs', *Medical History*, 35 (1991), 145–63.

59 This at least is the oft-cited conclusion of the folklore specialist Arnold Van Gennep, in *Manuel*, vol. 1, p. 156.

60 Herman W. Rodenburg, 'The Autobiography of Isabella de Moerloose', 522–4; Marc Soriano, 'From Tales of Warning to Formulettes: The Oral

Tradition in French Children's Literature', *Yale French Studies*, 43 (1969), 24–43; Hélias, *Horse of Pride*, pp. 6–7; 'Fritz Pauk, Cigar Maker', in Kelly, *German Worker*, pp. 399–427 (p. 401). See also Dekker, *Childhood, Memory and Autobiography*, pp. 81–7.

61   Peter N. Stearns and Timothy Haggerty, 'Role of Fear', 66–7.
62   Brunfels, *Von der Zucht und Underweisung der Kinder* (Strasbourg, 1525), p. D 2a, cited by Steven Ozment, *When Fathers Ruled*, p. 139.
63   David Hunt, *Parents and Children*, p. 133; Elizabeth W. Marvick, 'Childhood History and Decisions of State: The Case of Louis XIII', *History of Childhood Quarterly*, 2 (1975), 135–80 (152); eadem, *Louis XIII*, p. 30; Tomalin, *Parents and Children*, p. 15.
64   David Hunt, *Parents and Children*, p. 139; Locke, *Concerning Education*, p. 139; Greven, *Protestant Temperament*, pp. 38–43.
65   Conrad Sam, *Davids Eebruch* (Ulm, 1534), p. F 3b, cited by Ozment, *When Fathers Ruled*, p. 133; Locke, *Concerning Education*, p. 104.
66   David Hunt, *Parents and Children*, ch. 7; and Greven, *Protestant Temperament*, ch. 2.
67   David Hunt, *Parents and Children*, p. 134.
68   Morgan, *Puritan Family*, p. 103; Elizabeth Pleck, *Domestic Tyranny: The Making of Social Policy against Family Violence from Colonial Times to the Present* (New York: Oxford University Press, 1987), pp. 44–7, and 205–16; Genovese, *Roll, Jordan, Roll* (n. 10 above), pp. 509–11; Wright, *Black Boy*, p. 4.
69   Cited, among other places, in Antonia Gransden, 'Childhood and Youth in Medieval England', *Nottingham Medieval Studies*, 16 (1972), 3–19 (6–7); and McLaughlin, 'Survivors and Surrogates' (n. 4 above), p. 131.
70   Berkvam, *Enfance et maternité*, p. 61.
71   Caspar Huberinus, *Spiegel der Hauszucht* (Nuremberg, 1565), cited by Strauss, *Luther's House*, p. 93; Samuel Butler, *The Way of All Flesh*, pp. 117 and 297. For a dismal view of modern German child-rearing practices, with particular emphasis on vicious corporal punishments, see also Aurel Ende, 'Battering and Neglect: Children in Germany'.
72   Sereno E. Dwight (ed.), *The Works of President Edwards: With a Memoir of his Life* (New York, 1829), vol. 1, pp. 126–30, cited by Philip J. Greven (ed.), *Child-Rearing Concepts*, p. 77.
73   Schama, *Embarrassment of Riches*, p. 556 (though see also, Dekker, *Childhood*, ch. 10); Pleck, *Domestic Tyranny*, pp. 39–44; West, *Growing up*, pp. 158–60; Linda Gordon, *Heroes of their Own Lives: The Politics and History of Family Violence, Boston 1880–1960* (Harmondsworth: Penguin Books, 1989), p. 33; Paul Thompson, *The Edwardians: The Remaking of British Society* (2nd edn, London: Routledge, 1992), pp. 45–8.
74   Strauss, *Luther's House*, p. 93; Marie Jeanne Philipon, *Madame Roland de la Platière: An Autobiographical Sketch (c.1760)*, cited by Lorence, 'Eighteenth-Century Europe', 18–19; Robertson, 'Home as Nest: Middle-class Childhood in Nineteenth-Century Europe', in deMause, *History of Childhood*, pp. 407–31 (p. 416).
75   Butler, *Way of All Flesh*, p. 57.
76   Ibid.

Chapter 7 Relations with Parents and the Peer Group during the Third Phase of Childhood

1 David Hunt, *Parents and Children in History*, p. 180; Steven Mintz and Susan Kellog, *Domestic Revolutions: A Social History of American Family Life* (New York: Free Press, 1988), pp. 15 and 72; Jessica Tovrov, 'Mother–Child Relationships among the Russian Nobility', in Ransel, *The Family in Imperial Russia*, pp. 15–43 (p. 17).

2 Arnold Van Gennep, *Manuel de folklore français contemporain*, vol. 1, (Paris: Picard, 1972), pp. 166–7.

3 Tovrov, 'Mother–Child Relationships', pp. 25–6.

4 John F. Benton, *Self and Society in Medieval France: The Memoirs of Abbot Guibert of Nogent* (Toronto: University of Toronto Press, 1984), pp. 38, 74. The relationship between Guibert and his mother has aroused considerable attention: besides the Introduction by Benton, see also McLaughlin, 'Survivors and Surrogates', in deMause, *History of Childhood*, pp. 105–9; Jonathan Kantor, 'A Psycho-Historical Source: The Memoirs of Abbot Guibert of Nogent', *Journal of Medieval History*, 2 (1976), 281–304; M. D. Coupe, 'The Personality of Guibert de Nogent Reconsidered', *Journal of Medieval History*, 9 (1983), 317–29; Nancy F. Partner, 'The Family Romance of Guibert of Nogent: His Story/Her Story', in John Carni Parsons and Bonnie Wheeler (eds), *Medieval Mothering* (New York: Garland Publishing, 1996), pp. 359–79.

5 Berkvam, *Enfance et maternité*, pp. 128–9.

6 Elisabeth Badinter, *The Myth of Motherhood: An Historical View of the Maternal 'Instinct'*, transl. Roger DeGaris (London: Souvenir Press, 1981), pp. 64–7.

7 Benton, *Memoirs*, p. 41; Mary P. Ryan, *Cradle of the Middle Class: The Family in Oneida County, New York, 1790–1865* (Cambridge: Cambridge University Press, 1981), p. 162.

8 Engel, 'Mothers and Daughters' (see ch. 6 n. 6 above), p. 50. See also Houlbrooke, *English Family*, p. 187; and Ryan, *Family in Oneida County*, pp. 192–3.

9 Janet L. Nelson, *Charles the Bald* (London: Longman, 1992), pp. 79–80.

10 Jerome Cardan, *The Book of my Life*, transl. Jean Stoner (New York, 1930), p. 142, cited by James Bruce Ross, 'The Middle-Class Child in Urban Italy, Fourteenth to Early Sixteenth Century', in deMause, *History of Childhood*, pp. 183–228 (p. 213).

11 Trumbach, *Rise of the Egalitarian Family*, p. 254; see also John F. Walzer, 'A Period of Ambivalence: Eighteenth-Century American Childhood', in deMause, *History of Childhood*, pp. 351–82 (p. 368).

12 Cited in Levin L. Schücking, *The Puritan Family: A Social Study from the Literary Sources*, transl. Brian Battershaw (London: Routledge and Kegan Paul, 1969), pp. 60–1.

13 M. J. Tucker, 'The Child as Beginning and End: Fifteenth and Sixteenth Century English Childhood', in deMause, *History of Childhood*, pp. 229–57 (pp. 248–9).

14 Mintz and Kellog, *Domestic Revolutions* (n. 1 above), *passim*; Daniel Blake Smith, *Inside the Great House: Planter Family Life in Eighteenth-*

Century Chesapeake Society (Ithaca, NY: Cornell University Press, 1980), ch. 3; Ryan, *Cradle of the Family, passim*; Robert L. Griswold, *Fatherhood in America: A History* (New York: Basic Books, 1993), ch. 2.

15   Robert L. Griswold, ' "Ties that Bind and Bonds that Break": Children's Attitudes towards Fathers, 1900–1930', in West and Petrik, *Small Worlds*, pp. 255–74 (p. 273).

16   Behlmer, *Child Abuse*, p. 15.

17   Sylvia Schafer, *Children in Moral Danger*, p. 21.

18   Jacques Donzelot, *The Policing of Families*, transl. Robert Hurley (London: Hutchinson, 1980), chs 2–3; Rachel G. Fuchs, 'France in Comparative Perspective', in Elinor A. Accampo, Rachel G. Fuchs and Mary Lynn Stewart (eds), *Gender and the Politics of Social Reform in France, 1870–1914* (Baltimore: Johns Hopkins University Press, 1995), pp. 157–87 (p. 163); Schafer, *Third Republic France, passim*.

19   Key works include Jean S. Heywood, *Children in Care: The Development of the Service for the Deprived Child* (3rd edn, London: Routledge and Kegan Paul, 1978); Behlmer, *Child Abuse, passim*; Nick Frost and Mike Stein, *The Politics of Child Welfare: Inequality, Power and Change* (New York: Harvester Wheatsheaf, 1989), chs 3–4; Hendrick, *Child Welfare*, ch. 2; and Linda Mahood, *Policing Gender, Class and Family: Britain, 1850–1940* (London: UCL Press, 1998).

20   Dickinson, *The Politics of German Child Welfare*, ch. 1 (p. 27).

21   Ronald D. Cohen, 'Child-Saving and Progressivism, 1885–1915', in Hawes and Hiner, *American Childhood*, pp. 273–309; LeRoy Ashby, *Endangered Children: Dependency, Neglect, and Abuse in American History* (New York: Twayne Publishers, 1997), ch. 3; Linda Gordon, *Heroes of their Own Lives: The Politics and History of Family Violence, Boston, 1880–1960* (Harmondsworth: Penguin, 1989), chs 1–2.

22   Dickinson, *German Child Welfare*, p. 20; Hendrick, *England*, p. 54.

23   Paul Thompson, *The Edwardians: The Remarking of British Society* (2nd edn; London: Routledge, 1992), pp. 45–6. See also Pollock, *Forgotten Children, passim*.

24   Judith Rich Harris, 'Where Is the Child's Environment? A Group Socialization Theory of Development', *Psychological Review*, 102 (1995), 458–89; and eadem, *The Nurture Assumption: Why Children Turn out the Way they Do* (London: Bloomsbury, 1998). See also the review by Anthony Clare in the *Observer*, 13 December 1998.

25   François Lebrun, *La Vie conjugale sous l'ancien régime* (Paris: Armand Colin, 1975), p. 138.

26   Wright, *Black Boy*, p. 67.

27   Humphries, *Hooligans or Rebels?*, ch. 7; Geoffrey Pearson, *Hooligan: A History of Respectable Fears* (London: Macmillan, 1983), ch. 5; Bill Schwarz, 'Night Battles: Hooligan and Citizen', in Mica Nava and Alan O'Shea, *Modern Times: Reflections on a Century of English Modernity* (London: Routledge, 1996), pp. 101–28; Michael Mitterauer, *A History of Youth* (Oxford: Basil Blackwell, 1992), p. 200; Michelle Perrot, 'Dans la France de la Belle Epoque, "Les Apaches", premières bandes de jeunes', in *Les Marginaux et les exclus dans l'histoire* (Paris: Union générale d'éditions, 1979), pp. 387–407 (p. 390); James Marten, *The Children's Civil War*, p. 163.

28   Iona and Peter Opie, *Lore and Language of Schoolchildren*, ch. 8; Jean Drouillet, *Folklore du Nivernais et du Morvan* (5 vols, La Charité-sur-Loire: Thoreau, 1959), vol. 1, 88.

29   Louis Pergaud, *La Guerre des boutons* (Paris: Mercure de France, 1963), p. 265; Drouillet, *Folklore du Nivernais*, vol. 1, 89; Heywood, 'On Learning Gender Roles'.

30   Mitterauer, *History of Youth*, pp. 195–202; Humphries, *Hooligans*, p. 190.

31   Orme, 'Children and the Church', 571; Alexandre-Bidon and Didier Lett, *Les Enfants*, p. 173; Thomas, 'Children in Early Modern England', p. 52; idem, 'Age and Authority in Early Modern England', *Proceedings of the British Academy*, 62 (1976), 205–48 (218–19); Mary P. Ryan, *Cradle of the Middle Class: The Family in Oneida County, New York, 1790–1865* (Cambridge: Cambridge University Press, 1981), p. 164; and Georges Dumoulin, *Carnets de Route* (Lille: Editions de 'L'Avenir', 1937), p. 16. See also ch. 18, 'Pranks', in Opie and Opie, *Lore and Language*; Pearson, *Hooligan*, pp. 89–90; and Thompson, *The Edwardians* (n. 23 above), pp. 39–40.

32   Humphries, *Hooligans*, pp. 180–8; John R. Gillis, 'The Evolution of Juvenile Delinquency in England, 1890–1914', *Past and Present*, 67 (1975), 96–126 (99–100).

33   Maurice Crubellier, *L'Enfance et la jeunesse dans la société française, 1800–1950* (Paris: Armand Colin, 1979), p. 60.

34   Yvonne Verdier, *Façons de dire, façons de faire: la laveuse, la couturière, la cuisinière* (Paris: Gallimard, 1979), pp. 171–2; and Martial Chaulanges, *La Terre des autres*, vol. 3, *Les Rouges Moissons* (2nd edn, Paris: Delagrave, 1975), p. 16.

35   Iona and Peter Opie, *Children's Games in Street and Playground*, pp. 6–8.

36   For an interesting discussion of contemporary moralizing around children's games, as revealed in this and other pictures, see Schama, *Embarrassment of Riches*, pp. 497–516.

37   Thomas E. Jordan, *Victorian Childhood*, pp. 196–7; James, Jenks and Prout, *Theorizing Childhood*, pp. 28–30; and Jordanova, 'Children in History'.

38   Larcom, *New-England Girlhood*, pp. 30–1; David Vincent, *Literacy and Popular Culture* (Cambridge: Cambridge University Press, 1981), p. 57; John Clare, 'Prose on the Pleasures of Childhood', cited in James Walvin, 'Children's Pleasures', in John K. Walton and James Walvin (eds), *Leisure in Britain, 1780–1939* (Manchester: Manchester University Press, 1983), pp. 227–41 (p. 232); James Mellon (ed.), *Bullwhip Days: The Slaves Remember* (New York: Weidenfeld and Nicolson, 1988), p. 38. See also West, *Growing up*, pp. 101–4.

39   Victoria Bissell Brown, 'Golden Girls: Female Socialization among the Middle Class of Los Angeles, 1880–1910', in West and Petrik, *Small Worlds*, pp. 232–54; Davin, *Growing up Poor*, ch. 4; Alain Faure, 'Enfance ouvrière, enfance coupable', *Les Révoltes logiques*, 13 (1981), 13–35; Bernard Mergen, 'Made, Bought, and Stolen: Toys and the Culture of Childhood', in West and Petrick, *Small Worlds*, pp. 86–106 (p. 101).

40   Opie and Opie, *Children's Games*, passim; Strutt, *Sports and Pastimes*, ch. 4; Alice Bertha Gomme, *The Traditional Games of England*,

Scotland, and Ireland (2 vols, New York: Dover Publications, 1964 [1894–8]), *passim*; Heywood, *Childhood*, ch. 3.

41   Hélias, *Horse of Pride*, pp. 11–12, ch. 5; West, *Growing up*, pp. 110–12.

42   Walvin, 'Children's Pleasures', p. 240; and Davin, *Growing up Poor*, p. 65.

43   J. H. Plumb, 'The New World of Children', 85; Andrew Davies, 'Leisure in the "Classic Slum" 1900–1939', in Andrew Davies and Steven Fielding (eds), *Workers' Worlds: Cultures and Communities in Manchester and Salford, 1880–1939* (Manchester: Manchester University Press, 1992), pp. 102–32 (pp. 121–5); Foley, *Bolton Childhood*, p. 26.

44   John Springhall, 'Leisure and Victorian Youth'; David Nasaw, 'Children and Commercial Culture: Moving Pictures in the Early Twentieth Century', in West and Petrik, *Small Worlds*, pp. 14–25.

45   Ariès, *Centuries of Childhood*, pp. 353–7.

46   J. Hajnal, 'Two Kinds of Pre-Industrial Household Formation System', in Richard Wall, Jean Robin and Peter Laslett (eds), *Family Forms in Historic Europe* (Cambridge: Cambridge University Press, 1983), pp. 65–104. Hajnal defines north-west Europe as comprising Scandinavia, Britain, the Low Countries, the German-speaking area and northern France. See also Houlbrooke, *English Family*, p. 150; Michael Mitterauer, 'Servants and Youth', *Continuity and Change*, 5 (1990), 11–38; and Terence R. Murphy, "Woful Childe of Parents Rage"'.

47   Pierre Desportes, 'La Population de Reims au XVe siècle d'après un dénombrement de 1422', *Le Moyen Age*, 4th ser., 21 (1966), 463–509 (501); Ann Kussmaul, *Servants in Husbandry in Early Modern England* (Cambridge: Cambridge University Press, 1981), ch. 5; Richard Wall, 'The Age at Leaving Home', *Journal of Family History*, 3 (1978), 181–202; idem, 'Leaving Home and the Process of Household Formation in Pre-Industrial England', *Continuity and Change*, 2 (1987), 77–101; idem, 'Leaving Home and Living Alone: An Historical Perspective', *Population Studies*, 43 (1989), 369–89.

Chapter 8   Children at Work

1   Hugh Cunningham, 'The Employment and Unemployment of Children', 126. See also Ogilvie, 'Coming of Age in a Corporate Society'; and Walter I. Trattner, *Crusade for the Children*, pp. 25–6.

2   Zelizer, *Pricing the Priceless Child*, p. 3.

3   Hugh Cunningham, 'Child Labour in the Industrial Revolution', *The Historian* (spring 1987), 3–8; idem, *The Children of the Poor*, ch. 2; Trattner *Crusade for the Children*, pp. 11–12.

4   Michael Lavalette, *Child Employment in the Capitalist Labour Market* (Aldershot: Avebury, 1994), p. 223.

5   W. H. Hutt, 'The Factory System of the Early Nineteenth Century', in F. A. Hayek (ed.), *Capitalism and the Historians* (London: Routledge and Kegan Paul, 1926), pp. 160–88. For an extended critique of this latter work, see E. P. Thompson, *The Making of the English Working Class* (Harmondsworth: Penguin, 1968), pp. 366–84.

6 The evidence from different countries is summed up in Clark Nardinelli, *Child Labor*, ch. 6.

7 Howard P. Marvel, 'Factory Regulation: A Reinterpretation of Early English Experience', *Journal of Law and Economics*, 20 (1977), 379–402; Per Bolin-Hort, *Work, Family and the State*.

8 Myron Weiner, *The Child and the State in India: Child Labor and Education Policy in Comparative Perspective* (Princeton: Princeton University Press, 1991), ch. 6.

9 See e.g. Vincent, *Bread, Knowledge and Freedom*; West, *Growing up*; Hanawalt, *Medieval London*; Graff, *Conflicting Paths*; Maynes, *Taking the Hard Road*; Davin, *Growing up Poor*.

10 P. E. H. Hair, 'Children in Society', p. 47.

11 Eugene D. Genovese, *Roll, Jordan, Roll: The World the Slaves Made* (New York, Pantheon Books, 1974), pp. 502–3; James Mellon (ed.), *Bullwhip Days: The Slaves Remember* (New York: Weidenfeld and Nicolson, 1988), pp. 39–40.

12 This pattern has been noted at various periods and in numerous countries. See e.g. Hanawalt, *Ties that Bound*, ch. 10; David E. Vassberg, 'Juveniles in the Rural Work Force of Sixteenth-Century Castile', *Journal of Peasant Studies*, 11 (1983), 62–75; Ilana Krausman Ben-Amos, *Adolescence and Youth in Early Modern England* (New Haven: Yale University Press, 1994), ch. 2; Heywood, *Childhood*, ch. 2; Mary Neth, *Preserving the Family Farm: Women, Community, and the Foundations of Agribusiness in the Midwest, 1900–1940* (Baltimore: Johns Hopkins University Press, 1995), ch. 1.

13 Riché and Alexandre-Bidon, *L'Enfance*, p. 167.

14 George Ewart Evans, *Ask the Fellows Who Cut the Hay* (London: Faber and Faber, 1956), ch. 11.

15 Pamela Horne, *The Victorian Country Child* (Kineton: Roundwood Press, 1974), p. 81; Marguerite Audoux, *Marie-Claire* (Paris, 1910), p. 124. See also Mats Sjöberg, 'Working Rural Children. Herding, Child Labour and Childhood in the Swedish Rural Environment', in Coninck-Smith, Sandin and Schrumpf (eds), *Industrious Children*, pp. 106–28.

16 Vassberg, 'Sixteenth-Century Castile', 64–5.

17 Simonetta Ortaggi Cammarosano, 'Labouring Women in Northern and Central Italy in the Nineteenth Century', in John Davis and Paul Ginsborg, *Society and Politics in the Age of Risorgimento* (Cambridge: Cambridge University Press, 1991), pp. 152–83 (p. 171); René de Herdt, 'Child Labour in Belgium, 1800–1914', in Hugh Cunningham and Pier Paolo Viazzo (eds), *Child Labour* p. 24; Horn, *Country Child*, pp. 82–6; Jennie Kitteringham, 'Country Work Girls in Nineteenth-Century England', in Raphael Samuel (ed.), *Village Life and Labour* (London: Routledge and Kegan Paul, 1975), pp. 75–38 (pp. 98–112); W. A. Armstrong, 'Labour 1: Rural Population: Growth, Systems of Employment, and Incomes', in G. E. Mingay (ed.), *The Agrarian History of England and Wales*, vol. 6, '1750–1850' (Cambridge: Cambridge University Press, 1989), ch. 7 (pp. 685–6).

18 Leslie Howard Owens, *This Species of Property: Slave Life and Culture in the Old South* (New York: Oxford University Press, 1976), pp. 205–6.

19 Evans, *Ask the Fellows*, p. 27.

20   Neth, *Family Farm*, p. 23.
21   David Herlihy, *Opera Muliebria: Women and Work in Medieval Europe* (New York: Magraw-Hill, 1990), pp. 51–2; Bridget Hill, *Women, Work and Sexual Politics in Eighteenth-Century England* (Oxford: Basil Blackwell, 1989), p. 35; Lee A. Craig, *To Sow One Acre More: Childbearing and Farm Productivity in the Antebellum North* (Baltimore: Johns Hopkins University Press, 1993), ch. 2; Neth, *Family Farm*, ch. 1; West *Growing up*, chs 4 and 6.
22   Michael Mitterauer, 'Servants and Youth', *Continuity and Change*, 5 (1990), 11–38 (18–20). See above pp. 115–16.
23   Regina Schulte, 'Peasants and Farmers' Maids: Female Farm Servants in Bavaria at the End of the Nineteenth Century', in Richard J. Evans and W. R. Lee (eds), *The German Peasantry* (London: Croom Helm, 1986), pp. 158–73; Olwen Hufton, *The Prospect before Her: A History of Women in Western Europe*, vol. 1, '1500–1800' (London: HarperCollins, 1995), ch. 2.
24   Evans, *Ask the Fellows*, pp. 23–9.
25   Martial Chaulanges *La Terre des autres*, vol. 2, *Le Roussel* (Paris: Delagrave, 1972), p. 132.
26   Françoise Michaud-Frejaville, 'Bons et loyaux services: les contrats d'apprentissage en Orléanais (1380–1480)', *Annales de l'Est*, 34 (1982), 183–208 (190–4); Ben-Amos, *Adolescence* (n. 12 above), ch. 4; Joan Lane, *Apprenticeship in England, 1600–1914* (London: UCL Press, 1996), p. 14, ch. 4.
27   See e.g. Lionel Rose, *The Erosion of Childhood*, chs 3–11; and Jeremy P. Felt, *Hostages of Fortune*, ch. 6.
28   Davin, *Growing up Poor*, chs 9–10.
29   David Herlihy and Christiane Klapisch-Zuber, *Tuscans and their Families: A Study of the Florentine Catasto of 1427* (New Haven: Yale University Press, 1985), p. 136; Klapisch-Zuber, *Women, Family, and Ritual*, pp. 106–7; Hufton, *The Prospect*, ch. 2; Hill, *Women, Work*, ch. 8; Abel Chatelain, 'Migrations et domesticité féminine urbaine en France, XVIIIe–XXe siècle', *Revue d'histoire économique et sociale*, 47 (1968), 506–28 (515–16); E. H. Hunt, *British Labour History, 1815–1914* (London: Weidenfeld and Nicolson, 1981), table 1.2, p. 15.
30   Ben-Amos, *Adolescence*, pp. 47 and 83; Kelly, *German Worker*, pp. 252–68. See also Bruce Bellingham, 'Institution and Family: An Alternative View of Nineteenth-Century Child Saving', *Social Problems*, 33 (1986), 533–57.
31   Cunningham, *Children of the Poor*, pp. 51–64; Serge Chassagne, 'Le Travail des enfants aux XVIIIe et XIXe siècles', in Becchi and Julia (eds), *Histoire de l'enfance*, vol. 2, pp. 224–72 (pp. 233–6).
32   Harry Hendrick, *Images of Youth: Age, Class, and the Male Youth Problem 1880–1920* (Oxford: Clarendon Press, 1990), *passim*; Jacquelyn Dowd Hall, James Leloudis, Robert Korstad, Mary Murphy, Lu Ann Jones and Christopher B. Daly, *Like a Family: The Making of a Southern Cotton Mill World* (Chapel Hill: University of North Carolina Press, 1987), p. 15.
33   Alexander Hamilton, 'Report on Manufactures (1795)', cited in Fass and Mason, *Childhood in America*, p. 248.

34 E. H. Hunt, *Labour History*, p. 9. See also Ellen Jordan, 'Female Unemployment in England and Wales 1851–1911: An Examination of the Census Figures for 15–19 Year Olds', *Social History*, 13 (1988), 175–90; and, in the French context, Colin Heywood, 'The Market for Child Labour in Nineteenth-Century France', *History*, 66 (1981), 34–49 (35–6).

35 Sara Horrell and Jane Humphries, '"The Exploitation of Little Children"', 485–516; Claudia Goldin and Kenneth Sokoloff, 'Women, Children, and Industrialization'.

36 Thompson, *English Working Class*, p. 366; Heywood, 'Market for Child Labour', 37.

37 Hans Medick, 'The Proto-Industrial Family Economy: The Structural Function of Household and Family during the Transition from Peasant Society to Industrial Capitalism', *Social History*, 3 (1976), 291–315 (302).

38 Jean H. Quataert, 'Combining Agrarian and Industrial Livelihood: Rural Households in the Saxon Oberlausitz in the Nineteenth Century', *Journal of Family History*, 10 (1985), 145–62 (151); David Levine, *Family Formation in an Age of Nascent Capitalism* (New York: Academic Press, 1972), p. 28.

39 Daryl M. Hafter, 'The Programmed Brocade Loom and the "Decline of the Drawgirl', in Martha Moore Trescott (ed.), *Dynamos and Virgins Revisited* (Metuchen, NJ: Scarecrow Press, 1979), pp. 49–66 (p. 62); Heywood, *Childhood*, p. 134; Laura Strumingher, 'Les Canutes de Lyon (1835–1848)', *Le Mouvement social*, 105 (1978), 59–86.

40 Sally Alexander, 'Women's Work in Nineteenth-Century London: A Study of the Years 1820–50', in Juliet Mitchell and Ann Oakley (eds), *The Rights and Wrongs of Women* (Harmondsworth: Penguin, 1976), pp. 59–111 (pp. 80–3); C. H. Johnson, 'Economic Change and Artisan Discontent: The Tailors' History', in R. Price (ed.), *Revolution and Reaction: 1848 and the Second French Republic* (London: Croom Helm, 1975), pp. 87–114; Robyn Dasey, 'Women's Work and the Family: Women Garment Workers in Berlin and Hamburg before the First World War', in Richard J. Evans and W. R. Lee (eds), *The German Family* (London: Croom Helm, 1981), pp. 221–55; Felt, *Hostages of Fortune*, p. 141.

41 Bolin-Hort, *Work, Family*, p. 35; Serge Chassagne, 'La Naissance de l'industrie cotonnière en France: 1760–1840. Trois générations d'entrepreneurs', thesis, doctorat d'Etat, EHESS, 1986, p. 340. See also Mary B. Rose, *The Gregs of Quarry Bank Mill: The Rise and Decline of a Family Firm 1750–1914* (Cambridge: Cambridge University Press, 1986), chs 2–3.

42 Goldin and Sokoloff, 'Women, Children, and Industrialization', 742.

43 Herman Freudenberger, Frances J. Mather, and Clark Nardinelli, 'A New Look at the Early Factory Labor Force', *Journal of Economic History*, 44 (1984), 1085–90 (1086); Heywood, *Childhood*, pp. 101–2; Peter Scholliers, 'Grown-ups, Boys and Girls in the Ghent Cotton Industry: The Voortman Mills, 1835–1914', *Social History*, 20 (1995), 201–18 (209). For a more pessimistic conclusion, see Horrell and Humphries, '"Exploitation of Little Children"', *passim*, and 'Child Labour and British Industrialization', in Michael Lavalette (ed.), *A Thing of the*

Past? Child Labour in Britain in the Nineteenth and Twentieth Centuries (New York: St Martin's Press, 1999), pp. 76–100 (pp. 87–8).

44 Heywood, *Childhood*, p. 143.

45 These points are discussed in more detail in Colin Heywood, 'Age and Gender at the Workplace'.

46 Jane Humphries, 'Protective Legislation, the Capitalist State, and Working Class Men: The Case of the 1842 Mines Regulation Act', *Feminist Review*, 7–9 (1981), 1–33; Patricia Hilden, *Women, Work, and Politics: Belgium, 1830–1914* (Oxford: Clarendon Press, 1993), ch. 4; Judy Lown, *Women and Industrialization: Gender at Work in Nineteenth-Century England* (Cambridge: Polity, 1990), ch. 2.

47 Joy Parr, 'Disaggregating the Sexual Division of Labour: A Transatlantic Case Study', *Comparative Studies in Society and History*, 30 (1988), 511–33; William Lazonick, 'Industrial Relations and Technical Change: The Case of the Self-Acting Mule', *Cambridge Journal of Economics*, 3 (1979), 231–62.

48 Heywood, *Childhood*, p. 104, table 4.2; René de Herdt, 'Child Labour in Belgium', (n. 17 above), pp. 26–7.

49 This point is emphasized in Hugh Cunningham, 'The Decline of Child Labour: Labour Markets and Family Economies in Europe and North America since 1830', *Economic History Review*, 53 (2000), 409–28 (411–12).

50 Louis R. Villermé, *Discours sur la durée trop longue du travail des enfants dans beaucoup de manufactures* (Paris, 1837), pp. 60–1; idem, *Tableau de l'état physique et morale des ouvriers employés dans les manufactures de coton, de laine et de soie* (2 vols, Paris, 1840), *passim*.

51 Davin, *Growing up Poor*, pp. 207–8. See above, pp. 29–30.

52 Cunningham, *Children of the Poor*, p. 65; Marjorie Cruickshank, *Children and Industry*, ch. 1.

53 Villermé, *Tableau*, ch. 5; Horrell and Humphries, 'Child Labor', table 1, 491; Hendrick, *Child Welfare*, p. 68 n. 84; Claudia Goldin, 'Family Strategies and the Family Economy in the Late Nineteenth Century: The Role of Secondary Workers', in Theodore Hershberg (ed.), *Philadelphia: Work, Space, Family, and Group Experience in the Nineteenth Century* (New York: Oxford University Press, 1981), pp. 277–310 (p. 284); Michael R. Haines, 'Industrial Work and the Family Life Cycle, 1889–1890', *Research in Economic History*, 4 (1979), 289–356 (309, 319).

54 See Heywood, *Childhood*, p. 177; and Hendrick, *Child Welfare*, p. 68.

55 Louis R. Villermé, 'Mémoire sur la mortalité en France dans la classe aisée et dans la classe indigente', *Mémoires de l'Académie Royale de Médecine*, 1 (1828), 51–98 (80).

56 De Herdt, 'Child Labour in Belgium' (n. 17 above), pp. 29–31.

57 Popp, *Autobiography*, pp. 42–3; Foley, *Bolton Childhood*, p. 53.

58 For surveys of the impact of child labour on health, see e.g. Cruickshank, *Children and Industry, passim*; and Heywood, *Childhood*, ch. 6.

59 Colin Heywood, 'The Catholic Church and the Formation of the Industrial Labour Force in Nineteenth-Century France', *European History Quarterly*, 19 (1989), 509–33 (516–17).

60 Larcom, *New-England Girlhood*, chs 7–8; Harriet Robinson, *Loom and Spindle* (Boston, 1898), cited in Bremner, *Children and Youth*, vol. 2, pp.

600–3. See also Caroline F. Ware, *The Early New England Cotton Manufacture* (Boston: Houghton Mifflin, 1931), and Thomas Dublin, *Women at Work: The Transformation of Work and Community in Lowell, Massachusetts, 1826–1860* (New York: Columbia University Press, 1979).

61 Norbert Truquin, *Mémoires et aventures d'un prolétaire à travers la révolution* (Paris: François Maspéro, 1977 [1888]), pp. 50–1.

62 John Brown, *A Memoir of Robert Blincoe* (Derby: Derbyshire Archaeological Society, 1966 [1828–1832]). See also Stanley D. Chapman, *The Early Factory Masters: The Transition to the Factory System in the Midlands Textile Industry* (Newton Abbot: David and Charles, 1967), pp. 199–209; and A. E. Musson, 'Robert Blincoe and the Early Factory System', in *Trade Union and Social History* (London: Frank Cass, 1974), pp. 195–206.

63 Cammarosono, 'Labouring Women' (n. 17 above), p. 166.

64 Clark Nardinelli, 'Corporal Punishment and Children's Wages in Nineteenth-Century Britain', *Explorations in Economic History*, 19 (1982), 283–95. For a convincing counter-blast, there is Mary MacKinnon and Paul Johnson, 'The Case against Productive Whipping', *Explorations in Economic History*, 21 (1984), 218–23.

65 Rose, *Quarry Bank Mill*, pp. 106–9.

66 Ariès, *Centuries of Childhood*, p. 354. See below, pp. 156–7.

67 Heywood, *Childhood*, p. 201; Cathy L. McHugh, *Mill Family: The Labor System in the Southern Cotton Textile Industry, 1880–1915* (New York: Oxford University Press, 1988), p. 39.

68 Jules Reboul, *La Vie de Jacques Baudet, 1870–1930* (Privas, 1934), pp. 52–4; Virginia Yans-McLaughlin, *Family and Community: Italian Immigrants in Buffalo, 1880–1930* (Urbana: University of Illinois Press, 1982), p. 177; Claudia Goldin, 'Household and Market Production of Families in a Late Nineteenth Century American City' *Explorations in Economic History*, 16 (1979), 111–31; eadem, 'Family Strategies' (n. 53 above), *passim*. See also McHugh, *Mill Family*, pp. 66–70.

69 Maynes, *Taking the Hard Road*, p. 72; and Emilie Carlès, *Une soupe aux herbes sauvages* (Paris: Simoën, 1977), pp. 49–76. See also Mary Jo Maynes, 'Work or School? Youth and the Family in the Midi in the Early Nineteenth Century', in Donald N. Baker and Patrick J. Harrigan (eds), *The Making of Frenchmen: Current Directions in the History of Education in France, 1679–1979* (Waterloo, Ontario: Historical Reflections Press, 1980), pp. 115–33; and W. B. Stephens, *Education, Literacy and Society, 1830–70: The Geography of Diversity in Provincial England* (Manchester: Manchester University Press, 1987).

70 Clark Nardinelli, 'Child Labor and the Factory Acts', *Journal of Economic History*, 40 (1980), 739–55; and idem, *Child Labor*, ch. 5.

71 Goldin and Sokoloff, 'Women, Children', 747. See also Nardinelli, *Child Labor*, ch. 6.

72 See above, p. 123.

73 Hair, 'Children in Society', p. 47; Cunningham, 'Decline of Child Labour', 412–13; Michael Lavalette, 'The Changing Form of Child Labour *circa* 1880–1918', in Lavalette, *A Thing of the Past?* (n. 43 above), pp. 118–38; Trattner, *Crusade for the Children*, pp. 32–6; Heywood, *Childhood*, p. 100.

74 Nardinelli, *Child Labor*, pp. 124–5.
75 Howard P. Marvel, 'Factory Regulation: A Reinterpretation of Early English Experience', *Journal of Law and Economics*, 20 (1977), 379–402; and Weissbach, *Child Labor Reform, passim*.
76 Nardinelli, 'Child Labor', 742–3.
77 Myron Weiner, *The Child and the State in India: Child Labor and Education Policy in Comparative Perspective* (Princeton: Princeton University Press, 1991), p. 110.
78 Rousseau, *Emile*, p. 79; Harry Hendrick, 'Children and Childhood', *Refresh*, 15 (1992), p. 2. See above, pp. 23–7.
79 Heywood, *Childhood*, p. 311; Trattner, *Crusade for the Children*, pp. 39–40.
80 See e.g. Nardinelli, 'Child Labor', McHugh, *Mill Family*, pp. 53–4; and Heywood, 'The Market for Child Labour', *passim*.
81 Bolin-Hort, *Work, Family and the State, passim*.
82 On the importance of part-time child labour in modern Britain, and its pernicious influence on child welfare, see Lavalette, *Child Employment, passim*.
83 See the recent survey by Cunningham, 'Decline of Child Labour', 412–20.
84 Lavalette, *Child Employment* (n. 4 above), *passim*.

Chapter 9   Investing in the Future: Health and Education

1 Heywood, *Childhood*, p. 279.
2 St Augustine, *Confessions*, p. 31.
3 Roger Cooter, 'Introduction' to *In the Name of the Child: Health and Welfare, 1880–1940* (London: Routledge, 1992), p. 2; Strauss, *Luther's House*, p. 86.
4 Strauss, *Luther's House*, p. 86.
5 Sylvère, *Toinou*, pp. 100–1; 'Fritz Pauk, Cigar Maker', in Kelly, *German Worker*, pp. 399–427 (pp. 403–4); Popp, *Autobiography*, pp. 42–3.
6 Roberts, *A Ragged Schooling*, p. 39; Sylvère, *Toinou*, p. 100; Popp, *Autobiography*, p. 44; Hélias, *The Horse of Pride*, p. 83.
7 Floud, Wachter and Gregory, *Height, Health and History*, ch. 1.
8 P. B. Eveleth and J. M. Tanner, *Worldwide Variation in Human Growth* (Cambridge, 1976), p. 1, cited in Floud et al., *Height, Health and History*, p. 16. See also Richard H. Steckel, 'Height and Per Capita Income', *Historical Methods*, 16 (1983), 1–7. This is not to ignore genetic differences among populations, for these certainly interact with environmental ones during the growth period, but the recent consensus is that the environment has a greater impact on average heights.
9 J. M. Tanner, *A History of the Study of Human Growth* (Cambridge: Cambridge University Press, 1981), ch. 5; Floud et al., *Height, Health and History*, p. 182; Kenneth L. Sokoloff and Georgia C. Villaflor, 'The Early Achievement of Modern Stature in America', *Social Science History*, 6 (1982), 453–81; and Robert W. Fogel et al., 'Secular Changes in Ameri-

can and British Stature and Nutrition', *Journal of Interdisciplinary History*, 14 (1983), 445–81 (462–3).

10 John Komlos, 'Patterns of Children's Growth in East-Central Europe in the Eighteenth Century', *Annals of Human Biology*, 13 (1986), 33–48; idem, 'Stature and Nutrition in the Habsburg Monarchy: The Standard of Living and Economic Development in the Eighteenth Century', *American Historical Review*, 90 (1985), 1149–61; Roderick Floud and Kenneth W. Wachter, 'Poverty and Physical Stature: Evidence on the Standard of Living of London Boys 1770–1870', *Social Science History*, 6 (1982), 422–52 (433); Floud et al., *Height, Health and History*, pp. 166–9; Fogel et al., 'Secular Changes', 464.

11 Michael W. Flinn, *The European Demographic System, 1500–1820* (Brighton: Harvester Press, 1981), ch. 2; Michael Anderson, *Population Change in North-Western Europe, 1750–1850* (London: Macmillan, 1988), p. 32.

12 Roger Schofield and E. A. Wrigley, 'Infant and Child Mortality'; Flinn, *European Demographic System*, p. 133.

13 Jacques Vallin, 'Mortality in Europe from 1720 to 1914: Long-Term Trends and Changes in Patterns by Age and Sex', in R. Schofield, D. Reher and A. Beher, *The Decline of Mortality in Europe* (Oxford: Clarendon Press, 1991), pp. 38–67 (49–51); E. A. Wrigley and R. S. Schofield, *The Population History of England, 1541–1871: A Reconstruction* (London: 1981), p. 249; Yves Blayo, 'La Mortalité en France de 1740 à 1829', *Population* (1975), 123–42.

14 Michel Poulain and Dominique Tabutin, 'La Mortalité aux jeunes âges en Europe et en Amérique du Nord du XIXe à nos jours', in Paul Marie Boulanger and Dominique Tabutin (eds), *La Mortalité des enfants dans l'histoire* (Liège: Ordina Editions, 1980), *passim*; Richard A. Meckel, *Save the Babies*, p. 245 n. 9; Preston and Haines, *Fatal Years*, ch. 2; C. A. Corsini and P. P. Viazzo (eds), *The Decline of Infant Mortality in Europe: Four National Case Studies* (Florence: UNICEF, 1993) and *The Decline of Infant and Child Mortality*.

15 John Komlos, 'Height and Social Status in Eighteenth-Century Germany', *Journal of Interdisciplinary History*, 20 (1990), 607–21 (611–15); Tanner, *Human Growth*, pp. 106–12. For details of the numerous school surveys in Europe and America during the late nineteenth century, see Tanner, ch. 9.

16 Floud et al., *Height, Health and Nutrition*, p. 198; Fogel et al., 'Secular Changes', 480.

17 Tanner, *Human Growth*, ch. 7; Richard H. Steckel, 'Slave Height Profiles from Coastwise Manifests', *Explorations in Economic History*, 16 (1979), 363–80; and idem, 'A Peculiar Population: The Nutrition, Health, and Mortality of American Slaves from Childhood to Maturity', *Journal of Economic History*, 46 (1986), 721–41.

18 Emmanuel Le Roy Ladurie, Nicole Bernageau and Yvonne Pasquet, 'Le Conscrit et l'ordinateur. Perspectives de recherche sur les archives militaires du XIXe siècle français', *Studi Storici*, 10 (1969), 260–308 (297).

19 Edmonde Vedrenne-Villeneuve, 'L'Inégalité sociale devant la mort dans la première moitié du XIXe siècle', *Population*, 16 (1961), 665–98 (681).

20   Poulain and Tabutin, 'La Mortalité', p. 120; and F. B. Smith, *The People's Health, 1830–1910* (London: Croom Helm, 1979), p. 136.

21   R. I. Woods, P. A. Watterson and J. H. Woodward, 'The Causes of Rapid Infant Mortality Decline in England and Wales, 1861–1921, Part I', *Population Studies*, 42 (1988), 343–66; C. H. Lee, 'Regional Inequalities in Infant Mortality in Britain, 1861–1971: Patterns and Hypotheses', *Population Studies*, 45 (1991), 55–65; and Naomi Williams and Chris Galley, 'Urban–Rural Differentials in Infant Mortality in Victorian England', *Population Studies*, 49 (1995), 401–20; Alice Reid, 'Locality or Class? Spatial and Social Differentials in Infant and Child Mortality in England and Wales, 1895–1911', in Corsini and Viazzo, *European Experience*, pp. 129–54.

22   Thomas McKeown and R. G. Brown, 'Medical Evidence Related to English Population Changes in the Eighteenth Century', *Population Studies*, 9 (1955–6), 119–41; Thomas McKeown and R. G. Record, 'Reasons for the Decline of Mortality in England and Wales during the Nineteenth Century', *Population Studies*, 16 (1962–3), 94–122. McKeown later summed up his position in *The Modern Rise of Population* (London: Edward Arnold, 1976).

23   Thomas McKeown, R. G. Brown and R. G. Record, 'An Interpretation of the Modern Rise of Population in Europe', *Population Studies*, 26 (1972), 345–82.

24   McKeown and Record, 'Decline of Mortality', esp. 104–6.

25   I. A. Abt (ed.), *Abt–Garrison History of Pediatrics* (Philadelphia: W. B. Saunders, 1965), pp. 55–73; Biraben, 'Médecine et l'enfant', Marie-France Morel, 'The Care of Children: The Influence of Medical Innovation and Medical Institutions on Infant Mortality 1750–1914', in Schofield et al., *Decline of Mortality*, pp. 196–219 (p. 203).

26   Charles Dickens, *Oliver Twist* (Harmondsworth: Penguin, 1994 [1837–9]). p. 2.

27   Marcelle Bouteiller, *Médecine populaire d'hier et d'aujourd'hui* (Paris: Maisonneuve et Larose, 1966); Matthew Ramsey, *Professional and Popular Medicine in France, 1770–1830* (Cambridge: Cambridge University Press, 1988).

28   Morel, 'Care of Children', *passim*; J.-N. Biraben, 'Le Médecin et l'enfant au XVIIIe siècle: aperçu sur la pédiatrie au XVIIIe siècle', *Annales de démographie historique* (1973), 215–23.

29   Pierre-Jakez Hélias, *Le Cheval d'orgueil* (Paris: Plon, 1975), p. 120; Popp, *Autobiography*, pp. 21–8.

30   For example, Alfred Perrenoud, 'Mortality Decline in its Secular Setting', in T. Bengtsson et al., *Pre-Industrial Population Change* (Stockholm, 1984), pp. 41–69; Massimo Livi-Bacci, *Population and Nutrition: An Essay on European Demographic History*, transl. Tania Croft-Murray (Cambridge: Cambridge University Press, 1991); Simon Szreter, 'The Importance of Social Intervention in Britain's Mortality Decline c.1850–1914: A Re-interpretation of the Role of Public Health', *Social History of Medicine*, 1 (1988), 1–37.

31   Samuel H. Preston, 'The Changing Relation between Mortality and Level of Economic Development', *Population Studies*, 29 (1975), 231–48 (240); Roger Schofield and David Reher, 'The Decline of Mortality in

Europe', in Schofield et al., *Decline of Mortality* (n. 13 above), pp. 1–17 (p. 10).

32 Robert W. Fogel, 'Nutrition and the Decline in Mortality since 1700: Some Preliminary Findings', in Stanley L. Engerman and Robert E. Gallman (eds), *Long-Term Factors in American Economic Growth* (Chicago: University of Chicago Press, 1986), pp. 439–527 (p. 507); John Campbell, 'Work, Pregnancy, and Infant Mortality among Southern Slaves', *Journal of Interdisciplinary History*, 14 (1984), 793–812.

33 Samuel H. Preston and Etienne van de Walle, 'Urban French Mortality in the Nineteenth Century', *Population Studies*, 32 (1978), 275–97.

34 Useful comparative material can be found in Jane Jenson, 'Representations of Gender: Policies to "Protect" Women Workers and Infants in France and the United States before 1914', in Linda Gordon (ed.), *Women, the State, and Welfare* (Madison: University of Wisconsin Press, 1990), pp. 152–77; Rachel G. Fuchs, 'France in a Comparative Perspective', in Elinor A. Accampo, Rachel G. Fuchs and Mary Lynn Stewart (eds), *Gender and the Politics of Social Reform in France, 1870–1914* (Baltimore: Johns Hopkins University Press, 1995), pp. 157–87; Seth Koven and Sonya Michel, 'Womanly Duties: Maternalist Politics and the Origins of Welfare States in France, Germany, Great Britain, and the United States, 1880–1920', *American Historical Review*, 95 (1990), 1076–1108; eidem (eds), *Mothers of a New World: Maternalist Politics and the Origins of Welfare States* (New York: Routledge, 1993); and Alisa Klaus, *Every Child a Lion*.

35 See Beaver, 'Population, Infant Mortality and Milk', and the pessimistic riposte from P. J. Atkins, 'White Poison?'; Buchanan, 'Infant Feeding'; Anthony S. Wohl, *Endangered Lives: Public Health in Victorian Britain* (London: Dent, 1983), ch. 2; Preston and Haines, *Fatal Years*, pp. 23–4; Meckel, *Save the Babies*, *passim*.

36 See e.g. Anna Davin, 'Imperialism and Motherhood', *History Workshop*, 5 (1978), 9–65; Jane Lewis, *The Politics of Motherhood: Child and Maternal Welfare in England, 1900–1939* (London: Croom Helm, 1980); Karen Offen, 'Depopulation, Nationalism, and Feminism in Fin-de-Siècle France', *American Historical Review*, 89 (1984), 648–76; and Deborah Dwork, *War is Good for Babies*.

37 Cited in Dickinson, *The Politics of German Child Welfare*, p. 55.

38 Meckel, *Save the Babies*, p. 121; and Virginia Yans-McLaughlin, *Family and Community: Italian Immigrants in Buffalo, 1880–1930* (Urbana: University of Illinois Press, 1982), p. 154.

39 See above, pp. 72–3.

40 See Carol Dyhouse, 'Working-Class Mothers and Infant Mortality in England, 1895–1914', *Journal of Social History*, 12 (1978), 248–67.

41 Dwork, *War is Good for Babies*, pp. 164–6.

42 Assefa Bequele, 'Emerging Perspectives in the Struggle against Child Labour', in William E. Myers (ed.), *Protecting Working Children* (London: UNICEF, 1991), pp. 69–86 (77).

43 Carlo M. Cipolla, *Literacy and Development in the West* (Harmondsworth: Penguin, 1969), p. 33; James Bowen, *A History of Western Education*, vol. 3, pp. 161–2; R. A. Houston, *Literacy in Early Modern Europe*, pp. 48–50.

44 Karl A Schleunes, 'Enlightenment, Reform, Reaction: The Schooling Revolution in Prussia', *Central European History*, 12 (1979), 315–42; Peter Lundgreen, 'Industrialization and the Educational Formation of Manpower in Germany', *Journal of Social History*, 9 (1975–6), 64–80; Bowen, *Western Education*, vol. 3, *passim*.

45 See e.g. Carl F. Kaestle, '"Between the Scylla of Brutal Ignorance and the Charybdis of a Literary Education": Elite Attitudes toward Mass Schooling in Early Industrial England and America', in Lawrence Stone (ed.), *Schooling and Society*, pp. 177–91; Theodore Zeldin, 'Education and Hope', in *France 1848–1945*, vol. 2 (Oxford: Clarendon Press, 1977), pp. 139–204; Harvey J. Graff, *The Literacy Myth: Literacy and Social Structure in the Nineteenth-Century City* (New York: Academic Press, 1979), and idem, *Legacies of Literacy*.

46 See François Furet and Jacques Ozouf, *Reading and Writing: Literacy in France from Calvin to Jules Ferry* (Cambridge: Cambridge University Press, 1982), pp. 1–4.

47 Ivan D. Illich, *Deschooling Society* (Harmondsworth: Penguin, 1973), p. 18.

48 S. Crawford, *Childhood in Anglo-Saxon England*, p. 147. See also Berkvam, *Enfance et maternité*, p. 66.

49 David Nicholas, 'Child and Adolescent Labour in the Late Medieval City: A Flemish Model in Regional Perspective', *English Historical Review*, 110 (1995), 1103–31 (1108–10); O. Jocelyn Dunlop, *English Apprenticeship and Child Labour* (London: T. Fisher Unwin, 1912), ch. 1.

50 Ariès, *Centuries of Childhood*, pp. 186–7, 353–6, 395–7. See also above, pp. 138–9. For criticisms of Ariès on these points, see Adrian Wilson, 'Philippe Ariès', 140–3; Alexandre-Bidon and Lett, *Les Enfants*, p. 73.

51 Georges Duby, 'In Northwestern France: The Youth in Twelfth-Century Aristocratic Society', in Frederic L. Cheyette (ed.), *Lordship and Community in Medieval Europe: Selected Readings* (New York: Holt, Rinehart, and Winston, 1968), pp. 198–209 (p. 199); Pierre Riché, *Education and Culture*, pp. 65–7; Berkvam, *Enfance et maternité*, pp. 65–8; Nicholas Orme, *Childhood to Chivalry*, ch. 1; Riché and Alexandre-Bidon, *L'Enfance*, pp. 158–61; Alexandre-Bidon and Lett, *Les Enfants*, pp. 79–82; Crawford, *Anglo-Saxon England*, pp. 145–7.

52 Crawford, *Anglo-Saxon England*, p. 152.

53 This section relies on 'Education and Apprenticeship', in Allardyce Nicoll (ed.), *Shakespeare in his Own Age*, Shakespeare Survey, 17 (Cambridge: Cambridge University Press, 1964), pp. 53–72; Flandrin, *Families in Former Times*, ch. 3; Ann Kussmaul, *Servants in Husbandry in Early Modern England* (Cambridge: Cambridge University Press, 1981), *passim*; Stephen R. Smith, 'The Ideal and the Reality: Apprentice–Master Relationships in Seventeenth Century London', *History of Education Quarterly*, 21 (1981), 449–59; Houlbrooke, *English Family*, ch. 7; Bridget Hill, *Women, Work, and Sexual Politics in Eighteenth-Century England* (Oxford: Basil Blackwell, 1989), chs 5–6; Michel Mitterauer, 'Servants and Youth', *Continuity and Change*, 5 (1990), 11–38; Joan Lane, *Apprenticeship in England, 1600–1914* (London: UCL Press, 1996), *passim*.

54 Jean-Roch Coignet, *Les Cahiers du capitaine Coignet, 1799–1815* (Paris, 1883), p. 5.

55 Kussmaul, *Servants*, pp. 85–93.

56 Richard L. Kagan, *Students and Society in Early Modern Spain* (Baltimore: Johns Hopkins University Press, 1974), p. 9 n. 18.

57 See above, pp. 91–6, 104–6.

58 Egil Johansson, 'The History of Literacy in Sweden', in Harvey J. Graff, *Literacy and Social Development*, pp. 151–82.

59 Janet L. Nelson, *Charles the Bald* (London: Longman, 1992), ch. 4; John F. Benton, *Self and Society in Medieval France: The Memoirs of Abbot Guibert of Nogent* (Toronto: University of Toronto Press, 1970), pp. 45–50; Locke, *Concerning Education*, pp. 128–30; Kagan *Early Modern Spain*, p. 10.

60 Linda Pollock, '"Teach Her to Live under Obedience": The Making of Women in the Upper Ranks of Early Modern England', *Continuity and Change*, 4 (1989), 231–58 (237).

61 David Vincent, *Literacy and Popular Culture* (Cambridge: Cambridge University Press, 1990), ch. 3; Edward Shorter, 'The "Veillée" and the Great Transformation', in Jacques Beauroy, Marc Bertrand and Edward T. Gargan (eds), *The Wolf and the Lamb: Popular Culture in France from the Old Regime to the Twentieth Century* (Saratoga, Calif.: Anma Libri, 1977), pp. 127–40; Hans Medick, 'Village Spinning Bees: Sexual Culture and Free Time among Rural Youth in Early Modern Germany', in Hans Medick and David Warren Sabean (eds), *Interest and Emotion: Essays on the Study of Family and Kinship* (Cambridge: Cambridge University Press, 1984), pp. 317–39; Martin Nadaud, *Léonard, maçon de la Creuse* (Paris: Maspero, 1977), pp. 24–5.

62 Furet and Ozouf, *Reading and Writing* (n. 46 above), p. 3; Pollock, 'Teach her to Live', p. 235.

63 Jong, 'Growing up in a Carolingian Monastery'; eadem, *In Samuel's Image*, *passim*.

64 Works discussing medieval schools include Pierre Riché, *De l'éducation antique à l'éducation chevaleresque*; idem; *Education and Culture*; Nicholas Orme, *English Schools in the Middle Ages* (London: Methuen, 1973); Alexandre-Bidon and Lett, *Les Enfants*.

65 Heywood, *Childhood in Nineteenth-Century France*, pp. 211–12. For English parallels, see Jane Purvis, *Hard Lessons: The Lives and Education of Working-Class Women in Nineteenth-Century England* (Cambridge: Polity, 1989), pp. 79–81.

66 R. S. Schofield, 'Dimensions of Illiteracy, 1750–1850', *Explorations in Economic History*, 10 (1972–3), 437–54 (450). See also David Cressy, 'Levels of Illiteracy in England, 1530–1730', *Historical Journal*, 20 (1977), 1–23 (5–9).

67 Kenneth A. Lockridge, *Literacy in Colonial New England*, p. 23.

68 Kagan, *Early Modern Spain*, p. 14.

69 Lockridge, *Colonial New England*, p. 23; Georges Dupeux, *Aspects de l'histoire sociale et politique du Loir-et-Cher, 1848–1914* (Paris: Mouton, 1962), p. 165.

70 David Cressy, 'Educational Opportunity in Tudor and Stuart England', *History of Education Quarterly*, 16 (1976), 301–20 (309–11); Margaret

Spufford, 'First Steps in Literacy: The Reading and Writing Experiences of the Humblest Seventeenth-Century Spiritual Autobiographers', *Social History*, 4 (1979), 407–35.

71   Johansson, 'Literacy in Sweden', 172–3.

72   Paul F. Grendler, *Schooling in Renaissance Italy: Literacy and Learning 1300–1600* (Baltimore: Johns Hopkins University Press, 1989), p. 43.

73   Rousseau, *Emile*, book 5; J. H. Broome, *Rousseau* (London: Arnold, 1963), ch. 5.

74   Lockridge, *Colonial New England*, pp. 38–42; Cipolla, *Literacy*, table 30; Graff, *Legacies of Literacy*, pp. 342–3; David I. Macleod, *The Age of the Child*, p. 76; Furet and Ozouf, *Reading and Writing* (n. 46 above), ch. 1; Raymond Grew, Patrick J. Harrigan and James Whitney, 'The Availability of Schooling in Nineteenth-Century France', *Journal of Interdisciplinary History*, 14 (1983), 25–63. See also W. B. Stephens, *Education, Literacy and Society, 1830–70: The Geography of Diversity in Provincial England* (Manchester: Manchester University Press, 1987).

75   See Furet and Ozouf, *Reading and Writing*, pp. 1–2.

76   See above, pp. 32–4 for Puritan views on the nature of childhood. The quotation is cited by David Cressy, in *Literacy and the Social Order: Reading and Writing in Tudor and Stuart England* (Cambridge: Cambridge University Press, 1980), p. 4.

77   Useful surveys from a vast literature include Lawrence Stone, 'Literacy and Education in England, 1640–1900', *Past and Present*, 42 (1969), 69–139; Rosemary O'Day, *Education and Society 1500–1800: The Social Foundations of Education in Early Modern Britain* (London: Longman, 1982); Graff, *Legacies of Literacy*, chs 5–6; Houston, *Early Modern Europe, passim*; Nicholas Orme, *Education and Society in Medieval and Renaissance England* (London: Hambledon Press, 1989), ch. 1; Paul F. Grendler, 'Schooling in Western Europe'.

78   The two classic studies are Michael Sanderson, 'Literacy and Social Mobility in the Industrial Revolution in England', *Past and Present*, 56 (1972), 131–54; and François Furet and Jacques Ozouf, 'Literacy and Industrialization: The Case of the Département du Nord in France, *Journal of European Economic History*, 5 (1976), 5–44.

79   Graff, *Legacies of Literacy*, p. 239; James A. Leith, 'Modernisation, Mass Education and Social Mobility in French Thought, 1750–1789', in R. F. Brissenden (ed.), *Studies in the Eighteenth Century*, vol. 2 (Toronto, 1973), 223–38; Harvey Chisick, *The Limits of Reform in the Enlightenment: Attitudes towards the Education of the Lower Classes in Eighteenth-Century France* (Princeton: Princeton University Press, 1981), *passim*; Antoine Prost, *Histoire de l'enseignement en France, 1800–1967* (Paris: Colin, 1968), p. 13.

80   Grzegorz Leopold Seidler, 'The Reform of the Polish School System in the Era of the Enlightenment', in James A. Leith (ed.), *Facets of Education in the Eighteenth Century*, Studies on Voltaire and the Eighteenth Century, 13 (Oxford: Voltaire Foundation, 1977), pp. 337–58 (p. 350).

81   H. C. Barnard, *Education and the French Revolution* (Cambridge: Cambridge University Press, 1969), pp. 81–2.

82   C. A. Anderson, 'Patterns and Variability in the Distribution and Diffusion of Schooling', in C. A. Anderson and M. J. Bowman (eds), *Education and Economic Development* (London: Cass, 1966), pp. 314–46 (p. 314).

83   Schleunes, 'Schooling Revolution in Prussia', 334; Nipperdey, 'Mass Education', 162–5; Maurice Gontard, *L'Enseignement primaire en France de la Révolution à la loi Guizot, 1789–1833* (Paris: Belles Lettres, 1959), p. 533; idem, *Les Ecoles primaires de la France bourgeoise (1833–1875)* (Toulouse: Centre régionale de documentation pédagogique de Toulouse, 1957), p. 4; Kaestle, 'Elite Attitudes toward Mass Schooling', *passim*.

84   See e.g. Bowen, *History of Western Education*, vol. 3, ch. 9; Annmarie Turnbull, 'Learning her Womanly Work: The Elementary School Curriculum, 1870–1914', in Felicity Hunt (ed.), *Lessons for Life: The Schooling of Girls and Women, 1850–1950* (Oxford: Basil Blackwell, 1987), pp. 83–100 (p. 87); Davin, *Growing up Poor*, chs 7–8; Meg Gomersall, *Working-Class Girls*; Louis-Henri Parias (ed.), *Histoire générale de l'enseignement et de l'éducation en France*, vol. 3, Françoise Mayeur, 'De la Révolution à l'école républicaine' (Paris: G. V. Labat, 1981), pp. 120–34; Macleod, *Age of the Child*, p. 84.

85   Thomas Nipperdey, 'Mass Education and Modernization: The Case of Germany 1780–1850', *Transactions of the Royal Historical Society*, 27 (1977), 155–72 (161).

86   This point is made clear in, for example, Bengt Sandin, 'Education, Popular Culture'.

87   Rev. F. Watkin's report on the Northern District in *Minutes of the Committee of Council* (1847), cited in Anne Digby and Peter Searby, *Children, School and Society in Nineteenth-Century England* (London: Macmillan, 1981), pp. 119–21. See also Richard Johnson, 'Educational Policy and Social Control in Early Victorian England', *Past and Present*, 49 (1970), 96–119.

88   Larcom, *New-England Girlhood*, ch. 2.

89   T. W. Laqueur, 'Working-Class Demand and the Growth of English Elementary Education, 1750–1850', in Stone, *Schooling and Society*, pp. 192–205; J. Ruffet, 'La Liquidation des instituteurs-artisans', *Les Révoltes logiques*, 3 (1976), 61–76.

90   Agricol Perdiguier, *Mémoires d'un compagnon* (1854), English translation in Mark Taugott (ed.), *The French Worker: Autobiographies from the Early Industrial Era* (Berkeley: University of California Press, 1993), p. 120; 'Aurelia Roth, Glass Grinder' and Fritz Pauk, Cigar Maker', in Kelly, *German Worker*, pp. 389–98 (p. 390) and pp. 399–427 (p. 402). For American parallels, see Macleod, *Age of the Child*, p. 89.

91   One thinks of, say, Lucy Larcom in the United States, Robert Roberts in England and Pierre-Jakez Hélias in France.

92   'Ludwig Turek, Child Tobacco Worker', in Kelly, *The German Worker*, pp. 307–19 (p. 316).

93   Edward Eggleston, *The Hoosier Schoolmaster* (New York: Sagamore Press, 1957), pp. 11–12; West, *Growing up*, p. 203.

94   Riché, *Education and Culture*, ch. 10; Alexandre-Bidon and Lett, *Les Enfants*, pp. 219–48.

95   For more details, see Danièle Alexandre-Bidon, 'La Lettre volée. Apprendre à lire à l'enfant au Moyen Age', *Annales ESC*, 44 (1989), 953–92; Orme, *English Schools*, pp. 60–2; Cressy, *Literacy*, ch. 2; O'Day, *Education and Society*, ch. 4; Kagan, *Early Modern Spain*, pp. 9–13; Houston, *Culture and Education*, ch. 3.
96   Davin, *Growing up Poor*, p. 122.
97   Michel Foucault, *Discipline and Punish: The Birth of the Prison*, transl. Alan Sheridan (Harmondsworth: Penguin, 1977), *passim*.

Conclusion

1   Linda Hannas, *The English Jigsaw Puzzle, 1760–1890* (London: Wayland Publishers, 1972), p. 11.
2   Tamara K. Hareven, *Family Time and Industrial Time: The Relationship between the Family and Work in a New England Industrial Community* (Cambridge: Cambridge University Press, 1982), p. 167.

Select Bibliography

Alexandre-Bidon, Danièle, and Closson, Monique, *L'Enfant à l'ombre des cathédrales*, Lyons: Presses Universitaires de Lyon, 1985.

Alexandre-Bidon, Danièle, and Lett, Didier, *Les Enfants au Moyen Age: Ve–XVe siècles*, Paris: Hachette, 1997.

Ariès, Philippe, *Centuries of Childhood*, transl. Robert Baldick, London: Pimlico, 1996.

Arnot, Margaret L., 'Infant Death, Child Care and the State: The Baby-Farming Scandal and the First Infant Life Protection Legislation of 1872', *Continuity and Change*, 9 (1994), 271–311.

Ashby, LeRoy, *Endangered Children: Dependency, Neglect, and Abuse in American History*, New York: Twayne Publishers, 1997.

Atkins, P. J., 'White Poison? The Social Consequences of Milk Consumption, 1850–1930', *Social History of Medicine*, 5 (1992), 207–27.

Attreed, Lorraine C., 'From *Pearl* Maiden to Tower Princes: Towards a New History of Medieval Childhood', *Journal of Medieval History*, 9 (1983), 43–58.

Augustine, St, *Confessions*, transl. R. S. Pine Coffin, Harmondsworth: Penguin, 1961.

Avery, Gillian, and Briggs, Julia (eds), *Children and their Books*, Oxford: Clarendon Press, 1989.

Beaver, M. W., 'Population, Infant Mortality and Milk', *Population Studies*, 27 (1973), 243–54.

Becchi, Egle, and Julia, Dominique (eds), *Histoire de l'enfance en Occident*, Paris: Editions du Seuil, 1996.

Behlmer, George K., *Child Abuse and Moral Reform in England, 1870–1908*, Stanford Calif.: Stanford University Press, 1982.

Benton, John F., *Self and Society in Medieval France: The Memoirs of Abbot Guibert of Nogent*, Toronto: University of Toronto Press, 1984.

Berkvam, Doris Desclais, *Enfance et maternité dans la littérature française des XIIe et XIIIe siècles*, Paris: Honoré Champion, 1981.

Berkvam, Doris Desclais, 'Nature and *Norreture*: A Notion of Medieval Childhood and Education', *Mediaevalia*, 9 (1983), 165–80.

Biraben, Jean-Noël, 'La Médicine et l'enfant au Moyen Age', *Annales de démographie historique* (1973), 73–5.

Bolin-Hort, Per, *Work, Family and the State: Child Labour and the Organization of Production in the British Cotton Industry, 1780–1920*, Lund: Lund University Press, 1989.

Boswell, John, *The Kindness of Strangers: The Abandonment of Children in Western Europe from Late Antiquity to the Renaissance*, London: Allen Lane, 1988.

Bowen, James, *A History of Western Education*, 3 vols, London: Methuen, 1972–81.

Bremner, Robert (ed.), *Children and Youth in America: A Documentary History*, 3 vols, Cambridge, Mass.: Harvard University Press, 1970–4.

Burnett, John (ed.), *Destiny Obscure: Autobiographies of Childhood, Education and Family from the 1820s to the 1920s*, London: Allen Lane, 1982.

Burrow, J. A., *The Ages of Man: A Study in Medieval Writing and Thought*, Oxford: Clarendon Press, 1986.

Burton, Anthony, 'Looking forward from Ariès? Pictorial and Material Evidence for the History of Childhood and Family Life', *Continuity and Change*, 4 (1989), 203–29.

Butler, Samuel, *The Way of All Flesh*, Harmondsworth: Penguin, 1966.

Calvert, Karin, *Children in the House: The Material Culture of Early Childhood, 1600–1900*, Boston: Northeastern University Press, 1992.

Carron, Roland, *Enfant et parenté dans la France médiévale, Xe–XIIe siècles*, Geneva: Droz, 1989.

Censer, Jane Turner, *North Carolina Planters and their Children, 1800–1860*, Baton Rouge: Louisiana State University Press, 1984.

Coninck-Smith, Ning de, Sandin, Bengt, and Schrumpf, Ellen (eds), *Industrious Children: Work and Childhood in the Nordic Countries 1850–1990*, Odense: Odense University Press, 1997.

Cooter, Roger (ed.), *In the Name of the Child: Health and Welfare, 1880–1940*, London: Routledge, 1992.

Corsini, C. A., and Viazzo, P. P. (eds), *The Decline of Infant and Child Mortality. The European Experience: 1750–1990*, Florence: UNICEF, 1997.

Coveney, Peter, *The Image of Childhood*, rev. edn, Harmondsworth: Penguin, 1967.

Cox, Roger, *Shaping Childhood: Themes of Uncertainty in the History of Adult–Child Relationships*, London: Routledge, 1996.

Crawford, Patricia, '"The Sucking Child": Adult Attitudes to Child Care in the First Year of Life in Seventeenth-Century England', *Continuity and Change*, 1 (1986), 23–51.

Crawford, Sally, *Childhood in Anglo-Saxon England*, Stroud: Sutton Publishing, 1999.

Cruickshank, Marjorie, *Children and Industry: Child Health and Welfare in North-West Textile Towns during the Nineteenth Century*, Manchester: Manchester University Press, 1981.

Cunningham, Hugh, *The Children of the Poor: Representations of Childhood since the Seventeenth Century*, Oxford: Basil Blackwell, 1991.

Cunningham, Hugh, 'The Employment and Unemployment of Children in England, c.1680–1851', *Past and Present*, 126 (1991), 115–50.

Cunningham, Hugh, *Children and Childhood in Western Society since 1500*, London: Longman, 1995.

Cunningham, Hugh, and Viazzo, Pier Paolo (eds), *Child Labour in Historical Perspective, 1800–1985*, Florence: UNICEF, 1996.

Darton, F. J. Harvey, *Children's Books in England*, 3rd edn, Cambridge: Cambridge University Press, 1982.

Davin, Anna, *Growing up Poor: Home, School and Street in London, 1870–1914*, London: Rivers Oram Press, 1996.

Dekker, Rudolf, *Children, Memory and Autobiography in Holland: From the Golden Age to Romanticism*, London: Macmillan, 1999.

Demaitre, Luke, 'The Idea of Childhood and Child Care in Medical Writings of the Middle Ages', *Journal of Psychohistory*, 4 (1977), 461–90.

DeMause, Lloyd B. (ed.), *The History of Childhood*, London: Souvenir Press, 1976.

Demos, John, *A Little Commonwealth: Family Life in Plymouth Colony*, London: Oxford University Press, 1970.

Dickinson, Edward Ross, *The Politics of German Child Welfare from the Empire to the Federal Republic*, Cambridge, Mass.: Harvard University Press, 1996.

Dreitzel, Hans Peter (ed.), *Childhood and Socialization*, New York, Macmillan, 1973.

Dunae, Patrick A., 'Penny Dreadfuls: Late Nineteenth-Century Boys' Literature and Crime', *Victorian Studies*, 22 (1989), 133–50.

Dwork, Deborah, *War is Good for Babies and Other Young Children: A History of the Infant and Child Welfare Movement in England, 1898–1918*, London: Tavistock, 1987.

Dyhouse, Carol, *Girls Growing up in Late Victorian and Edwardian England*, London: Routledge and Kegan Paul, 1981.

Elias, Norbert, *The Civilizing Process*, vol. 1, *The History of Manners*, transl. Edmund Jephcott, Oxford: Basil Blackwell, 1978 [1939].

Ende, Aurel, 'Battering and Neglect: Children in Germany, 1860–1978', *Journal of Psychohistory*, 7 (1979–80), 249–79.

Enfance abandonné et société en Europe, XIVe–XXe siècle, Rome: Ecole française de Rome, 1991.

'L'Enfant au moyen-âge', special issue of *Sénéfiance*, 9 (1980).

Ezell, Margaret J. M., 'John Locke's Images of Childhood', *Eighteenth-Century Studies*, 17 (1983–4), 139–55.

Fass, Paula S., and Mason, Mary Ann (eds), *Childhood in America*, New York: New York University Press, 2000.

Felt, Jeremy P., *Hostages of Fortune: Child Labor Reform in New York State*, Syracuse, NY: Syracuse University Press, 1965.

Fildes, Valerie A., *Breasts, Bottles and Babies: A History of Infant Feeding*, Edinburgh: Edinburgh University Press, 1986.

Fildes, Valerie A., *Wet Nursing: A History from Antiquity to the Present*, Oxford: Basil Blackwell, 1988.

Flandrin, Jean-Louis, 'Enfance et société', *Annales ESC*, 19 (1964), 322–9.

Flandrin, Jean-Louis, *Families in Former Times: Kinship, Household and Sexuality*, transl. Richard Southern, Cambridge: Cambridge University Press, 1979.

Floud, Roderick, Wachter, Kenneth, and Gregory, Annabel, *Height, Health and History: Nutritional Status in the United Kingdom, 1750–1980*, Cambridge: Cambridge University Press, 1990.

Foley, Alice, *A Bolton Childhood*, Manchester: Manchester University Extra-Mural Department, 1973.

Formanek-Brunell, Miriam, *Made to Play House: Dolls and the Commercialization of American Girlhood 1830–1930*, New Haven: Yale University Press, 1993.

Forsyth, Ilene H., 'Children in Early Medieval Art: Ninth through Twelfth Centuries', *Journal of Psychohistory*, 4 (1976), 31–70.

Frenken, Ralph, 'Changes in German Parent–Child Relations from the Fourteenth to the Middle of the Seventeenth Century, *Journal of Psychohistory*, 27 (2000), 228–72.

Fuchs, Rachel Ginnis, *Abandoned Children: Foundlings and Child Welfare in Nineteenth-Century France*, Albany: State University of New York Press, 1984.

Garnier, F., 'L'Iconographie de l'enfant au moyen âge', *Annales de démographie historique* (1973), 135–40.

Gavitt, Philip, *Charity and Children in Renaissance Florence: The Ospedale degli Innocenti, 1410–1536*, Ann Arbor, University of Michigan Press, 1990.

Gélis, Jacques, *History of Childbirth: Fertility, Pregnancy and Birth in Early Modern Europe*, transl. Rosemary Morris, Cambridge: Polity, 1991.

Gélis, J., Laget, M., and Morel, M.-F., *Entrer dans la vie: naissances et enfances dans la France traditionnelle*, Paris: Gallimard/Julliard, 1978.

Gittins, Diana, *The Child in Question*, London: Macmillan, 1998.

Goldin, Claudia, and Sokoloff, Kenneth, 'Women, Children, and Industrialization in the Early Republic: Evidence from the Manufacturing Censuses', *Journal of Economic History*, 42 (1982), 741–74.

Gomersall, Meg, *Working-Class Girls in Nineteenth-Century England*, London: Macmillan, 1997.

Goodich, Michael, 'Bartholomaeus Anglicus on Child-Rearing', *History of Childhood Quarterly*, 3 (1975), 75–84.

Gorham, Deborah, 'The "Maiden Tribute of Modern Babylon" Re-Examined: Child Prostitution and the Idea of Childhood in Late-Victorian England', *Victorian Studies*, 21 (1978), 353–79.

Gorham, Deborah, *The Victorian Girl and the Feminine Ideal*, London: Croom Helm, 1982.

Graff, Harvey J. (ed.), *Literacy and Social Development in the West: A Reader*, Cambridge: Cambridge University Press, 1981.

Graff, Harvey J. (ed.), *Growing up in America*, Detroit: Wayne State University Press, 1987.

Graff, Harvey J., *The Legacies of Literacy: Continuities and Contradictions in Western Culture and Society*, Bloomington: Indiana University Press, 1987.

Graff, Harvey J., *Conflicting Paths: Growing up in America*, Cambridge, Mass.: Harvard University Press, 1995.

Grendler, Paul F., 'Schooling in Western Europe', *Renaissance Quarterly*, 43 (1990), 775–87.

Greven, Philip J. (ed.), *Child-Rearing Concepts, 1628–1861*, Itasca, Ill.: F. E. Peacock, 1973.

Greven, Philip J., *The Protestant Temperament: Patterns of Child-Rearing, Religious Experience, and the Self in Early America*, New York: Alfred A. Knopf, 1977.

Grylls, David, *Guardians and Angels: Parents and Children in Nineteenth-Century Literature*, London: Faber and Faber, 1978.

Haas, Louis, *Renaissance Man and his Children: Childbirth and Early Childhood in Florence, 1300–1600*, London: Macmillan, 1998.

Hair, P. E. H., 'Children in Society, 1850–1980', in Theo Barker and Michael Drake (eds), *Population and Society in Britain, 1850–1980*, London: Batsford, 1982, pp. 34–61.

Hanawalt, Barbara A., 'Childrearing among the Lower Classes of Late Medieval England', *Journal of Interdisciplinary History*, 8 (1977), 1–22.

Hanawalt, Barbara A., *The Ties that Bound: Peasant Families in Medieval England*, New York: Oxford University Press, 1986.

Hanawalt, Barbara A., *Growing up in Medieval London: The Experience of Childhood in History*, New York, Oxford University Press, 1993.

Hardyment, Christina, *Dream Babies: Child Care from Locke to Spock*, London: Jonathan Cape, 1983.

Hawes, Joseph M. and Hiner, N. Ray, *American Childhood: A Research Guide and Historical Handbook*, Westport, Conn.: Greenwood Press, 1985.

Hawes, Joseph M. and Hiner, N. Ray (eds), *Children in Historical and Comparative Perspective: An International Handbook and Research Guide*, New York: Greenwood Press, 1991.

Hélias, Pierre-Jakez, *The Horse of Pride: Life in a Breton Village* transl. June Guicharnaud, New Haven: Yale University Press, 1978.

Henderson, John, and Wall, Richard (eds), *Poor Women and Children in the European Past*, London: Routledge, 1994.

Hendrick, Harry, *Child Welfare: England, 1872–1989*, London: Routledge, 1994.

Hendrick, Harry, *Children, Childhood and English Society, 1880–1990*, Cambridge: Cambridge University Press, 1997.

Herlihy, David, 'Medieval Children', in Bede Karl Lackner and Kenneth Roy Philp (eds), *Essays on Medieval Civilization: The Walter Prescott Webb Memorial Lectures*, Austin: University of Texas Press, 1978, pp. 109–41.

Heywood, Colin, *Childhood in Nineteenth-Century France: Work, Health and Education among the 'Classes Populaires'*, Cambridge: Cambridge University Press, 1988.

Heywood, Colin, 'On Learning Gender Roles during Childhood in Nineteenth-Century France', *French History*, 5 (1991), 451–66.

Heywood, Colin, 'Age and Gender at the Workplace: The Historical Experiences of Young People in Western Europe and North America', in Margaret Walsh (ed.), *Working out Gender: Perspectives from Labour History*, Aldershot: Ashgate, 1999, pp. 48–65.

Higonnet, Anne, *Pictures of Innocence: The History and Crisis of Ideal Childhood*, London: Thames and Hudson, 1998.

Hoffer, Peter C., and Hull, N. E. H., *Murdering Mothers: Infanticide in England and New England, 1558–1803*, New York: New York University Press, 1981.

Hoffert, Sylvia D., *Private Matters: American Attitudes toward Childbearing and Infant Nurture in the Urban North, 1800–1860*, Urbana: University of Illinois Press, 1989.

Holmes, Urban T., 'Medieval Childhood', *Journal of Social History*, 2 (1968–9), 164–72.

Horrell, Sara, and Humphries, Jane, ' "The Exploitation of Little Children": Child Labor and the Family Economy in the Industrial Revolution', *Explorations in Economic History*, 32 (1995), 485–516.

Houlbrooke, Ralph A., *The English Family, 1450–1700*, London: Longman, 1984.

Houston, R. A., *Literacy in Early Modern Europe: Culture and Education 1500–1800*, London: Longman, 1988.

Hoyles, Martin (ed.), *Changing Childhood*, London: Writers and Readers Publishing Cooperative, 1979.

Humphries, Stephen, *Hooligans or Rebels: An Oral History of Working-Class Childhood and Youth 1889–1939*, Oxford: Basil Blackwell, 1981.

Hunt, David, *Parents and Children in History: The Psychology of Family Life in Early Modern France*, New York: Harper Torchbooks, 1972.

Hunt, Peter, *An Introduction to Children's Literature*, Oxford: Oxford University Press, 1994.

Hunt, Peter (ed.), *Children's Literature: An Illustrated History*, Oxford: Oxford University Press, 1995.

Hürlimann, Bettina, *Three Centuries of Children's Books in Europe*, transl. Brian W. Alderson, London: Oxford University Press, 1967.

Jackson, Mark, *New-Born Child Murder: Women, Illegitimacy and the Courts in Eighteenth-Century England*, Manchester: Manchester University Press, 1996.

Jackson, Mary V., *Engines of Instruction, Mischief, and Magic: Children's Literature in England from its Beginnings to 1839*, Lincoln: University of Nebraska Press, 1989.

James, Allison, and Prout, Alan (eds), *Constructing and Reconstructing Childhood: Contemporary Issues in the Sociological Study of Childhood*, London: Falmer Press, 1990.

James, Allison, Jenks, Chris, and Prout, Alan, *Theorizing Childhood*, Cambridge: Polity, 1998.

Jasper, A. S., *A Hoxton Childhood*, London: Barrie and Rockliff, 1969.

Johansson, S. Ryan, 'Centuries of Childhood/Centuries of Parenting: Philippe Ariès and the Modernization of Privileged Infancy', *Journal of Family History*, 12 (1987), 343–65.

Jong, Mayke de, 'Growing up in a Carolingian Monastery: Magister Hildemar and his Oblates', *Journal of Medieval History*, 9 (1983), 99–128.

Jong, Mayke de, *In Samuel's Image: Child Oblation in the Early Medieval West*, Leiden: E. J. Brill, 1996.

Jordan, Thomas E., *Victorian Childhood*, Albany, NY: State University of New York Press, 1987.

Jordanova, Ludmilla, 'Children in History: Concepts of Nature and Society', in Geoffrey Scarre (ed.), *Children, Parents and Politics*, New York: Cambridge University Press, 1989, pp. 3–24.

Jordanova, Ludmilla, 'New Worlds for Children in the Eighteenth Century: Problems of Historical Interpretation', *History of the Human Sciences*, 3 (1990), 69–83.

Kagan, Jerome, *The Nature of the Child*, New York: Basic Books, 1984.

Kelly, Alfred (ed.), *The German Worker: Working-Class Autobiographies from the Age of Industrialization*, Berkeley: University of California Press, 1987.

Kern, Stephen, 'Freud and the Discovery of Child Sexuality', *History of Childhood Quarterly*, 1 (1973), 117–41.

Kertzer, David I., *Sacrificed for Honor: Italian Infant Abandonment and the Politics of Reproductive Control*, Boston: Beacon Press, 1993.

Kessen, William, 'The American Child and Other Cultural Inventions', *American Psychologist*, 34 (1979), 815–20.

Kiefer, Monica, *American Children through their Books, 1700–1835*, Philadelphia: University of Philadelphia Press, 1948.

Kincaid, James R., *Child-Loving: The Erotic Child and Victorian Culture*, London: Routledge, 1992.

Klapisch-Zuber, Christiane, *Women, Family, and Ritual in Renaissance Italy*, transl. Lydia Cochrane, Chicago: University of Chicago Press, 1985.

Klaus, Alisa, *Every Child a Lion: The Origins of Maternal and Infant Health Policy in the United States and France, 1890–1920*, Ithaca, NY: Cornell University Press, 1993.

Kroll, Jerome, 'The Concept of Childhood in the Middle Ages', *Journal of the History of the Behavioural Sciences*, 13 (1977), 384–93.

Kuefler, Mathew S., '"A Wryed Existence": Attitudes toward Children in Anglo-Saxon England', *Journal of Social History*, 24 (1990–1), 823–34.

Larcom, Lucy, *A New-England Girlhood*, Williamstown, Mass.: Corner House Publications, 1985.

LeRoy Ladurie, Emmanuel, *Montaillou: Cathars and Catholics in a French Village, 1294–1324*, transl. Barbara Bray, Harmondsworth: Penguin, 1980 [1978].

Leverenz, David, *The Language of Puritan Feeling: An Exploration in Literature, Psychology and Social History*, New Brunswick, NJ: Rutgers University Press, 1980.

Lindemann, Mary, 'Love for Hire: The Regulation of the Wet-Nursing Business in Eighteenth-Century Hamburg', *Journal of Family History*, 6 (1981), 379–95.

Locke, John, *Some Thoughts Concerning Education*, ed. John W. and Jean S. Yelton, Oxford: Clarendon Press, 1989.

Lockridge, Kenneth A., *Literacy in Colonial New England: An Enquiry into the Social Context of Literacy in the Early Modern West*, New York: W. W. Norton, 1974.

Lorence, Bogna W., 'Parents and Children in Eighteenth-Century Europe', *History of Childhood Quarterly*, 2 (1974), 1–30.

Macfarlane, Alan, *The Family Life of Ralph Josselin: A Seventeenth-Century Clergyman*, Cambridge: Cambridge University Press, 1970.

Macleod, David I., *The Age of the Child: Children in America, 1890–1920*, New York: Twayne Publishers, 1998.

McMillan, Sally G., *Motherhood in the Old South: Pregnancy, Childbirth, and Infant Rearing*, Baton Rouge: Louisiana State University Press, 1990.

Marten, James, *The Children's Civil War*, Chapel Hill: University of North Carolina Press, 1998.

Martindale, Andrew, 'The Child in the Picture: A Medieval Perspective', in Diana Wood (ed.), *The Church and Childhood*, Oxford: Blackwell Publishers, 1994, pp. 197–232.

Marvick, Elizabeth W., *Louis XIII: The Making of a King*, New Haven: Yale University Press, 1986.

Maynes, Mary Jo, *Taking the Hard Road: Life Course in French and German Workers' Autobiographies in the Era of Industrialization*, Chapel Hill: University of North Carolina Press, 1995.

Meckel, Richard A., *Save the Babies: American Public Health Reform and the Prevention of Infant Mortality 1850–1929*, Baltimore: Johns Hopkins University Press, 1990.

Murphy, Terence R., ' "Woful Childe of Parents Rage": Suicide of Children and Adolescents in Early Modern England', *Sixteenth-Century Journal*, 17 (1986), 257–70.

Nardinelli, Clark, *Child Labor and the Industrial Revolution*, Bloomington: Indiana University Press, 1990.

Nelson, Claudia, 'Sex and the Single Boy: Ideals of Manliness and Sexuality in Victorian Literature for Boys', *Victorian Studies*, 32 (1989), 525–50.

Nelson, Janet L., 'Parents, Children, and the Church in the Earlier Middle Ages', in Diana Wood (ed.), *The Church and Childhood*, Oxford: Blackwell Publishers, 1994, pp. 81–114.

Nicholas, David, *The Domestic Life of a Medieval City: Women, Children and the Family in Fourteenth-Century Ghent*, Lincoln: University of Nebraska Press, 1985.

Ogilvie, Sheilagh C., 'Coming of Age in a Corporate Society: Capitalism, Pietism and Family Authority in Rural Württemberg, 1590–1740', *Continuity and Change*, 1 (1986), 279–331.

Okenfuss, Max J., *The Discovery of Childhood in Russia: The Evidence of the Slavic Primer*, Newtonville, Mass.: Oriental Research Partners, 1980.

Opie, Iona, and Opie, Peter, *The Lore and Language of Schoolchildren*, Oxford: Clarendon Press, 1959.

Opie, Iona, and Opie, Peter, *Children's Games in Street and Playground*, Oxford: Clarendon Press, 1969.

Orme, Nicholas, *From Childhood to Chivalry: The Education of the English Kings and Aristocracy 1066–1530*, London: Methuen, 1984.

Orme, Nicholas, 'Children and the Church in Medieval England', *Journal of Ecclesiastical History*, 45 (1994), 563–87.

Orme, Nicholas, 'The Culture of Children in Medieval England', *Past and Present*, 148 (1995), 48–90.

Ozment, Steven, *When Fathers Ruled: Family Life in Reformation Europe*, Cambridge, Mass.: Harvard University Press, 1983.

Panter-Brick, Catherine, and Smith, Malcolm T. (eds), *Abandoned Children*, Cambridge: Cambridge University Press, 2000.

Paterson, Linda, *The World of the Troubadours: Medieval Occitan Society, c.1100–c.1300*, Cambridge: Cambridge University Press, 1993.

Pattison, Robert, *The Child Figure in English Literature*, Athens: University of Georgia Press, 1978.

Pinchbeck, Ivy, and Hewitt, Margaret, *Children and English Society*, 2 vols, London: Routledge and Kegan Paul, 1969–83.

Plumb, J. H., 'The New World of Children in Eighteenth-Century England', *Past and Present*, 67 (1975), 64–95.

Pollock, Linda, *Forgotten Children: Parent–Child Relations from 1500 to 1900*, Cambridge: Cambridge University Press, 1983.

Pollock, Linda, *A Lasting Relationship: Parents and Children over Three Centuries*, Hanover: University Press of New England, 1987.

Popp, Adelheid, *The Autobiography of a Working Woman*, transl. F. C. Harvey, London: T. Fisher Unwin, 1912.

Preston, Samuel H., and Haines, Michael R., *Fatal Years: Child Mortality in Late Nineteenth-Century America*, Princeton: Princeton University Press, 1991.

Ransel, David I. (ed.), *The Family in Imperial Russia*, Urbana: University of Illinois Press, 1978.

Ransel, David L., *Mothers of Misery: Child Abandonment in Russia*, Princeton: Princeton University Press, 1988.

Riché, Pierre, *De l'éducation antique à l'éducation chevaleresque*, Paris: Flammarion, 1968.

Riché, Pierre, *Education and Culture in the Barbarian West, Sixth through Eighth Centuries*, transl. John J. Contreni, Columbia: University of South Carolina Press, 1976.

Riché, Pierre, and Alexandre-Bidon, Danièle, *L'Enfance au Moyen Age*, Paris: Editions du Seuil, 1994.

Roberts, Robert, *A Ragged Schooling: Growing up in the Classic Slum*, London: Flamingo, 1984.

Rodenburg, Herman W., 'The Autobiography of Isabella de Moerloose: Sex, Childrearing and Popular Belief in Seventeenth Century Holland', *Journal of Social History*, 18 (1984–5), 517–40.

Rose, Lionel, *The Erosion of Childhood: Child Oppression in Britain, 1860–1918*, London: Routledge, 1991.

Rousseau, Jean-Jacques, *Emile, or On Education*, transl. Allan Bloom, Harmondsworth: Penguin, 1991.

Sandin, Bengt, 'Education, Popular Culture and the Surveillance of the Population in Stockholm between 1600 and the 1840s', *Continuity and Change*, 3 (1988), 357–90.

Schafer, Sylvia, *Children in Moral Danger and the Problem of Government in Third Republic France*, Princeton: Princeton University Press, 1997.

Schama, Simon, *The Embarrassment of Riches: An Interpretation of Dutch Culture in the Golden Age*, London: Fontana, 1991.

Schnucker, R. V., 'The English Puritans and Pregnancy, Delivery and Breast Feeding', *History of Childhood Quarterly*, 1 (1974), 637–58.

Schofield, Roger, and Wrigley, E. A., 'Infant and Child Mortality in England in the Late Tudor and Early Stuart Period' in Charles Webster (ed.), *Health, Medicine and Mortality in the Sixteenth Century*, Cambridge: Cambridge University Press, 1979, pp. 61–95.

Schultz, James A., *The Knowledge of Childhood in the German Middle Ages, 1100–1350*, Philadelphia: University of Pennsylvania Press, 1995.

Sears, Elizabeth, *The Ages of Man: Medieval Interpretations of the Life Cycle*, Princeton: Princeton University Press, 1986.

Setten, Henk van, 'Album Angels: Parent–Child Relations as Reflected in 19th-Century Photos, Made after the Death of a Child', *Journal of Psychohistory*, 26 (1999), 819–34.

Shahar, Shulamith, *Childhood in the Middle Ages*, London: Routledge, 1990.

Shorter, Edward, *The Making of the Modern Family*, London: Fontana/Collins, 1977.

Sieder, Reinhard, '"Vata, derf i aufstehn?": Childhood Experiences in Viennese Working-Class Families around 1900', *Continuity and Change*, 1 (1986), 53–88.

Snyders, Georges, *La Pédagogie en France aux XVIIe et XVIIIe siècles*, Paris: Presses Universitaires de France, 1965.

Sommerville, C. John, *The Rise and Fall of Childhood*, Beverly Hills, Calif.: Sage Publications, 1982.

Sommerville, C. John, *The Discovery of Childhood in Puritan England*, Athens: University of Georgia Press, 1992.

Springhall, John, 'Leisure and Victorian Youth: The Penny Theatre in London, 1830–1890', in John Hurt (ed.), *Childhood, Youth and Education in the Late Nineteenth Century*, London: History of Education Society, 1981, pp. 101–24.

Stearns, Peter N., and Haggerty, Timothy, 'The Role of Fear: Transitions in American Emotional Standards for Children, 1850–1950', *American Historical Review*, 96 (1991), 63–94.

Steedman, Carolyn, *Childhood, Culture and Class in Britain: Margaret McMillan, 1860–1931*, London: Virago, 1990.

Steedman, Carolyn, *Strange Dislocations: Childhood and the Idea of Human Interiority, 1780–1930*, Cambridge, Mass.: Harvard University Press, 1995.

Stone, Lawrence (ed.), *Schooling and Society: Studies in the History of Education*, Baltimore: Johns Hopkins University Press, 1976.

Stone, Lawrence, *The Family, Sex and Marriage in England, 1500–1800*, London: Weidenfeld and Nicolson, 1977.

Strauss, Gerald, *Luther's House of Learning: Indoctrination of the Young in the German Reformation*, Baltimore, Johns Hopkins University Press, 1978.

Strickland, Charles, 'A Transcendentalist Father: The Child-Rearing Practices of Bronson Alcott', *History of Childhood Quarterly*, 1 (1973), 4–51.

Sussman, George D., *Selling Mother's Milk: The Wet-Nursing Business in France, 1715–1914*, Urbana: University of Illinois Press, 1982.

Sylvère, Antoine, *Toinou: le cri d'un enfant auvergnat*, Paris: Plon, 1980.

Thane, Pat, 'Childhood in History', in Michael King (ed.), *Childhood, Welfare and Justice*, London: Batsford, 1981, pp. 6–25.

Thomas, Keith, 'Children in Early Modern England', in Gillian Avery and Julia Briggs (eds), *Children and their Books: A Celebration of the Work of Iona and Peter Opie*, Oxford: Clarendon Press, 1989, pp. 45–77.

Thompson, Thea, *Edwardian Childhoods*, London: Routledge and Kegan Paul, 1981.

Tomalin, Claire, *Parents and Children*, Oxford: Oxford University Press, 1982.

Trattner, Walter I., *Crusade for the Children: A History of the National Child Labor Committee and Child Labor Reform in America*, Chicago: Quadrangle Books, 1970.

Trumbach, Randolph, *The Rise of the Egalitarian Family: Aristocratic Kinship and Domestic Relations in Eighteenth-Century England*, New York: Academic Press, 1978.

Tucker, Nicholas, *What is a Child?*, London: Fontana/Open Books, 1977.

Ulbricht, Otto, 'The Debate about Foundling Hospitals in Enlightenment Germany: Infanticide, Illegitimacy, and Infant Mortality Rates', *Central European History*, 18 (1985), 211–56.

Vann, Richard T., 'The Youth of *Centuries of Childhood*', *History and Theory*, 21 (1982), 279–97.

Vincent, David, *Bread, Knowledge and Freedom: A Study of Nineteenth-Century Working-Class Autobiography*, London: Europa Publications, 1981.

Weinstein, Donald, and Bell, Rudolph M., *Saints and Society: The Two Worlds of Western Christendom, 1000–1700*, Chicago: University of Chicago Press, 1982.

Weissbach, Lee Shai, *Child Labor Reform in Nineteenth-Century France: Assuring the Future Harvest*, Baton Rouge: Louisiana State University Press, 1989.

West, Elliott, *Growing up with the Country: Childhood on the Far West Frontier*, Albuquerque: University of New Mexico Press, 1989.

West, Elliott, and Petrick, Paula (eds), *Small Worlds: Children and Adolescents in America, 1850–1950*, Lawrence: University Press of Kansas, 1992.

Wilson, Adrian, 'The Infancy of the History of Childhood: An Appraisal of Philippe Ariès', *History and Theory*, 19 (1980), 132–53.

Wilson, Stephen, 'The Myth of Motherhood a Myth: The Historical View of European Child-Rearing', *Social History*, 9 (1984), 181–98.

Wilson, Stephen, 'Infanticide, Child Abandonment, and Female Honour in Nineteenth-Century Corsica', *Comparative Studies in Society and History*, 30 (1988), 762–83.

Wright, Richard, *Black Boy*, London: Longman, 1970.

Wrightson, Keith, *English Society, 1580–1680*, London: Hutchinson, 1982.

Zelizer, Viviana A., *Pricing the Priceless Child: The Changing Social Value of Children*, New York: Basic Books, 1985.

Index